DOPED

THE REAL LIFE STORY OF THE
1960s RACEHORSE DOPING GANG

Jamie Reid

RACING POST

Paperback edition published in 2014 by Racing Post Books
Axis House, Compton, Newbury, Berkshire, RG20 6NL

First published in Great Britain in 2013

10 9 8 7 6 5 4 3 2

ISBN 978-1-909471-51-1

Cover designed by Jay Vincent
Text designed by SoapBox
www.soapboxcommunications.co.uk

Printed and bound in the UK by CPI Group (UK) Ltd, Croydon, CR0 4YY

www.racingpost.com/shop

PICTURE ACKNOWLEDGEMENTS
Cover
Front top and bottom: Getty Images.
Back top left and top right: PA Archive/Press Association; bottom left Daily Herald Archive/NMEM/Science and Society Picture Library.

Plate section
Daily Herald Archive/NMEM/Science and Society Picture Library: 2
Getty Images: 4 top and bottom, 5 top Mirrorpix: 3 top
NI Syndication: 1 top
PA Archive/Press Association: 5 bottom, 6, 7 top and bottom, 8 top

RACING POST BOOKS
Doped

'An explosive real life story ... a real page turner.'
The Sun

'He has captured the Sixties milieu to a tee and served up a richly enjoyable slice of Turf history.'
Independent on Sunday

'Impeccably-researched and furiously-paced ... unput-downable ... a breathless story of greed and corruption that shocked the nation.'
Sport magazine

'A marvellous evocation of the period with late night stable visits by dopers, Soho gangsters, milk bars and Ford Zephyrs.'
The Sunday Times

'Doped superbly evokes a lost world of seedy glamour when spivs, racketeers and glamour pusses rubbed shoulders with aristocratic high-rollers.'
The Independent

'... a galloping page turner. Place your bets now.'
Vanity Fair

For Sara

Contents

Cast of Characters

THE DOPING GANG

Bill Roper – *Bookmaker and professional gambler.*

Micheline Lugeon – *Bill's Swiss lover.*

Edward 'Teddy' Smith – *Nicknamed 'The Witch Doctor'.*

Charlie Mitchell – *Bookmaker, gambler and hard man.*

Joe Lowry – *Professional punter and 'earwigger'.*

Edward 'Jackie' Dyer – *Bookmaker, punter and 'earwigger'.*

Emmanuel Lipman Leonard 'Darkie' Steward – *Former stable lad and apprentice jockey.*

Jack Stiles – *Former stable lad turned bad boy.*

Richard McGee – *Tablet Production Manager at Bayer Laboratories.*

Alexander 'Harry' Field – *Professional burglar and locksmith.*

Brian Perry – *A foolish friend of Darkie Steward.*

Sylvia Cross – *Daughter of an antiques dealer and Darkie Steward's girlfriend.*

Elaine Grande – *Auburn-haired stripper and Harry Field's girlfriend.*

May Kibble – *Unmarried mother of four young children. Ted Smith's lady.*

Jimmy Cronin – *Former stable lad.*
Johnny Barnham – *Former boxer turned black cab driver.*

THE LOYAL WIFE
Doris Roper, nee Doris Curd – *The official Mrs Roper and mother of Bill's two sons.*

THE BOOKMAKERS
Max Parker – *Owner of the family business and chairman of Ladbrokes.*
Harry 'Snouty' Parker – *Maxie's older brother.*
Cyril Stein – *Snouty and Maxie's nephew.*
William Hill – *Max Parker's arch rival.*
Bernie Howard – *Surrey-based bookmaker and punter.*

THE GANGSTERS
Albert Dimes – *Also known as 'Italian Albert'. Owner of a credit bookmaking business in Frith Street.*
Billy Hill – *Predecessor and ally of Dimes.*
Jack Spot – *So called 'King of the Underworld' until forced out by Hill and Dimes.*
Billy Howard – *Ex prize fighter and club owner.*
The Kray Brothers – *Charlie Mitchell's business partners in the 1960s.*
The Sabinis – *Racecourse racketeers in the 1920s and 30s.*

THE TRAINERS
Flat:

Noel Murless – *The top trainer in Britain in the 1950s and 1960s. Based at Warren Place stables in Newmarket.*

Captain Cecil Boyd-Rochfort – *Murless's Newmarket neighbour and rival.*

Jack Waugh – *Trained at Heath House stables, Newmarket.*

Jack Watts – *Trained at Fairway House, Newmarket.*

Major Dick Hern – *Trained from 1957 to 1962 at La Grange stables, Newmarket.*

Henri Jellis, Fergie Sutherland and Reg Day – *Newmarket-based trainers.*

Willie Smyth – *Private trainer to the Duke of Norfolk at Arundel in Sussex.*

Dermot 'Boggy' Whelan – *Popular Irish trainer based in Epsom.*

Harold Wallington – *Gambling trainer based at Hillcrest stables, Epsom.*

Peter and Dick Thrale – *Father and son trainers based at Downs House stables, Epsom.*

Farnham Maxwell – *Irish trainer based in Lambourn.*

Bob Read – *Journeyman trainer based in Lambourn.*

Jumps:

Major Peter Cazalet – *Owner of Fairlawne in Kent. Trained for the Queen Mother.*

Captain Ryan Price – *Brilliant, rogueish, piratical trainer, based at Findon in Sussex.*

Arthur Thomas – *Official licence holder at Guy's Cliffe stables near Warwick. Stooge for the Irish trainer, Paddy Sleator.*

TF 'Fred' Rimell – *Based at Kinnersley in Worcestershire.*

Roy Whiston – *Based near Hodnet in Shropshire.*

Tim Molony –*Based at Wymondham in Leicestershire.*

Captain Neville Crump –*Based at Middleham in Yorkshire.*

WA 'Arthur' Stephenson – *Based at Leasingthorne near Bishop Auckland.*

Major Calverley Bewicke – *Known as 'Verley'. Based at Shawdon Hall in Northumberland.*

C H Bell – *Based at Hawick in Scotland.*

Ken Oliver – *Based at Hawick in Scotland.*

Chris Nesfield – *Based at Charing in Kent.*

THE JOCKEYS

Flat:

Gordon, later Sir Gordon, Richards – *Champion jockey 26 times between 1925 and 1954. Later became a trainer.*

Lester Piggott – *Sir Gordon's successor and stable jockey to Noel Murless.*

Arthur 'Scobie' Breasley – *Australian-born jockey who rode for Gordon Smyth and the Duke of Norfolk.*

Geoff Lewis – *Stable jockey to Harold Wallington.*

Dandy McGreevy – *An apprentice in Epsom in the 1950s.*

Jumps:

Fred Winter – *Stable jockey to Ryan Price.*

Bill Rees and David Mould – *Stable jockeys to Major Peter Cazalet.*

Bobby Beasley – *Stable jockey to Arthur Thomas and Paddy Sleator.*

David Nicholson – *Nicknamed 'The Duke'.*
Derek Ancil – *Oxfordshire-based trainer and jockey.*
Terry Biddlecombe – *Stable jockey to Fred Rimell.*
Johnny Lehane, Harry East, Jimmy Fitzgerald, Johnny
Leech and Tommy Barnes – *Northern based jockeys in
the early 1960s.*

THE STABLE LADS
Philip 'Snuffy' Lawler – *One of Noel Murless's top lads.*
Michael Heffernan and Kenny Santus – *Worked in
Newmarket for Fergie Sutherland.*
Jimmy Hilliard – *Worked in Newmarket in the 1950s and
1960s.*
Norman Pope – *Worked in Epsom in the 1950s.*

THE JOCKEY CLUB
Lord Rosebery – *Harry Rosebery, the 6th Earl. Owner, breeder
and punter.*
Duke of Norfolk – *Bernard Marmaduke Fitzalan-Howard.
The Crown's Ascot representative from 1945 until 1972.*
Major General Sir Randle Fielden – *A former managing
director of the NAAFI.*
Lord Crathorne – *The former Conservative cabinet minister,
Sir Thomas Dugdale.*
Edward Weatherby – *Secretary to the Jockey Club.*
Colonel Neville Blair – *Jockey Club head of security.*
Bob Hill – *Former Metropolitan Police Detective Sergeant
recruited by Colonel Blair.*

THE LAW

Sir Ranulf Bacon – *Metropolitan Police commissioner.*

Richard Jackson – *Assistant commissioner and head of CID.*

Detective Chief Superintendent George Davis – *Nominal head of the doping enquiry.*

Detective Chief Inspector Ernest Barnett – *Head of CID at West End Central and effective leader of the doping enquiry.*

Detective Inspector Bob Anderson – *Flying Squad.*

Detective Inspector Terence O'Connell – *Flying Squad.*

Detective Sergeant Pat Sughrue – *Flying Squad.*

Detective Chief Inspector George Dunstan – *Head of Brighton CID.*

PC Charles Pickin – *Newmarket beat bobby.*

Prologue

FAIRLAWNE

THE MYSTERIOUS young Frenchwoman in the sealskin coat arrived at Fairlawne on a misty November afternoon in 1961. She came in a black Ford Zephyr saloon that turned in through the lodge gates about half past three. Cock pheasants were scuttling around in the undergrowth beside the drive and there was a smell of wood smoke in the air where some estate workers were making a bonfire of brush and old leaves.

The car came to a halt on the gravel apron in front of the big house and a young chauffeur, smartly suited and wearing a peaked cap, got out and rang the bell. After a while the butler, Bradbrook, came to the door. The chauffeur explained that his passenger was Mademoiselle Rosemarie Laumaine from Paris. She had met Major Cazalet at the races the previous week and had expressed an interest in sending him a couple of horses to train. They had talked on the telephone and the Major had suggested that, if she was ever passing, she should drop in and look around the yard. Mademoiselle was on her way to Dover to take the ferry back to France and this had seemed like the perfect opportunity. The butler, who was not expecting visitors, explained that the Major and Mrs Cazalet were not at home and not expected back from Newbury until 6 p.m. at the earliest. But someone in the stable yard – which was down the hill to the left, out of sight of the main house – might be able to help. The chauffeur nodded politely and Bradbrook watched as the car drove slowly down the hill between the box hedges and into the stable yard at the bottom.

In Cazalet's absence his head lad Jim Fairgrieve had been left in charge and his staff were already busy with the routine chore of evening stables, feeding the horses and cleaning out their stalls. The chauffeur approached the tall, redheaded Scotsman and went through his story once again. The head lad later admitted that he found the details puzzling. The Major was a martinet who ran his stable on military lines. He had made no mention of a possible new owner who might drop by. But when the lady in question got out of the car and walked towards him, smiling warmly, hand outstretched, Fairgrieve's doubts were swept away. Mademoiselle Laumaine was stunningly attractive. She had dark brown bouffant hair and dark eyes and she wore red lipstick and a silk scarf around her neck. She carried a pair of black gloves and a black leather handbag and beneath her fur coat Fairgrieve caught a glimpse of what looked like an expensive suit and elegantly stockinged legs. She apologised for disrupting Fairgrieve's work and offered him a cigarette from her silver cigarette box. The head lad, who would have loved one, said that Major Cazalet didn't approve of smoking in the yard. Mademoiselle, who spoke English well though with a pronounced French accent, put her cigarette box away and said how excited she was to be at the famous Fairlawne. She would so love to have a brief look around if she could as she wasn't sure when she would next be in England though she would love to come back when the Major was at home.

Fairgrieve knew that Cazalet's last runner at Newbury, Jaipur, owned by Queen Elizabeth the Queen Mother, had been due to contest the Halloween Novices Chase at 3 p.m. The Major might still be on the course in the weighing room or the royal box or he might already have left. But, with no mobile phones available in 1961, there was no way for Fairgrieve to check Mademoiselle's story and in the circumstances it would have been awkward bordering on impertinent to refuse her request. The Sixties' satire boom had just begun and *Beyond The Fringe* was playing to packed houses in London's West End. But horse racing was still run on hierarchical and deferential lines and a mere stable employee, even a head lad like Fairgrieve, knew his place.

Besides, Mademoiselle Laumaine was such a charming and enthusiastic guest that it was no effort to give her a brief tour. So Fairgrieve showed her around the Queen Anne style stable block with the gabled roof and the small pond with the fountain in the middle and the pump house beyond. Estate cottages stood around the edge of the stabling area and there was a lads' dormitory on the upper floor above the tack room. Fairgrieve escorted Mademoiselle down a line of boxes, horses' heads looking out over the dark wooden doors and Mademoiselle patted a few heads and stroked a few manes and gazed inside at the whitewashed interiors with the high ceilings. Her chauffeur strolled along behind her, making notes as he went. They saw some of Cazalet's best steeplechasers including the Queen Mother's pair Double Star and Laffy, a five-year-old French-bred gelding purchased that summer by the Polish Colonel Bobinski and about to embark on a career over fences. Mademoiselle Laumaine seemed particularly interested in the box numbers and which horse was where although Fairgrieve explained that they moved them around quite often. As the tour continued, Fairgrieve noticed her effect on the lads who were also smiling and patting their charges and generally scurrying this way and that, working that little bit harder and more conspicuously than might usually be the case on a dull Wednesday afternoon.

After they'd seen the stables, Fairgrieve took Mademoiselle up the track that led to the parkland where they exercised the horses each morning. The Queen Mother frequently stood with Cazalet beneath those giant oak and horse chestnut trees – and once a shivering Noël Coward had stood there too – and watched her horses on the gallops. From the park there was a perfect view of the beautiful south-facing side of the house, of the cupola and bell tower and the glass-fronted conservatory and of the svelte green lawn where the Major sometimes played croquet with his royal patron. And behind the kitchen gardens they could see the deep woods of West Kent stretching away towards Ightham Mote and Knole.

Fairgrieve asked if Mademoiselle would like to go back up to the house and have a cup of tea before she left but his visitor regretfully declined, explaining that she'd already caused enough trouble and that she really ought to go. But she did say how much she looked forward to coming back to Fairlawne soon and meeting all the stable lads again and they agreed how much they all looked forward to seeing her again too.

The Ford Zephyr didn't go back up past the house but left by the service drive. Fairgrieve's last sight of Mademoiselle Laumaine was of her waving to him from the back seat of the car. The chauffeur turned left on to the A227 through the village of Shipbourne and within ten minutes they were on the outskirts of Tonbridge. The lights were on now in all the shops and schoolchildren were queuing for buses or trudging back across muddy rugger pitches on their way to a boarding house tea. The quickest way to Dover would have been to take the A26 towards Maidstone and Ashford but, instead, the Zephyr turned right at the Star and Garter and took the main road north through Hildenborough and Sevenoaks. By the time the car had climbed River Hill the chauffeur and his passenger felt able to relax. The chauffeur had taken off his cap and she had lit them both a cigarette. Mademoiselle Laumaine unbuttoned her fur coat and stretched out comfortably in the back seat. She liked the role-playing and the dressing up and she felt a sense of physical, almost sexual, satisfaction about a job well done. Another stable visit. Another reconnaissance mission. She was the best spy in the business.

It was after 7 p.m. when Cazalet got back to Fairlawne. The Major, who always dressed for dinner, had stopped off in his office on his way to his bath when Jim Fairgrieve rang him from the stable yard and told him about the glamorous Mademoiselle. Cazalet exploded. He had met no such person as this Rosemarie Laumaine, not at Sandown or Kempton or anywhere else and he most certainly hadn't invited her to drop in to the stable whenever she was passing. But he had heard racecourse rumours about an extremely attractive young Frenchwoman who, as he now explained to a mortified Fairgrieve, was to be avoided at all costs.

By now the attractive young woman was safely ensconced in fifth-floor luxury in a penthouse flat in Stafford Court, overlooking Kensington High Street. The black Ford was locked away in a garage at the back of the building and the 'chauffeur' had hurried off to his bedsit in the seedier purlieus of Notting Hill. Mademoiselle Laumaine, whose real name was Micheline Emilienne Lugeon and who wasn't French but Swiss, was enjoying a celebratory drink with a deeply appreciative man who was old enough to be her father. William John Roper – better known as Bill Roper or Mr Racing – was a bookmaker and professional gambler. In the summer of 1955 Micheline had come from Geneva to work as an au pair in Bill's marital home in North London. By 1961 Roper and Lugeon were lovers. They were also the central figures in one of the biggest doping and gambling conspiracies in the history of British racing.

Bill and Micheline didn't know it at the time but that seemingly successful visit to Fairlawne was to mark a turning point in their fortunes. Up until then almost all their bets had been winning ones. But within a month of the trip to the royal stable there would be a special Scotland Yard team on their trail. . . . and the police weren't the only ones interested in their activities.

As Roper sipped his Scotch and admired Micheline walking across the bedroom in her underwear, he was trying not to think about his wife and sons in Mill Hill. And he was trying even harder not to think about the spiralling costs of his life and how to meet them. The only way, it seemed, was to send his gang back out to a stable in the dead of night – he never went himself – where they would wake up a sleeping racehorse, twist its upper lip with a tourniquet or 'twitch' and force barbiturates down its throat. The following day, the same horse would start favourite for a race with a small number of runners and Bill and his bookmaking associates would lay it at several points over the odds and back the second or third favourite to win the race or combine them in a reverse forecast. It was a dirty but extremely profitable business and Bill Roper and Micheline Lugeon had reached a point where to go back would have been even more dangerous than to carry on.

This is their story.

1

A COLOURFUL BUT CUTTHROAT WORLD

AS FAR back as he could remember, Bill Roper had always wanted to be a bookmaker. Bill was a South London boy, born in Catford in 1905 and brought up in a Victorian two-up two-down, in one of a grid network of streets built to accommodate the families of bookkeepers and clerks commuting to the City.

Roper got his formal education at the LCC School on Brownhills Road, and he was an able pupil. Attentive, bright and with a particularly good grasp of English and mathematics. Not that boys like Bill were expected to stay on at school and sit their matriculation certificate. They were expected to go out to work and help support their family and that's what Roper did in 1920 at the age of 15. He was employed, initially as an office boy, by the South London property developer and punter Bernard Sunley, and by the early 1930s he had been promoted to the role of office manager. But the dry recording of property surveys, contracts and accounts was far from the limit of Bill Roper's interest in financial affairs.

In 1942 Roper volunteered for the RAF. The 37-year-old was too old to join a bomber crew. But being six feet tall, fit and strong, he was deemed a suitable recruit for the Military Police and he served as a redcap corporal and sergeant at bases in Lincolnshire until he was honourably discharged in 1946. A fine war record maybe, but Bill did have weaknesses and it was generally agreed that they revolved around money and women. By the mid-1940s Roper had married one woman and then fallen in love with another. The spouse declined to give him a divorce but in 1947 his new paramour, Doris Lillian Curd, changed her name to Roper and proceeded to live very happily as his wife and the mother of his two sons, born in 1951 and 1952, even though the couple were never officially married. Supporting and satisfying two women and dividing his time between their different households didn't seem to be a problem for Bill who flitted between them as charming as could be and still had energy to spare for his other consuming passion.

From the summer of 1922, when the 17-year-old saw Steve Donoghue win the Derby on Captain Cuttle, Roper had been fascinated by the speculative world of horse racing. The Bernard Sunley offices closed every year on the first Wednesday in June allowing their staff to head to London Bridge for the race specials down to Epsom and Tattenham Corner, the carriages humming with wit and banter and the traditional high spirits of Londoners embarking on their great day out. Roper loved the noise and passion of the crowds on Epsom Downs, the hurdy-gurdy of the funfair and the unforgettable sight of thoroughbred horses racing over the uniquely undulating course. But what really intrigued him were the smart clothes and confident manners of the men who laid the bets and the thick wads of the folding stuff he saw changing hands between them. If that's what a bookmaker and professional gambler looked like, Bill wanted to be one.

He got a further taste of racecourse excitement at Brighton in August. There were no Derby winners on show. It was holiday fare for a holiday crowd but the London bookmakers were there and the biggest of them were staying at the Metropole and the Grand. Bill, celebrating a winner with oysters and splash, thought this could become a way of life. Being a streetwise boy, he may also have noticed the gangsters in the backgound like the Sabini brothers who wielded cutthroat razors and extorted money from some bookies in return for letting them bet. Not that Bill had any intention of becoming a racketeer's stooge. Not then, at least.

Roper was intelligent and ambitious with an inborn business instinct. If he had been growing up in New York instead of South London, the dynamic nature of American society might have permitted him to become a Wall Street banking tycoon, or a bootlegger, or both. If he had been a young man in London in 1987, the Big Bang might have transformed him into a budding Nick Leeson and striped jacketed trader on the floor of the Financial Futures Exchange. But in the Britain of the 1920s and '30s, class and economic barriers made it almost unthinkable for a Catford boy to work in the City in anything other than a clerical capacity. The quick-witted world of gambling and bookmaking, however – which in the view of one unsentimental old timer 'was fundamentally not about horses and dogs but about buying and selling money' – presented no such obstacles.

In post-war Britain, off-course cash betting was officially illegal (and had been since 1853) but punters with the means to do so could have telephone credit accounts with as many bookies as they wished. Some of them sent bets and cheques in the post or relayed their selections by telegram. But working-class punters who were not creditworthy, and couldn't afford the time or the money to go racing, were still dependent on their local illegal street bookie. It was a business that was technically forbidden and yet widely tolerated and the police and judiciary generally adopted a benign, not to say comically two-faced, attitude to the booming trade. 'You was nicked by appointment,' says the former bookmaker's clerk Bobbie Edwards. 'The other 364 days of the year they just looked the other way.'

Bill Roper had done a bit of street bookmaking in Catford before the war. He carried on laying the odds in the RAF and then again in South London after he was demobbed. He had soon discovered that he preferred to be the man who sets the odds than the man who takes them. But what Bill really wanted was to branch out into the altogether more exotic world of the racecourse and before the end of the decade he got his chance. Bill had taught himself tic-tac – the ingenious language of hand signals and codes by which betting money used to be shunted around a racetrack – and in 1948 he was taken on as a tic-tac and 'outside man' by the diminutive Max Parker who owned one of the biggest credit bookmaking firms in the country. Maxie was an East Ender and his main office was in Whitechapel on the Commercial Road. It was from there that he kept in touch with his representatives on course, using the specially installed bookmaker's telephone service or 'blower' and they phoned back, relaying bets and information. Bill Roper rarely had to go to the office in person. His new workplace was Epsom, Ascot, Newmarket and Hurst Park and he loved every minute of it.

The popular impression of Britain in the late 1940s is of an exhausted, bombed-out and bankrupt country in the grip of austerity and shortages. But on the racecourses life wasn't like that at all. The late Geoffrey Hamlyn, a *Sporting Life* starting price reporter for 56 years and one of the Turf's most cherishable observers, used to say that the 1940s and '50s were a golden age of horse racing and gambling. The tracks were awash with great bundles of black market money and, with no betting duty or levy or costly overheads to worry about, the bookmakers played for high stakes.

The public, longing for entertainment and distraction after six years of war, flocked to the big meetings in unprecedented numbers. An estimated crowd of 200,000 turned out at Aintree for the 1946 Grand National and at Chester in May 100,000 came to watch the Chester Cup. It was a similar story a month later when a teeming mass of humanity, many of them just glad to be alive, cheered home Airborne, the appropriately named 50-1 winner of Epsom's first post-war Derby.

Not everyone was happy. The new Labour government toyed with the idea of closing racing down for a while due to the disastrous state of the nation's economy and Nye Bevan, the fiercely socialist health minister, was in favour of a permanent shutdown. Fortunately for the Turf, Lord Rosebery was on hand to fight its corner. The sixth Earl, who had won every classic race and twice owned and bred the Derby winner, had served briefly in Churchill's outgoing cabinet that had allowed racing to continue even at the height of the hostilities. He was also an enthusiastic punter and he was incensed when he heard of Labour's plans. He went straight to see the Prime Minister, Clement Attlee, and demanded that the proposal be scrapped. Attlee complied although big races like the Derby were temporarily moved to a Saturday and Rosebery persuaded the editor of *The Sporting Life*, Ben Clements, not to publish detailed betting reports in the paper until 1950 as it was felt that racing's image would be damaged if the full scale of the massive wagering that was taking place could be read every day.

The dominant figure in the betting ring was William Hill who bet on the racecourse in person from 1941 to 1955 and regularly accepted four- and five-figure wagers. Max Parker was Hill's biggest rival and Bill Roper's new guvnor and his clan had a reputation as the craftiest bookmakers of them all. There were four brothers: Harry, the eldest, born in 1895 and sometimes referred to as Dick but more often as Snouty, Max, Jack and Isaac. Their parents were Russian Jewish émigrés who had settled in London in the late-nineteenth century and their family name was Stein.

In the 1920s and '30s, Snouty was a big deal in the street bookmaking fraternity and he had dozens of pitches in Whitechapel and Bethnal Green. He laid huge bets on the racecourse too and one of his biggest wins was on Royal Mail in the 1937 Grand National when he was said to have made nearly £100,000, the equivalent of £5million in modern money. But then Snouty, Maxie and their confreres were never short of readies. Norman Pegg, who for 35 years was 'Gimcrack', the racing correspondent of the *Daily Herald*, never forgot the sight of them playing cards in a first-class carriage on a train returning from Salisbury to Waterloo in May 1940. It was just before Dunkirk and the nation was facing the gravest peril but racing had continued all the same and Snouty Parker had made a killing backing the future Derby winner, Owen Tudor, first time out. 'They must have had hundreds of pounds worth of banknotes floating around on the table,' wrote Pegg. 'And every time you looked up, soldiers earning £1 a week had their noses glued to the windows of the compartment.'

Things went downhill for Snouty from that point on. In 1941 he was 'warned off' – or banned from all racecourse premises – for four years by the Jockey Club for allegedly paying a jockey for information. In 1945 he died of a heart attack just before he was due to return. Max Parker had already taken over the business, keeping his brother's clients and the credit office on the Commercial Road, and it was Maxie that Bill Roper teamed up with three years later.

In the betting and racing culture that Bill was now a part of, information was the oxygen of the trade. The bookies gleaned intelligence from their customers who were often owners, trainers, jockeys – or their putters on – and stable lads as well as from the shrewder professional punters. Some stables were easy to penetrate but others guarded their secrets every bit as closely as the layers and cheated regularly with their runners until the day when the money was down. Not that either side complained unduly. There was no whining about 'transparency' or 'accountability' as there would be today. Geoffrey Hamlyn took the view that 'in matters of sin on the racecourse it was about a 50–50 split between the bookmakers on the one side and trainers and jockeys on the other'.[1]

Many of the top jockeys, although officially not allowed to bet, were regular and even compulsive gamblers. Mostly they did their best for their retained stable but sometimes they rode for a bookmaker or favoured their own money.

It was a colourful but cutthroat world and it made Bill Roper in its image. Max Parker shared Al Pacino's view as Michael Corleone in *The Godfather Part Two*, when he advises Frankie Pentangeli to 'keep your friends close and your enemies closer'; Maxie and Bill remained close to all the top gambling jockeys – providing them with cash, girls and hospitality – even when they suspected they'd stitched them up. Bill often organised private planes to take the jockeys to evening meetings in summer. The riders would be flown from course to course and then home again, all expenses paid

1 'We all knew they were at it,' recalls Charlie Maskey, a veteran associate of the Victor Chandler bookmaking firm, 'and they all knew we knew.'

by the Max Parker firm, and if they cared to chat about their prospects on the way, so be it. Bill and Max were equally close to the top gambling trainers and the whole circus of bookmakers, punters, owners, trainers, jockeys and racing correspondents would all congregate together whenever they went away from home for the big meetings.

The racing calendar in the 1940s and '50s had a rather different look to today and, outside of the classic races and Royal Ascot, was dominated by the big betting handicaps like the Lincoln and the Grand National which were known as the Spring Double. After hours it was all tremendously social and everyone – Bill Roper included – had the time of their lives. When they went up for the Lincoln in March they stayed at Woodhall Spa, for the St Leger they went to the Majestic in Harrogate, for Cheltenham they were at Droitwich Spa. Max Parker would take a suite and the trainers, jockeys and journalists would all be there too. They'd meet for drinks and dinner and then afterwards they'd go down to the billiard room and play chemin-de-fer for big money until the early hours.

'Racing was a wonderful life back then,' remembers Bobbie Edwards, 'if you treated it as fun, and for the first five or ten years after the war, bookmaking was a good way to make a living.'

2

THE SWISS AU PAIR GIRL

MICHELINE LUGEON dreamed of the good life too and, being intelligent and enterprising as well as pretty, was prepared to work hard to attain it. Lugeon was born in Geneva on 30 December 1936 and her father was the cemetery superintendent at Pierreplaine on the banks of the Rhône. Hers was a respectable middle-class background and she attended the Swiss Protestant equivalent of a grammar school, graduating with distinction at the age of 17. But there was to be no question of university. Micheline had other plans. At the time she left school she could already speak a modicum of English but she had decided that a proper command of the language was essential for her future career. 'I must learn English to succeed in business,' she told her school friends. And what better way to learn it properly than to go to London and live there.

The concept of the au pair girl, who was meant to be a member of the household and not just a domestic servant, was particularly attractive in Britain after the war – especially to couples who were no longer able to afford the kitchen staff and housemaids who might have worked for their parents in the 1920s and '30s. The au pair, who would receive 50 shillings a week plus board, would learn English and enhance her employment and marriage prospects while helping out around the home.

By the Swinging Sixties the very idea of young Swiss, French or Scandinavian girls doing their best to be accommodating was a titillating euphemism for promiscuity and sex. But in 1955 young girls like Micheline, who all had to have an aliens card and were not permitted to work more than 25 hours a week, were regarded as a cross between Heidi and Mary Poppins. Demure and sensible, they were expected to blend in seamlessly with their hosts and share meals and everyday life with them. In that respect Micheline drew a winning ticket when the employment agency in Geneva placed her with a bookmaker's family in Mill Hill.

Mainstream Britain in 1955 was nowhere near as colourful or awash with funds as the racing world. Rationing had only officially come to an end the year before and unappetising items like Libby's Pork Luncheon Meat, tinned fruit and soggy, overcooked vegetables remained the staples of many everyday meals. And despite the advent of the NHS and the Welfare State, good health, comfort and longevity were by no means guaranteed for most citizens. The Big London Smog of December 1952 – a toxic pea souper comprised of coal smoke, traffic fumes and industrial pollution – killed almost 4,000 people while families still went in fear of diseases like polio and TB. There were repressive undercurrents in the air too, despite the national reputation for tolerance and fair play, and nothing fed the appetite like a good sex scandal or murder.

In May 1954 the future Lord Montagu of Beaulieu and the *Daily Mail* journalist Peter Wildeblood were among a group of gay men prosecuted and imprisoned for 'inciting acts of gross indecency' even though the acts in question had all taken place in private and among consenting adults. And on 13 July 1955 – only ten days before Micheline arrived in London – Ruth Ellis was executed at Holloway Prison. The 28-year-old platinum blonde, the last woman to be hanged in Britain, had pumped five bullets into the body of her faithless lover, the racing driver David Blakeley, who had repeatedly beaten her up.

By comparison with these grim events, Bill and Doris Roper's home at Number 16 Uphill Drive, just around the corner from Mill Hill Broadway, was cheerful, easygoing and well stocked with material comforts. Number 16 (now sub-divided into flats), was a large, post-war, double-fronted detached house with gardens front and back. Nowadays the A1 practically starts outside the door but in the mid-1950s the Watford Way was still a two-lane arterial road and the green playing fields and parkland of Mill Hill School began just beyond it. Thanks to Bill's profitable dealings on the racecourse the Ropers had a car, two telephone lines, an automatic washing machine, a drinks cabinet and a new fifty-eight-guinea television set with teak surround. The cigarette boxes were always full, the larder and refrigerator were kept liberally supplied and every weekend there was a slap-up Sunday lunch, the sound of *Two Way Family Favourites* echoing around the house.

On the comparatively rare occasions when Bill took time off from the racecourse he took his family on outings to the seaside and Billy Smart's Circus and when he went away to a big meeting in the north, like Manchester or Aintree, he always brought presents on his return. Coty perfume and stockings for Doris. Toy soldiers and train sets for the boys. And maybe a new Beaver shaving brush or Jaeger dressing gown for himself to go with his Lentheric aftershave and his Daks and Vantella jackets and shirts.

There was a long, late summer in 1955 and the warm weather continued into the autumn. Micheline's days were spent largely with the children. There were trips to the shops on Mill Hill Broadway. To the butcher's and the greengrocer and the Tudorbethan sweet shop and the Copper Kettle café for tea and cakes; sometimes there were walks up to the top of Mill Hill where the boys were destined to start prep school when they were eight years old.

From Mondays to Saturdays, Micheline didn't see much of Bill but neither did his wife and children. Roper was earning £20 a week, plus commission, working for Max Parker and on top of that he was gambling increasingly on his own behalf. The more embedded he became in the betting ring the more knowledge he acquired and the more skilful he became at exploiting it to his own and Maxie's advantage. 'If a stable wanted a large commission [a big bet placed on one of their horses], say £5,000, they would give it to Max,' Bill explained years later. 'We worked commissions for most of the big owners and trainers.'

If Max Parker was at the races in person he might tell Bill

how much he wanted him to put on a horse and Bill would get it on with various other high-stakes bookies. If Max wasn't there, Bill's job would include hanging around the weighing room, the private boxes and the members' bar, mingling with owners and trainers and asking what business they wanted to do that day. He would then phone the details back to Max using their blower connection and, if the client was a shrewd one, Max would tell Bill how much money to invest on the horse for the firm and on Max's personal account and Bill would subsequently add a sum for W.J. Roper too.

Bill put on £10,000 (£183,000 in today's money) for the Scottish racehorse owner Ian Murray whose best horse, Tudor Treasure, trained by Eric Cousins, won the Victoria Cup at Hurst Park, and, at the peak of his trading in the late 1950s and early '60s, he would sometimes get on as much as £15,000 (nearly £275,000 today) for a single client. His success at attracting the custom of the high rollers lay in his skill at getting the total amount on to a decent average without depressing the market. The wagers, which were all on credit, had to be spread out with different firms. Bill wouldn't just go up to a bookmaker and attempt to get all the money on in a single bet. The bookie might only be prepared to accept part of the stake at his top price and the rest at a much shorter price and, by the time the negotiations were over, the odds would've contracted elsewhere in the ring. To circumvent the problem, Roper had up to ten trusted 'faces' or putters-on who would step in simultaneously at a given signal, each of them wagering a part of the stake money at the bigger odds. Bill's tic-tac skills told his men when to move but the essence of the operation was organisation and pinpoint timing.

The highly specialised role of the commission agent, which was what Bill called himself, has vanished in the mists of racing history. But in the 1940s and '50s, when it was still unthinkable for a steward or Jockey Club member to go up to a bookmaker in person, they performed a valued service. They were the trusted intermediaries between the occupants of stately homes, city offices and historic studs and stables on the one side and the grubby but irresistible world of racecourse commerce on the other.

Handling a powerful client like Lord Rosebery, who did all his betting with the Parker firm, was not without its headaches. Rosebery expected, indeed demanded, to be accommodated at certain odds and when he wasn't questioning the prices his agents had taken for him, he was not above putting pressure on the SP returners themselves. On one occasion at lowly Leicester races in the early 1950s he complained bitterly to Geoffrey Hamlyn that one of his winners had been returned at 15-8 instead of the 9-4 he'd assured all his friends they'd be paid out at.

They could be a nuisance, these aristocratic clients, but then so could their more spivvish counterparts and, in an age when gambling debts were unenforceable by law, at least the gentlemen – or the Rich Charlies, as the bookies called them – were generally good for the money. As the future Clermont Club owner, John Aspinall, realised when he started hosting private gaming parties in London in the mid-1950s, there was still a large pool of feckless toffs in Britain with inheritances to play with. The club owner or bookmaker who hooked them on the end of his line could, if he was patient, play them for all they were worth. That's why Max Parker bought Ladbrokes.

The flamboyant Scottish bookmaker, John Banks, once said that 'punters shouldn't be angry when Ladbrokes refuse to lay them a bet. They should be worried when they do.' That comment was made in the 1970s when Ladbrokes was a public company and on the way to becoming the biggest and most successful betting shop chain in the world. But, back in the 1920s and '30s, the Ladbrokes brand was so upmarket and socially exclusive that it was said you practically needed a stately home and a double-barrelled name even to think of opening an account with them.

The business was run from Six Old Burlington Street, a beautiful four-storey Queen Anne house that had previously belonged to Weatherby and Sons, the civil servants to the Jockey Club. The building, which was demolished in 1963, had oak panelling and a magnificent oak staircase and became the most well-heeled bookmaking quarters in London.[2] The louche directors and their friends treated Number Six as their club and ate lunch there regularly in the front office. The food was said to be excellent and often included smoked salmon sent down by train from Scotland by one of the clients. The teatime scones and sandwiches

2 The then Ladbrokes chairman Arthur Bendir was born in South London, like Bill Roper, but by the 1930s he owned a house in Mayfair and also bought Medmenham Hall in Buckinghamshire where the 18th-century Hellfire Club used to conduct their bacchanalian orgies.

were also a favourite and some gentleman punters dropped round each day to partake, rather like elderly backwoodsmen turning up at the House of Lords to claim their attendance allowance and enjoy the currant buns.

Working practices were quaint to say the least. When one of the aristocratic punters rang up to place a wager, a clerk would scurry into a booth and draw a curtain around it so that the details of the conversation would remain private. The same clerk, who had to stand up as sitting down would have been impolite to the customer, then had to enter the transaction in a ledger sitting on a high stool and using a quill pen.

It was inimitable, comical and charming but by 1956 business was demonstrably in decline, the old ways no match for leaner competitors. One of the directors offered to try and negotiate a sale and the racehorse owner and colossal gambler, Dorothy Paget, and Bill Roper's former employer, Bernard Sunley, were both interested. But it was the gimlet-eyed Max Parker who eventually agreed a price.

There was something of a social rockface between the Commercial Road and the typical Ladbrokes clientele and to begin with Maxie, who punctuated his conversation with expletives at the best of times, was far from convinced of the wisdom of his new purchase. 'What do I want to take that fucking lot on for?' he'd say. 'All those old accounts. All those fucking rich boys who never pay. All those debts. What fucking use is it to me?' Fortunately for Max, his 28-year-old nephew Cyril, who was Jack Stein's son but happy to use his grandfather's surname, was on hand to advise him. Cyril could see the potential and that with aggressive modern management and a broader client base, Ladbrokes could become as big as William Hill if not bigger.

Max said he paid £100,000 to acquire Ladbrokes, paying by instalments, although Cyril later claimed the figure was closer to £250,000. Geoffrey Hamlyn once described Cyril Stein as having 'a mind like a whetted razor' and, shortly after the deal was done in June 1956, the razor's edge was turned on the antiquated practices at Six Old Burlington Street. 'It was straight out of a Dickens novel,' Stein told the *Daily Mirror*'s Noel Whitcomb in an interview in 1967. 'The directors were mostly knocking on 70 and wouldn't open an account for a man with humble beginnings. A grocer who had become rich wouldn't be welcome as a client – not even if he usually lost.' Cyril, who had been to grammar school and business college and had no such snobbish inhibitions, cleared out the old boys and brought in hungry young clerks, a forest of telephones and an electronic accountancy system. He also began advertising discreetly for new customers, which would have been regarded as unforgivably vulgar if it had been made public.

Maxie was now chairman of Ladbrokes and Cyril was on the board but the chairman had also retained his own business. Bill Roper always maintained that he worked primarily for the uncle not his nephew although, as the 1950s wore on, the distinction blurred and the clients, trades and secrets of the two firms began increasingly to overlap.

It all resulted in a lot more work for Bill and a lot more hobnobbing with the quality and, as the commission rolled in, it meant a lot more money too. Ladbrokes used to distribute betting cards to the occupants of the private boxes in Ascot's old stand and, come the royal meeting, it now became part of Bill Roper's job to go up to the boxes before each race and collect the clients' bets whether they were with Ladbrokes or Max Parker. 'Right Boy. Eleven hundred pound to four. Sir Percy Lorraine. Hyphen. Five hundred pounds to two. Down to His Lordship. My Pal. Nine thousand pound to one. Frank Vogel.'

There was still cash beneath the top hats, as both Bill and John Aspinall could testify, and having sometimes taken bets of a sizeable nature, Roper would then have to dash back down the stairs and fight his way through the crowds to see his men on the rails before the off.

Micheline Lugeon was entertained in a private box at Ascot in June 1959 and it enabled her to form a picture of Bill in his professional capacity. By then she had long since ceased to be an au pair girl. As far as Micheline had been concerned there had been many attractions to life with the Ropers but, for an ambitious and determined young woman, impatient to get on, there was one major drawback. The two boys were only four and three years old in 1955 and needed a lot of attention but the time-consuming business of childcare was not what Micheline had come to England to learn. So in the summer of 1956 she moved on, very amicably, to work for a doctor's household in Highgate and then the year after that she was employed by a barrister in Hampstead. In each case the family had children but they were older and often away at boarding school.

All the time Micheline was busy trying to improve her English and, by 1957, her liguistic skills had improved sufficiently for her to take a part-time course in beauty culture. Then, in 1958, she left the au pair agency behind and was employed as a beautician and saleswoman in the cosmetics department at Selfridges earning £7.10s a week. So persuasive and *charmante* was the pretty and hard working young Swiss girl that within six months she'd moved on to a similar but better paid job at Fortnum & Mason and was by now living in her own flat in Marylebone. But she yearned to be a lot more than just a salesgirl. She wanted to start a business of her own. After work was over each day she began giving facials and other treatments at home to a few select clients. Some of them were friends or friends of friends she had made at work. Others were women who dropped by the store regularly and wanted the occasional longer and more personal consultation than the Fortnums' or Selfridges' shopfloor permitted. Especially if they had a big occasion to go on to and wanted to look their best for a husband or a lover.

Micheline's dream was to become another Elizabeth Arden or Helena Rubinstein and she had already decided that the colour scheme and packaging for her products would be white and gold. She began to evolve her own line of cosmetics, experimenting in her kitchen by heating materials in saucepans and moulding her own lipsticks. She also thought continually of how she could possibly raise the capital to get her business off the ground. In May 1959, mindful of what the future might bring, she registered the name Michelle de Paris as a trademark and then a few weeks later she went to the races and was fatefully reunited with Bill Roper, the cash-rich bookie.

3

MR RACING

ROYAL ASCOT 1959 began on Tuesday 16 June before an even bigger crowd than usual and in glorious weather. The sun shone through the morning with a light breeze blowing and throughout the afternoon scarcely a cloud crossed the sky. As a result of the prolonged dry spell the grass in the centre of the heath was a parched yellow but the course itself was a healthy green after heavy watering. The Duke of Norfolk, the Queen's Ascot representative, might not have approved of the policemen in shirt sleeves directing the crowds on their way up from Ascot station but, once inside the racecourse, it seems that everyone conformed to the strict dress code.

There was to be no royal procession that year as the Queen, although racing on the first two days, was to be packed off on an official visit to Canada on the Thursday morning. But in all other respects it seems it was Royal Ascot at its best and *The Times* racing correspondent was particularly impressed. 'Under the competent direction of the Duke of Norfolk and General Dawnay (the clerk of the course),' he wrote, 'everything from the luncheon rooms and bars to the weighing room and the conduct of the racing was meticulous and it was a pleasure to walk in the well-groomed enclosures.' The tipster Prince Monolulu wore his usual feathered headdress and the starter, Mr Alec Marsh, cut a dash in a black silk topper and black morning coat in which he rode down to the start on horseback. But otherwise there was a preponderance of grey top hats among the male racegoers and a great swathe of flowered prints and conventional petal hats among the women.

For Micheline Lugeon, aspiring beautician and guest of clients and friends who had signed her royal enclosure application voucher, it was all new and exciting and a seeming confirmation of everything she had worked for since coming over from Switzerland at the age of 18. One of the high points of her day was to be a reunion with her former employer whom she had not spoken to in the flesh for four years. Micheline was far from being just a pretty face. She was an intelligent and perceptive young woman who had learned a lot about England in a short time and she understood that at Ascot, as elsewhere in the country, there were certain demarcation lines designed to allow some people in and keep others out. But she also sensed that in the racing world there were moments and situations when those distinctions might be blurred.

There were no bookmakers in the royal enclosure at Ascot. The cash or boards bookies stood on their boxes in Tattersalls ring next door while the elite rails or credit bookmakers, many of whose punters were royal enclosure regulars, stood along the Tattersalls side of the railings that divided the two areas. The idea that the bookies all went around in loud check suits and spotted bow ties was an Ealing Studios cliché. Most of the rails bookies wore lounge suits but extremely smart, tailored Savile Row suits and their shirts and shoes were all handmade too. To complete the uniform they sported a brown trilby hat from Locks. It was often said of the impeccably dressed Bill Roper that he could easily have passed for a bank manager or a 'respectable' businessman. But then, as Bobbie Edwards recalls, 'It was half the game back then to wear a different suit each day. And they'd have all been horrified at the way most racecourse bookies dress now.'

One or two of Bill's colleagues, like the Ladbrokes' representative Dickie Gaskell and Victor Chandler's father Victor senior, were former public schoolboys. Others were enormously wealthy self-made men. No matter how prosperous or well turned out they may have been, from the perspective of the royal enclosure these bookmakers weren't 'gentlemen' and never would be. But this social impediment didn't prevent many senior Jockey Club members from availing themselves of their services. As a collective regulatory body the Jockey Club showed an almost complete lack of interest in betting and bookmaking until the late 1960s but numerous individual stewards, who were also leading owners, were regular punters and Bill Roper did business with most of them. Bill was not just smartly dressed but courteous, attentive and extraordinarily quick with odds, numbers and percentages. And as he would one day boast in public he 'laid bets to everyone from Lord and Lady Rosebery to the Newmarket postman'.

Edward 'Jackie' Dyer, a racecourse bookmaker who worked closely with Roper and knew him well, remembers him as 'an unbelievable man. Brilliant. It was like he had two brains. And he was such a character. He could talk to anybody.'

Charm and sartorial flair may have been part of Bill's image but he had no illusions about the main purpose of bookmaking which was to skin the punter. Max Parker had taught him that a good client only lasted three years. After that they had either gone broke, or seen the error of their ways and stopped gambling, or they had become very clever and had started winning which was no good for the business that was laying their bets.

You had to be sharp to survive and Bill was sharper than most. He frequently employed the bookmaking technique known as the 'knock-out', a crafty but legitimate practice first devised by Snouty Parker in the 1930s. Then, as now, all bets on racing were settled at what is known as the 'starting price' or SP. This is, literally, the last price available about a horse with the on-course market before a race gets underway. Bill had contacts in all the top stables and always knew when a horse was 'off'. If he fancied it, he would back it with his fellow layers – or use decoys to back it for him – and stipulate that he wanted his bets settled at SP. He would then stand up on his pitch on the rails and loudly offer prices on the horses he'd backed – but not necessarily accept bets on them – at several points over the odds. He was hoping that the official SP returners, like Geoffrey Hamlyn, would hear him and return the horse at the bigger price, thus maximising his profit if it won. Sometimes his bookmaking colleagues, anxious to hang on to their share of the market, would push the horse's odds out anyway to keep pace with the Parker firm.

Bill was equally dextrous in his use of the 'blower' and was in constant touch with the Whitechapel office. Whatever bets he took at the track on a horse he'd backed, he'd phone through to the London HQ and then, a few minutes before the off, the office would phone them over to other credit bookies, requesting that they be settled at SP too. If Bill took £2,000 in bets on the rails at an average of 4-1 and laid them off at an SP of 5-1, he'd make a £2,000 profit every time. Even if the horse lost, he'd only have to pay to the offices the two grand he'd taken at the track.

Micheline could hardly fail to have been impressed when she met Bill again. He seemed so knowledgeable about racing and bookmaking and so well informed. Everyone, it seemed, knew Mr Roper. He had been at the racecourse since half past seven that morning, one of a select group of bookmakers and journalists watching Baron de Waldner's Wallaby II, the main French challenger for the Ascot Gold Cup, do a mile-and-a-half gallop on the track. Bill said he thought the Frenchie would prove too strong for the Newmarket-based favourite, Alcide, whose trainer Captain Cecil Boyd-Rochfort trained for the Queen. He told Micheline and her friends what to back and what not to back that afternoon and, on a difficult card which included four long-priced winners, they ended up with a double on the Irish two-year-old, Martial, in the Coventry Stakes and the Queen's colt, Above Suspicion, who won the St James's Palace Stakes which closed the programme. He also gave them a tip for the following afternoon: Faultless Speech trained at Epsom by Harold Wallington and apparently strongly fancied for the Royal Hunt Cup.

It had been a halcyon June day and after the racing was over Bill joined them all for a drink. Roper was 54 years old, a married man with a receding hairline and two children under ten. He was, as they say, no oil painting although those who remember him describe a confident, chirpy personality brimming with energy and appetites. Micheline was 23 years old and looked like a petite Ava Gardner. Chatting away vivaciously in the car park and offering the other women her advice about lipsticks, mascara and face cream, she took Bill's breath away. Before they parted Roper asked her for her private telephone number and Micheline gave it to him.

Micheline had met all kinds of men in London. Nice men, sexy men, chinless young men she could wrap around her little finger and a kind but hard-up student who wanted her to go with him to Ban The Bomb demonstrations and went everywhere by bus when she longed to be driven around London in a smart car. There were handsome but impractical men, men with no business instinct and older married men who wanted her to be their little bit of Swiss fluff they could install in a mews flat in Bayswater or St John's Wood where she would be available for supper and seduction twice a week. None of them really comprehended the extent of her hard work and ambition. None of them was as shrewd or as business savvy as Bill Roper. And none was as generous or as much fun to be with either.

Like so many couples in that period, Bill and Micheline's first date after Ascot took place not in a pub or restaurant but in a coffee bar. It was that era when it was first considered cool and even slightly risqué to sip glass cups of frothy Espresso – or Expresso as some British proprietors insisted on calling it – in neon lit Italian-style cafés. The film *Expresso Bongo*, based on a West End musical and starring Laurence Harvey as a music business hustler and Cliff Richard as his hot signing, would open the following year. To identify Harvey's raffish characteristics, his character wore a pork pie hat and was frequently seen with a cigarette in one hand and a coffee cup in the other. Fashionable coffee bars like Fantasie on the King's Road and Moka Express – which had been opened by Gina Lollobrigida – on Frith Street had Formica-topped tables, a Gaggia machine, some pastries under a glass case on the counter and a jukebox in the corner.

Micheline loved the atmosphere and Bill Roper was not too old or too square to enjoy it too. Bill was amused by Micheline's stories about her clients. He loved her anecdotes, her tales of North London hostesses determined to use too much nail polish and hairspray and her views on the kind of fixtures and carpets that should one day grace her salon. She was becoming a minor celebrity too. Shortly after Ascot she had begun giving a series of three-minute talks on an afternoon BBC television programme called *Fashion and Beauty*. She had been booked by the husband of a client who was a TV producer and she got paid 12 guineas a session. Bill was impressed and for their next few encounters he took her to some of his favourite places. Expensive grown-up restaurants like L'Epicure and the Coq d'Or where the waiters wore tails and were all French, or pretended to be, and served chateaubriand and crêpe Suzette flambéed at their table. Micheline dressed up and he bought her flowers and pressed jewellery into her hands and over the caviar and champagne he told her something of his life story and the world that he worked in. Afterwards he took her on to places like the Pigalle Club in Piccadilly, where the owner and resident comedian, Al Burnett – 'the ham they could not cure' – still did the same schtick every night, or to every gangster's favourite nightclub, the Astor near Berkeley Square.

At some point in the autumn of 1959 Roper and Micheline became, in the coy language of the time, 'intimate'. Bill was determined to be discreet. He didn't want to upset Doris and the children and he didn't want to embarrass 'Mickey', as he called her, by showing up at her flat when her landlady might be around. But, like a number of his amorous bookmaking and racing colleagues, he'd long since made arrangements for situations like this. He owned a serviced flat in Stafford Court overlooking Kensington High Street – an extremely comfortable penthouse flat on the fifth floor. The singer Alma Cogan was one of his neighbours and had become a friend. It was the ideal setting for an affair and, despite the age difference and for all her strict Swiss upbringing, Micheline seems to have taken to the relationship with enthusiasm. Roper was often in the West End now after racing, reporting to Max or Cyril or both and it was easy to ring Doris and say that he was going to stay over in town rather than drive back out to Mill Hill. When he was returning late from the racecourse it was intoxicating to imagine getting back to Stafford Court and undressing his lovely young mistress, tangling with her high heels, her lipstick and her bouffant hair.

Roper was infatuated but he wasn't stupid. He didn't want to give the impression of being an old fool, losing his head over a much younger woman. He knew that what Micheline wanted was premises of her own, investment to develop her stock and publicity to launch it. Bill understood and said he would find her the money. The 54-year-old felt it was a price worth paying to continue to enjoy her youth and beauty. Roper was in an expansionary mood on his own account too, like much of the country as Prime Minister Harold Macmillan's consumer boom took hold. Change was in the air in the gambling community. High-stakes legal gaming clubs were starting to proliferate in the West End and, at the same time, bookmakers' representatives were in negotiations with the Home Office over the possible legalisation of off-course cash betting.[3]

Bill was beginning to think it would be a good time to strike out on his own. Max Parker had been ill for much

3 The bookmaking team was led by Archie Scott, an independent layer and Old Etonian who was related by marriage to the Ascot clerk of the course, General Dawnay.

of 1958 and Bill couldn't be sure how long he would go on or what kind of future he could expect under Cyril Stein. So why not try and profit directly from all his upmarket contacts and from all those Mayfair and Knightsbridge telephone numbers and clients with private boxes? A friend, Alex Willmore, who worked on the rails for the bookmaker Laurie Wallis, had already come to Bill with a proposal for a partnership that would combine a credit SP office with a rails pitch and would include a third investor. But serious money would be needed to fund both his own and Micheline's plans. He couldn't borrow against the house in Mill Hill. He had Doris's security and the boys' education to consider. But there were other ways a betting and racing man could raise cash, especially one as well informed as Mr Roper.

One of Bill's earliest formative experiences in Max Parker's employ came at Ascot in the autumn of 1948. The Clarence House Stakes, run on 23 September, was a race for two-year-olds only over six furlongs. It was considered a prestigious contest in its own right and also a stepping-stone to bigger things. There were only four runners that year but one of them, Royal Forest, was a son of the 1938 Derby winner Bois Roussel. The colt was owned by the whisky distilling Jockey Club member Reginald McDonald-Buchanan and trained at Beckhampton by Noel Murless. The then 38-year-old Murless – a future father-in-law of Sir Henry Cecil – would go on to the famous Warren Place stables in Newmarket and be recognised as one of the greatest British racehorse trainers of the 20th century. Murless was not a big punter himself but the beautifully bred horses in his care were often the subject of hefty support – and rumour and gossip – in the ring.

Royal Forest had an exalted reputation. He had won the Coventry Stakes at the royal meeting in June and such were the reports of his prowess on the gallops that he was sent off at an incredible 1-25, or 25 to one on, for the Clarence House. The odds meant that punters would have to place £25 on him just to win £1 and the bookies were betting 33-1 and upwards the rest. The ring couldn't see him getting beaten and the unbelievably short odds seemed designed to discourage all wagering. But one man, an owner and punter called Harold Dickson, decided to step in. He asked for a bet – all on credit – of £25,000 to win £1,000 and Maxie Parker accommodated him.

When the race got underway the Duke of Norfolk's horse Burpham made the running with Royal Forest a close second on the outside. The favourite's jockey was the number one man Gordon Richards, the gentle parfait knight of the weighing room who was nicknamed 'Moppy' by the bookies because of his shock of black hair. Richards seemed confident enough but, as they came past the two furlong pole, Burpham still leading, he tried to bustle up the favourite and nothing happened. Royal Forest didn't change gear and pull away as expected. He began to struggle. Richards had his whip out now but there was no response to that either. To the shock and incredulity of the racegoers in the stands, Burpham maintained his advantage all the way to the line. Royal Forest was a length and a half behind in second place. As the runners passed the winning post, one of the bookies turned in Harold Dickson's direction and called out, 'You had the £25,000, Harold. What did you need the extra grand for?' There was ribald laughter all around the ring – and Bill Roper and Max Parker may well have joined in – but the episode taught Roper an invaluable lesson.

Some punters would plunge on short-priced favourites no matter what and the bookmaker who was prepared to take them on could make a killing. Especially if he knew in advance that the favourite couldn't possibly win.

4

PHARMACEUTICAL ASSISTANCE

THERE WERE numerous instances of doping on British racecourses in the early 20th century. There were a number of American trainers and jockeys based in Newmarket at the time and their methods were innovative in more ways than one. The Jockey Club didn't get around to officially prohibiting dope, or what would nowadays be called performance-enhancing medication, until 1904 and the visitors, following practices that were widespread in the USA, regularly gave their runners a speedball of Benzedrine and cocaine when the money was down. Jockeys like the brothers Lester and Johnny Reiff, Skeets Martin and Tod Sloan allegedly rode to order for shadey US gamblers like *Boardwalk Empire*'s Arnold Rothstein who fixed baseball's 1919 World Series and always liked to have everything in his favour.

Most of the Yanks went home after the First World War but rumours about doping lived on and, in the 1940s and '50s, a lot of the stories involved the French. Bookmakers were illegal in France, although this didn't prevent the existence of several illegal high-stakes layers, and then, as now, the unfortunate French public had to make do with the indifferent service of the state-run Tote or PMU.[4] But the leading owners all had accounts with bookmakers in England and they loved to try and catch out Max Parker or William Hill with a craftily plotted coup in an English race, be it a classic at Epsom or a humble 'seller'.[5]

For their part, the bookies were philosophical about the French pulling off a touch with a horse that was winning on its merits even if that ability had been disguised in the run-up to the race. Plenty of English trainers got up to those sort of tricks. But what really exercised the gambling fraternity and members of the press, was the suspicion that the Frogs were sometimes inclined to give their horses a little pharmaceutical assistance to make them run faster.

The Sporting Life's man, Geoffrey Hamlyn, had no doubt he'd witnessed something dodgy at Doncaster in 1951 when there was a massive raceday gamble on the French colt Talma II in the St Leger. The horse, who was named after a famous French actor of the Napoleonic era, was owned by the textile tycoon Marcel Boussac and trained at Chantilly by Charlie Semblat. He had little worthwhile form to his name but Boussac's horses were winning everywhere at the time and that alone seemed to justify the market confidence.

---

4 Bookmakers were outlawed in France in 1891 and all legal betting there on horse racing is with the Paris Mutuel Urbain or PMU.

5 A selling race is traditionally the lowest class of contest on the Turf. The winner is automatically put up for auction straight after the race.

In the half-hour before the off, Talma was backed to win an astonishing £100,000 (or over £3million in 2013 money) and he started 7-1 second favourite. His supporters never had a moment's worry. The race was a procession, the French challenger winning by ten lengths in a lather of sweat. 'There is no doubt that a dope test would've been ordered today,' said Hamlyn in 1994. 'Although starting favourite for the next two Ascot Gold Cups, Talma never won another race in England, nor, I believe, anywhere else.'

Jackie Dyer says the bookies were all equally convinced that Talma had been buzzed up. 'They flew him in to Doncaster late that morning and he went straight back on the plane as soon as the race was over. Everyone in the ring was talking about it and it wasn't only the French horse there were stories about.'

Some post-war English trainers got hold of stimulants too and when a hurdler called Woolpack fell at Doncaster in 1948, killing his jockey, he was found to have traces of Benzedrine in his system. But the thing about doping to win was that it only really benefited those punters and connections who were in on the plot. Whereas when a horse was nobbled, it was invariably the bookmakers, those stern scourges of French impropriety, who were at the root of it. The bookies were rarely caught but, from time to time, some gambling jockey or stable lad who had lent them his assistance would be made an example of.

In the spring of 1960, an ageing stableman called Bert 'Bandy' Rogers blew his brains out with a shotgun after being quizzed by Scotland Yard detectives investigating the doping of horses at the stable of Sir Gordon Richards – as he was now – at Ogbourne Maizey near Marlborough. The 66-year-old Rogers feared that he would either have to lie on oath or incriminate his co-conspirators who included a chemist's dispenser from Staffordshire. He faced ruin either way. The case came to trial at Gloucester Assizes in October 1960 and two of the defendants were sent to prison. But the Rogers gang were amateurs and the sums of money they won would barely have covered Max Parker's monthly telephone bill.

By comparison, the massive conspiracy that began in 1953, fuelled initially by the obsessions and fascinations of Edward 'Teddy' Smith, nicknamed 'The Witch Doctor', and subsequently masterminded by Bill Roper, would rock British horse racing to its roots.

Ted Smith's natural habitat was the urban-suburban borderland of Surrey and South West London. New Malden. Worcester Park. Motspur Park. England in the early 1950s. Fog and rain. Bus stops and train strikes. Drab parades of pre-war shops and mock Tudor barns of pubs like the Toby Jug on Kingston Bypass. Billiard Halls. Station Caffs. Chip shops. Not the sort of places that Lord Rosebery or the Duke of Norfolk would ever be seen in. But a home from home for Teddy Boys and market traders. Juvenile delinquents and stable lads. Ted liked the smoky interiors of the pubs and the billiard parlours and he liked betting on horses and greyhounds. He was a Hurst Park man. An Epsom, Kempton and Sandown regular and he liked an evening at the dogs too. Ted had his moments as a punter. Good times and drunken pleasures, easy money and powerful friends, and, had it not been for one drunken, boastful afternoon at Brighton races in August 1962 he might have lived a lot longer to enjoy them.

Smith, who was born in 1925, was a tall, gaunt man and prematurely grey. He was employed for a while as a male nurse at Roehampton psychiatric hospital but then, in 1953, he started work as a laboratory clerk at Bayer Products, a manufacturing chemist in West Molesey. The lab was part of the old industrial estate on Central Avenue, one of a row of square brick buildings surrounded by dimly lit streets equidistant from the Island Barn Reservoir and the Thames at Hurst Park. It was the kind of suburban no man's land where black marketeers might safely park hijacked lorries full of cigarettes or nylons and where determined men could go about their business after dark with little fear of detection.

The tablet production manager at Bayer was Richard McGee, a 40-year-old ex-grammar school boy who had a wife and four children and a house in Harlesden in North West London. In 1953 McGee's marriage collapsed and his wife left him for another man. Ted Smith offered friendship and support to his older colleague. He became his regular drinking companion and the two men engaged in long, late-night sessions that sometimes ended with McGee sleeping on the sofa in Smith's Surbiton flat. There was later speculation, unconfirmed, that their relationship was more than just platonic. This was an era when a married man like McGee, even a cuckolded one, would have flinched from revelations that might have endangered his position at work, as well as placing him outside the law. But the pair were indisputably close and Smith's support, affection even, when his friend's life seemed to be at its lowest ebb, appears to have left McGee feeling that he was eternally in Teddy Smith's debt.

A staple topic of conversation during the coffee breaks and lunch hours at Bayer was horse and dog racing and Ted Smith, who read the *Life* and *Sporting Chronicle* every day, was always full of gossip and theories. He would look at the photographs of racing and gambling big shots, like Prince Aly Khan and his new wife Rita Hayworth, and he'd read the adverts by amenable sounding tipsters with names like the 'The Major' and 'The Investor' and he'd think, 'Why shouldn't a couple of decent fellows like Ted Smith and Dick McGee have a shot at winning a few bob too?'

Over a snooker session at the Charter pub on Epsom High Street, Smith had got to know an apprentice jockey called 'Dandy' McGreevy who worked at Peter Thrale's stable on Epsom Downs. Dandy was a young Irish tearaway who wanted to improve his financial prospects and didn't fancy his chances of ever getting the leg up on a Derby winner. He told Smith about the stories he'd heard about ingenious strokes and gambles, including thieving French gambles, and they both talked about the big winning bets that, since 1950, were reported in the *Life* every day.

If the Frenchies could get hold of cocaine and Benzedrine, reasoned Dandy McGreevy, then why couldn't English and Irish lads do the same? But Ted Smith wasn't interested in doping to win. As he explained to Dandy, he'd always thought there was a lot more money to be made if you had the means to make a racehorse lose. A well-backed favourite for example. Imagine what a bookmaker would pay for that knowledge?

Smith went back to Bayer and shared his thoughts with Richard McGee who was an expert on the effects of tablets. McGee suggested phenobarbitone which had soporific and hypnotic qualities and depressed the central nervous system. It was manufactured at Bayer under its trade name, Luminal, along with other drugs whose base was phenobarbitone including luminal sodium, a particularly quick acting form of the barbiturate. At Smith's behest, McGee stole a small quantity of Luminal, and despite the laboratory's security checks – or more probably because the security was so lax – smuggled it out and into the hands of his grateful friend. A few nights later Smith showed the goods to Dandy McGreevy in the gents in the Charter and Dandy, ignoring the dictum that too much contact with the gambling fraternity can be prejudicial to a young jockey's health, phoned his friendly local bookie.

Bernard Howard was the self-styled Mister Big of New Malden and cock of the suburban walk. He had a credit betting office, a nice house on Buxton Drive, not far from Malden Golf Club, and seems to have aspired to Bill Roper's lifestyle but on a smaller scale. Gerry Parker, a former boxer and betting ring face who once worked for the gangster Jack Spot, knew Howard well and describes him as 'a lovely fella. A diamond'.

Bernie had pitches at Epsom, Kempton and Sandown Park and after the war he had enjoyed a reputation as a high-stakes layer at the old pony-racing course at Hawthorn Hill. He had contacts in the West End too. Not as socially impressive as Roper's or Max Parker's maybe, but wealthy men like the bookmaker Jack Swift who had an office on Dover Street and who was known facetiously as 'Chuckles' due to his grouchy demeanour. Swift's son Brian, a future trainer, went on to marry Loretta Breasley, the daughter of the great Australian jockey Arthur 'Scobie' Breasley who duelled regularly with Lester Piggott and rode some of the best horses in training.

Howard set up a discreet evening meeting with Smith and McGreevy and, after being shown the luminal sodium, he named a horse in Peter Thrale's stable that he would be happy to see lose next time out. Dandy duly doped the horse on the day of its next race, mixing – as McGee had advised – two level tablespoons of Luminal with four tablespoons of water and giving it to the unfortunate horse by mouth. It seemed to work all right because the horse lost and an appreciative Bernie Howard, who had laid it at a point or two over the odds to his unsuspecting punters, gave Smith £50 (£1,000 today), which he shared with McGee, along with a further £25 for Dandy McGreevy.

Over the next two years the trio colluded in half a dozen more dopings and, each time, Howard bet against the doped horses on course and shared his information, at a price, with a few select bookies like Jack Swift. But in the devious and Masonic world that Max Parker, Bill Roper and the rest of the boys were trading in, it's probable that they too would have known about Bernie's little scams before long and been able to adjust their books accordingly.

During the course of 1954 and 1955, Ted Smith received

around £700 from Bernie Howard while Dandy McGreevy earned in the region of £200. All this at a time when many teenage stable lads were on a basic rate of two shillings and sixpence a week. Dandy began living not wisely but too well and, at the end of 1955, he was dismissed from Thrale's employ and drifted out of racing altogether. But other stable lads were keen to take his place.

Norman Pope, who also worked for Thrale and had heard rumours about the mysterious Ted Smith and his magic potions, sought out Smithie in the Charter and told him that he'd like to make some money. Ted told him to give him the names of some more fancied local horses and, after consulting with Bernie Howard, a few of them were doped. But Norman Pope was from the Norman Wisdom school of racecourse racketeering and one evening, travelling back to Epsom on the bus after meeting Ted Smith at his place in Surbiton, he thought it would be fun to try some of the drugs himself. He proceeded to taste the crystals of luminal sodium on his tongue and then swallowed the lot. Even a mild phenobarbitone overdose is enough to cause hypertension, hyperthermia and a slowing of all bodily functions and, by the time Pope got out on Epsom High Street he was feeling 'a bit peaky'. So he popped into the Charter and had a couple of Brown Ales. But unfortunately they didn't improve things. By now Pope was sweating profusely and when he looked at his face in the mirror he was so alarmed by his appearance that he stumbled round to Dorking Road Hospital where he told the doctors he thought he 'might be going down with something'. He was behaving oddly enough for the hospital to keep him in under observation for three days and when he was discharged he took to his bed for a month, staying well clear of Ted Smith and the Charter pub.

That was the end of Pope the Dope's role in race fixing and, for the time being, it was the end of Bernard Howard too. In July 1956, Diamond Bernie ended up in the dock at the Old Bailey but not for defrauding punters or bribing stable lads. Bernie was charged with fiddling his tax returns by falsifying the daily record sheets in his racecourse ledger. According to the prosecution, Howard and his clerk, Richard Silver of Kingston Vale, had understated Bernie's earnings by £41,000 over a five-year period, defrauding the Inland Revenue of £32,000 in tax. On one occasion a profit of £900 that the book had made on a day's racing was written up as a loss of £114 by the simple ruse of entering fake losing bets that had never been struck.

Bernie was compelled to disclose the contents of his bank account which showed a credit balance of £38,000 compared to just £400 five years before. He tried to claim that his increased wealth was all down to successful punting which would not have been taxable and, of course, he was betting successfully against Teddy Smith's doped horses but he couldn't reveal that to the authorities. On 20 July 1956 he was sentenced to 18 months' imprisonment and fined £5,000 while Dick Silver got nine months and a £1,000 fine.[6]

6 Bernie Howard spent part of his sentence on the Isle of Sheppey where he met and befriended George Walker, brother of the boxer Billy Walker and a future owner of the William Hill betting shop chain. Walker, who also went on to found Brent Walker, was inside for stealing a lorryload of nylons.

With Howard out of circulation, Ted Smith had lost his backer and when, in April 1957, the West Molesey laboratory suddenly closed, it appeared that he had lost his supplier too. Bayer's work was transferred to the Winthrop laboratory at Fawdon in Newcastle Upon Tyne and Richard McGee went with the business, moving home to the North East and hoping to start a new life.

Ted Smith could have gone to work for Winthrop in Newcastle too but he decided to accept a cash pay-off and stay in his native Surrey and South West London. There may have been no doped horses to bet on during the summer of 1957 but the newly unemployed Ted, with funds in his pocket, spent more time than ever around Epsom's racing pubs, drinking his brown and mild and breathing in the talk about tips, plots and coups which hung as heavy in the air as the smoke from the lads' Woodbines and Players Number Six.

It was the monochrome underside of Bill Roper's world, populated by the thriftless but the ever hopeful and they were all big winners in the pub after five or six pints. But one day Ted met a charming, sly, cockney jockey who, like Dandy McGreevy and Norman Pope, was out for what he could get and prepared to go a whole lot further to achieve it.

Emmanuel Lipman Leonard Steward, nicknamed 'Darkie', was born in Bethnal Green in December 1932. Evacuated from London during the Blitz, he left school in Sheerness in Kent at the age of 14, and began working as an apprentice at Harold Wallington's yard in Epsom. He did a ten-year stint at the Burgh Road stable, riding his share of winners around the gaffe tracks and acquiring his nickname after a horse kicked him in the eye. The rogue colt didn't damage Darkie's confidence or good looks but, whether due to a lack of talent or luck or application or all three, he was unable to break through to the next level.

On one occasion he rode the favourite for Peter Thrale in a two-horse race at Folkestone. The trainer's instructions as he mounted up were short and to the point. 'Whatever you do, don't finish in front of the other one.' Darkie did as he was told and the trainer duly won his bet but the runner-up's owner was furious and demanded that Darkie never ride for him again. Maybe the cynicism of that episode was the tipping point but, by the mid-1950s, Darkie was growing tired of the hard graft of an apprentice jockey's life which, in many yards, was still positively feudal.

The jump jockey David Mould, who rode with great distinction for Peter Cazalet and the Queen Mother at Fairlawne, began, like Darkie Steward, as a 14-year-old apprentice on the flat. Mould, whose father was a horse dealer, was at Staff Ingham's yard in Epsom – a near neighbour of Harold Wallington – and when he started out in 1954 he weighed four-and-a-half stone. In common with Willie Carson, who started work at 14 at Gerald Armstrong's stable in North Yorkshire, young Mould was paid half a crown a week for a working day that began with mucking out at five o'clock every morning and he got one half-day off a fortnight. At least Mould had a hostel to sleep in. Some lads bunked down on a straw-filled mattress on the floor or even in the stalls of the horses they looked after. Others could still expect to be subjected to regular thrashings by tyrannical trainers who believed it was the only way to turn boys into men.

In the 1950s and '60s the majority of the owners that Mould and Carson rode for were men of great wealth and power including Jockey Club members and rich industrialists. Their seeming indifference to the conditions of their staff is hard to reconcile with basic notions of workplace decency. But it was also monumentally counter-productive. It must be stressed that there were hundreds of stable lads who toiled away honourably for years despite the harsh environment, giving a lifetime of uncomplaining service to their employers and, in particular, to the beloved horses in their care. But at the bottom of the pyramid there was a pool of hungry and disaffected labourers who had negligible rights or representation and gambled regularly to supplement their income and, as the bookmakers realised, many of them were ripe for grooming by smooth-talking chancers offering them a shot at easy money.

In 1957 Darkie Steward took a year out from stable life, working on a building site in Epsom and sharing digs with a nice boy called Brian Perry who shared Darkie's fantasies about Italian suits and scooters but was only about half as intelligent. In the evenings and at weekends, the pair went to dance halls, pubs and dog tracks together and one night in the Toby Jug in Kingston, Darkie met Ted Smith and discovered that the two of them had interests and friends in common. When Darkie was working at Harold Wallington's yard he often used to go around with Dandy McGreevy and he had also given Norman Pope driving lessons. Darkie met

Ted's new lady, May Kibble, an unmarried mother of four young children, and Smith met Darkie's girlfriend, Sylvia Cross, the glamorous daughter of an antiques dealer.

In 1958 Darkie went back to work as a stable lad and, over the next 18 months, he moved from trainer to trainer, never lasting long with any of them. But wherever he went, on course and off, he heard stories about Teddy Smith and the gear he was rumoured to carry around with him in his pockets as if he was dealing Bennies and Purple Hearts. The Epsom lads had a name for him now. They called him 'The Witch Doctor'. Anything you desired to fix a race and straighten a horse, Ted Smith could make your dreams come true. But when Darkie eventually asked Smith what he could give him to make a horse win, the Witch Doctor had a problem. He only had stopping drugs in Surbiton, barbiturates like luminal sodium, and, with McGee up in Newcastle, it might not be easy to get his hands on anything else.

Ted rang his old drinking companion at his new office and asked his advice. McGee initially baulked at the idea of getting Ted drugs from Winthrop's lab. He'd rather hoped that phase of his life was behind him and he didn't want to start stealing Benzedrine or cocaine. So, in all seriousness, he suggested to Ted Smith that he went out and bought a bottle of Metatone and that's what Ted did, paying three shillings and sixpence for it in a chemist in Stoneleigh. He went home and poured it into a plain bottle and then a few days later he sold it to Darkie Steward for £5 at Lingfield races. Darkie slipped a dose to one of Harold Wallington's runners that Saturday and the horse ran well but finished outside the first four.

If Steward was aware that the miracle elixir he had acquired was in fact a standard high street tonic, he was careful not to say so to his two new friends, well-connected friends, who had supplied him with the £5 note. Joe Lowry and Jackie Dyer were proper punters and racecourse faces. They wore bespoke suits and camel hair coats. They knew Bernie Howard, who was a free man again and making a book at Wimbledon dogs, and, more importantly, they were associates of and regular putters-on for Mr William Roper.

Lowry, who was 45 in 1959, was another East Ender like Darkie Steward and Max Parker and, like the Parker/Stein boys, he hailed from Forest Gate. He officially described himself as a stallholder in the Queen's Road Market in Upton Park but, when he wasn't involved in minor acts of villainy – and by the late 1950s he already had 12 previous convictions, including three years for office breaking in 1946 – he made his living from betting on the racecourse. Joe – who was the spitting image of the comedian and *Carry On* actor Sid James – was what the milieu referred to as an 'earwigger' which meant that he was always hanging around the rails, ears open for news and information. Everyone liked Joe. You couldn't dislike him. He was friendly, generous and an incorrigible punter and, among the big betting ring players, he had particular regard for Bill Roper, a man he 'admired and looked up to'.

Jackie Dyer, who was born in 1924 and came from West London, was a bookmaker through and through. He began working as a bookie's clerk when he was 12 years old and he had retained the plump face and boyish smile of a perennial Artful Dodger. In his teens he was taking bets for a street bookie in Fulham and in 1953 he got 12 months for running an illegal betting shop. In 1958 he was ill and lost a kidney but he'd continued working as a racecourse bookmaker at all the big tracks around London and the south of England and he also called the odds at White City, Stamford Bridge and Catford dog stadiums.

Joe and Jackie were typical of many men in 1959 who would have chosen no other life but bookmaking and racing. Jackie still looks back fondly to the camaraderie of the old betting ring. 'You went early. You mixed. You had a drink. If someone was ill or had a bad day, there was a whip round. It's not like that now.' But they also believed that you couldn't be too particular if you wanted to show a profit and, when an opportunity arose, you had to have the nerve and the inclination to go for it.

According to Bernie Howard's old friend Gerry Parker, Jackie 'sometimes carried a gun' although more for protection than first use. If he had a weakness it was a tendency to bet on everything, even when the odds weren't in his favour. It was said that he wanted to back every winner and lay every losing favourite but his indiscriminate approach proved costly in the long run.

Bill Roper saw Jackie and Joe on a weekly and even daily basis. They were his crew: he used Jackie to help him get money on when he was working a commission in the ring and he paid Joe to keep him supplied with information.

Lowry was free with his tips and opinions, advising Roper that such and such a horse 'stays longer than the mother-in-law' and would be a good bet in a long-distance handicap whereas a short-priced rival 'wouldn't get the trip in a taxi'. And as for some Fancy Dan trainer from the Lambourn area, he was so crooked that 'he couldn't lay straight in bed at night'. Bill would laugh and shake his head but the drinks were on him when the right horse won.

Joe specialised in cultivating jockeys and stable lads, especially in Newmarket which was his favourite racecourse. Indeed he popped up so often in the headquarters of British racing that other faces used to joke that he was the bookmakers' official Newmarket correspondent. Friday and Saturday nights and any nights after a local meeting, Joe would be there in the regular watering holes, buying drinks all round, dispensing cigarettes and bonhomie and insuring that everyone knew he was their friend, generous with it and the kind of man you'd want to keep onside.

With the information at his disposal, Joe wanted to try and engineer a result in his and Jackie's favour and, in the summer of 1959, Darkie Steward (who had been putting himself about along the rails and was also known to Bill Roper) set up a meeting between them and Ted Smith at Ted's Surbiton flat. The two men, who were charming to May Kibble and brought gifts for her youngest daughter, explained to Smith in private that there was serious money to be made, much more than Bernie Howard had given him, if he could keep them regularly supplied.

The following day Ted rang Richard McGee in Newcastle and told him of his new clients. His friend was in financial difficulties again. It was proving costly to keep up with his children while they were down in London and he was living in the North East. The prospect of earning £20 a month for raiding the Winthrop Laboratory store cupboard was just too tempting. So, with a heavy heart, McGee agreed to send Ted a fresh consignment of luminal sodium in the post.

The Witch Doctor was back in business.

5

AN UNFOLDING CONSPIRACY

THROUGHOUT 1959 Micheline Lugeon had continued working at Fortnum & Mason by day despite her long evenings teaching students and developing her own products. From time to time Bill Roper dropped in on her at work. He loved the sensual and tactile atmosphere of the Fortnums' perfumery department. The racecourse betting ring was a tactile place, all grabbing hand gestures and fistfuls of money, but it was a hoarse-throated, masculine atmosphere reeking of spirits and cigar smoke. Walking across the thick pile carpet at Fortnums and breathing in the scent of Balmain, Arpège and Givenchy, Bill felt himself drenched by an intoxicating aura of femininity and sex.

If there was no racing that afternoon, Bill might join Micheline for a quick lunch in Fortnums' Patio Restaurant which was situated, unusually, in the travel department and served smoked trout, chicken pancakes and ice cream. But in the evenings they continued to go to L'Epicure or Chez Victor in Wardour Street where you could eat very well for about £5 (£90) for two and Bill knew the maitre d' and supplied him with tips.

On the night of Saturday 8 August 1959 there was good cause to celebrate. Faultless Speech, the Harold Wallington-trained horse that had been a winning tip of Bill's in the Royal Hunt Cup at Ascot in June, won the William Hill Gold Cup at Redcar and it seems that everyone was on. Not just Bill and Micheline and Max Parker but Darkie Steward and Joe Lowry and Jackie Dyer and a number of grateful and influential men in the Old Compton Street area. Some say it was a fixed race and that the horse was doped to win with a Benzedrine-based supplement. Others insist it was just 'a good thing at the weights', meaning it was the form pick, laid out for the race since Ascot and, in betting ring parlance, 'off for its life'. Either way, Darkie Steward, the former Wallington employee, knew the inside track. The mile contest, worth nearly £7,000 to the winner, which was twice the prize for the Hunt Cup, was one of three valuable handicaps run at Redcar each season and there had been a lively betting market. Faultless Speech was returned at 11-8 on course having been available at 3-1 in places and Bill Roper's money had gone on early. The jockey Geoff Lewis, who was making his first ever visit to Redcar, held his mount up for the first three-quarters of a mile and then quickened into the lead inside the final furlong and won well.

Roper had topped up Micheline's bet and there was another few hundred quid to go towards her shop while Micheline could splash out on new Bear Brand pure silk stockings from Selfridges, iron-grey suede gloves from the Glove Shop in Bond Street and a new Hardy Amies camel hair and wool short coat and matching skirt for the autumn. Darkie Steward could afford to go shopping too. Roper gave him a 'monkey' (£500) for his information and Lowry and Dyer paid him £300 each.

Bill would have had a double cause to celebrate that weekend had one other plot gone according to plan. Roper had been advised by Joe Lowry and Jackie Dyer that a horse called Providence should be opposed in the one mile Bunbury Stakes which was the last race on the card at Newmarket at 5 p.m. The three-year-old, trained locally by Fergie Sutherland, was to be the first doping job organised by Lowry, Dyer and Steward with a little help from Ted Smith. To get at Providence, they were dependent on the co-operation of one of Sutherland's stable lads, Michael Heffernan, who had worked in Newmarket for 20 years, and another younger lad called Jimmy Hilliard who worked for a neighbouring trainer. Heffernan and Hilliard were to share £20 each for giving Providence 'something that would make it lose' and to make it easier for them the dope was disguised in a toffee bar. But when Heffernan went into Providence's box at 1 a.m. on the Friday night, Hilliard keeping guard outside, his nerve failed him and his clumsiness spooked the horse. Providence spat out the dope and so far from losing the Bunbury Stakes, for which he started 6-4 favourite, he made all the running and won easily by three lengths.

Jackie Dyer was unhappy afterwards. He had laid Providence on course and lost money. Bill Roper had lost on the race too but he was philosophical about it. He'd no sooner have tipped off the authorities than he'd have applied to become a Mercury astronaut but he knew that Michael Heffernan – to his credit, in Bill's view – had been uneasy about doping a horse he'd cared for. So Roper suggested to Joe Lowry that he pop up to Newmarket and have a chat with Heffernan at his home, Number 38 Lisburn Road, which in the 1950s was a rather tatty, terraced street of two-up two-down houses with lavatories in the back garden. Ironically Newmarket police station was only just around the corner. Heffernan asked along his friend Jimmy Hilliard and he suggested they invite another lad, Philip 'Snuffy' Lawler who worked for Noel Murless, Newmarket's number one man. For Lowry and Dyer, getting close to a trusted employee at Murless's blue chip yard was like wartime German spies getting wind of the Allies' invasion plans. But Joe, an old hand at bribery and corruption, knew that they had to be patient with their sources and work on them step by step.

Over the beers and the Smiths' Crisps, Lowry chatted away amiably about the intricacies of doping, comporting himself like a cross between a kindly careers officer and the fox in Pinocchio. He assured the lads that the dope they'd be using would do the horses no long-term harm, which was true in some cases but not in others, and that the horses would feel no fear or pain, which was a lie. He told them that on the flat, at least, there was no danger to the jockey, which was also a lie, and he promised that no trainer would want to admit that one of his runners had been got at because he'd be frightened of the reaction of the stewards, which was true.

At the time the Jockey Club's policy on doping was draconian but ineffectual. The Club held that a trainer was solely responsible for the safe custody of his horses and any trainer whose charges tested positive for drugs, no matter how innocent he might be, was automatically warned off and had his licence withdrawn. When a trainer was warned off, notice of his exclusion would be printed in the *Racing Calendar* and might be reported in newspapers like *The Times*. In 1931 a trainer called Clive Chapman was so aggrieved at being warned off after a horse of his failed a dope test, and so upset at having his name posted in the press like a criminal, that he sued the Jockey Club for libel. He was initially successful but the Club managed to get the verdict overturned on appeal. When Chapman attempted to re-apply for his licence a few years later his temerity in challenging the Club was held against him by Lord Rosebery in particular who ruled, as only he could, 'that man took us on. He shall not come back.'

The situation was compounded by the lack of any consistent or automatic dope testing of either winners or well-backed losers. Those official dope-testing procedures that did exist were often inaccurate and misleading with analysts seemingly incapable of distinguishing between traces of substances that might have been prescribed quite legitimately by a recognised vet and stimulants or depressants designed to fix a race. This lack of scientific rigour and consistency, allied to the Jockey Club's pig-headed and vindictive approach towards often innocent men, made things a whole lot easier for Joe Lowry, Jackie Dyer, Darkie Steward and their friends.

With not just one but three Newmarket stable lads now recruited to the gang, Lowry and Dyer went back to see Teddy Smith who had received the fresh luminal sodium in the post from McGee. It was Smith's job to make up the doses of the drug, each one ground into a bolus, wrapped in silver paper and then bound with elastic bands. The packaging was designed to delay, by about 12 hours, the process by which the horse's digestive juices broke down the dope, slowly releasing it into the system and leaving the rubber bands to be passed out as droppings.

Ted got £25 a dose. For a horse weighing 1,000lbs, McGee had advised that a sufficient dose to 'switch it off' would be 20 to 25 grains. Ted often used 80 grains. McGee said that the drug worked in around half to three-quarters of an hour and the effect would last up to four hours. So the doping would have to be done by the stable lads themselves on the day of the race, probably in the horsebox or at the racecourse stables.

Saturday 12 September was the Variety Club's Charity Raceday at Sandown Park. The guests of honour were Jayne Mansfield and Gina Lollobrigida and Bill Roper was there too with his special guest Miss Micheline Lugeon, the Mayfair beautician. For Micheline it was a welcome break from work and another taste of the seductive and escapist world of horse racing. Other guests who knew about Bill's complicated domestic arrangements were too polite to ask about the long-suffering Doris (who was at home in Mill Hill) and the couple enjoyed champagne and lunch in the Variety Club tent, hosted by the holiday camp king Billy

Butlin. It was a warm, dry, late-summer day and during the afternoon Roper had a word or two in the betting ring with Joe Lowry and Jackie Dyer who had not been invited to lunch at the Variety Club.

Lowry told Roper he'd had a phone call that morning from Michael Heffernan in Newmarket, following a chat with Snuffy Lawler. It was standard practice for the local trainers to work their horses on Wednesday and Saturday mornings and two eye-catchers that weekend had been Open Sky and Off Key who were both trained by Noel Murless. The colt Open Sky was entered at Yarmouth the following Wednesday while Off Key was expected to contest a two-year-old race at Brighton on the same day. Off Key had run in the Coventry Stakes at Royal Ascot in June and the Brighton event represented a sharp drop in class. Lowry and Dyer already had the Brighton card under consideration. It was expected that a course specialist called Accompanist, trained in Lambourn by the spry Irishman Farnham Maxwell, would run in the five-furlong sprint at the end of the afternoon. But according to Darkie Steward, Dick Thrale – cousin of Peter – might have a fancied runner in that one too.

Lowry and Dyer made their plans. Open Sky, Off Key and Accompanist would all be doped on the day of the races with Snuffy Lawler taking care of things in Newmarket and Darkie catching up with Accompanist with the help of an old Epsom friend who now worked down at Maxwell's yard. Jackie Dyer, who was going to Brighton, would lay the doped horses at over the odds and back Indigenous, the Thrale runner in the Brighton sprint, with his own and his firm's money. Bill Roper would also lay the doped horses on course and through Max Parker's credit office and back Indigenous on his own account.

There had been a prolonged dry spell in the south and the ground at Brighton was as hard as paving stones. Conditions were little better at Yarmouth and losing punters may have attributed their misfortune to the going. But, from the dopers' perspective, it was a very satisfactory day and the stable lads all did their jobs as instructed. Open Sky led for the first mile at Yarmouth but then weakened quickly and finished second to last. Off Key was a well-beaten third at Brighton, having been backed into 5-2 second favourite and then, in the last race, the five-furlong Southwick Handicap, Accompanist, the 11-8 favourite, was a disappointing fourth. Indigenous won all right and was returned at 9-4 but the jockey, one R. Podmore, almost cocked it up. Told to come late by connections, he went to the front three furlongs from home and his mount was tiring rapidly near the line.

There are no records and no oral testimony to tell exactly how much Roper, Dyer, Lowry and the others won from mug punters outside the bookmaking loop that fine September Wednesday. Brighton and Yarmouth were second division 'gaffe' tracks and the on-course market not on a par with a major metropolitan course like Ascot. But three horses had been nobbled on the same day and three races profitably fixed and the dopers had the satisfaction of knowing that, thanks to Teddy Smith's gear, it could be done again. Next time they'd aim for a much bigger target and next time Bill

Roper would commit serious money for himself and Max Parker.

The unfolding conspiracy had already moved on from a purely Epsom perspective to Newmarket and beyond and now news of it was beginning to reach the West End. The area around Frith Street and Old Compton Street in 1959/60 was Soho's own version of the Brooklyn neighbourhood depicted in Martin Scorsese's film *Goodfellas*, with Albert Dimes, bookmaker and racing enthusiast, taking the role of the Robert De Niro alpha male.

'Italian Albert', as he was sometimes called, was born in 1915 and his family name was Dimeo. Tall, dark and handsome, he had taken over the mantle of the Sabinis who had been the dominant mobsters in London in the 1920s and '30s. Albert was a close associate of the celebrity gangster Billy Hill (not to be confused with William), and the pair had been involved in a power struggle with the Jewish gang leader Jack Spot, Gerry Parker's old pal and the one-time 'King of the Underworld'. At stake was the control of bookmaking pitches on racing and point-to-point tracks throughout southern England. When Spot was forced to 'retire' and Hill backed out of the picture, it was Italian Albert who, like Mr Colleoni in *Brighton Rock*, emerged as the bookmakers' new patron and protector.

Dimes ran a legal, credit bookmaking business from an office in Frith Street, and dozens of illegal, street bookmaking pitches in the West End.

He also controlled the pitches at a number of racetracks including Epsom, where he had all the business on the

Downs, the lower and Silver Ring at Newmarket and Lingfield and the so-called free side at places like Lewes, Brighton and Salisbury. At Epsom, which was the biggest money-spinner, Albert paid the council directly and, as one of his old employees puts it, 'he saw [to it] there were no welshers'.[7]

There were rules, naturally. If Albert's pitches were going 6-4 about a horse, another firm couldn't go 7-4. And if another bookmaker, or a professional gambler, was trying to engineer a coup at one of Albert's tracks, like Brighton, it was expected that, out of courtesy, he would inform Albert in advance so that he could take advantage. The bookies were all men of the world and they didn't need a detailed explanation of what might happen to them if they flouted the convention.

Dimes had a penchant for talking business in Soho cafés and he was to be found ensconced in one every morning. He relished the cakes in the Patisserie Valerie (the original on Old Compton Street, not the modern chain version) and he also liked to go to the Italian café, the 2i's, which was just around the corner from his office. Lonnie Donnegan used to do skiffle sessions in the basement at lunchtimes but, mid-morning, Albert might be in there studying the form with villains like Franny Daniels and Frankie Fraser. Sometimes the actor Stanley Baker would be there too: he

---

7 Stan Davis, now in his 90s, worked for Albert Dimes and put up the bookmakers' joints – meaning the equipment with which they plied their trade from their pitches in the ring – the night before a race meeting.

was mad keen about racing and he and Albert were very good friends.

Darkie Steward was another of Albert's good friends. He was passing on tips and information for the occasional reward, including the positive message about Faultless Speech before the William Hill Gold Cup for which an appreciative Albert paid him £100. He was also playing a leading role in Joe Lowry and Jackie Dyer's enterprise and it was almost certainly Darkie who tipped off Albert about Accompanist. As the autumn of 1959 rolled on, Darkie and his friends were planning their next doping job and Albert would have to be told about that one too. It was to be a major scam in which Bill Roper would be a fully fledged accomplice, sharing the laying of the doped favourite and dividing up the spoils.

6

CROSSING THE LINE

ONE OF the challenges facing Micheline Lugeon in her relationship with Roper was, if not to match, then at least to share his interest in horse racing. Bill was giving her tutorials on the leading owners, trainers and jockeys and, in the autumn of 1959, he may well have told her about the unprecedented run of Noel Murless whose stable had amassed £117,000 in winnings with almost two months of the season still to go.

Murless had the best horses such as the brilliant grey filly, Petite Etoile, who was owned and bred by the Aga Khan and his son Prince Aly,[8] and another of his leading patrons was the 77-year-old Sir Victor Sassoon, an immensely rich baronet and banker whose career and financial interests stretched from Shanghai to the Bahamas. In 1959 Sir Victor

---

8 Prince Aly Khan, father of the present Aga Khan, was an ardent betting and racing enthusiast and one of Europe's leading owner-breeders. He died in a car crash in Paris in May 1960.

was living in retirement on Cable Beach with his American wife Barnesie (his former nurse, Evelyn Barnes), but his stud farm near Newmarket continued to breed top-quality thoroughbreds. Sassoon's peacock blue and old gold colours had already been carried to victory in the Derby on three occasions – leading him to joke that 'the only race better than the Derby is the Jewish race' – and hopes were high at Warren Place that St Paddy, a bay colt by the Queen's stallion Aureole, could make it four.

Murless was renowned for not rushing his horses and St Paddy didn't see a racecourse until the Acomb Stakes at York on 18 August. It was the first day of the prestigious Ebor meeting and all the high rollers were there. St Paddy's reputation had preceeded him and he opened up at 5-2 in the ring but then drifted out to 5-1 before being backed back in to 3-1 at the off. Prince Aly Khan placed a bet of £4,000 on him with Ladbrokes, having been assured by Noel Murless that this was his Derby horse for the following year.

The big two-year-old pulled hard on his way down to the start and when the race got under way, Lester Piggott attempted to settle him some way off the pace. But there were 18 runners in the six-furlong contest and, when Piggott tried to make up ground, the gaps wouldn't come. St Paddy was allowed to coast home in his own time without ever coming under serious pressure.

It was clear that the York race had been an educative experience for a still immature horse. Next time out was expected to be very different as Noel Murless told Aly Khan and as St Paddy's stable lad, Snuffy Lawler, told

Michael Heffernan who, helpfully, informed Joe Lowry. And that's when the gang decided that St Paddy should be doped.

For his next run the bay colt was scheduled to line up in the Royal Lodge Stakes over a mile at Ascot on Friday 25 September. The race was one of the leading juvenile events of the season and Murless regularly targeted it with his best two-year-old. There was a small but select field for the 1959 renewal, a mere five runners, and for the dopers it seemed the perfect race. They'd lay St Paddy, who was expected to start favourite, and make a profit at the expense of their unfortunate punters, including hedging bookies out of the loop, who backed Lester Piggott's mount. They'd also back the second and third favourites in a reverse forecast, which means they'd win providing their selections finished first and second in either order.

The crucial role in the operation belonged to Snuffy Lawler and Joe Lowry had another meeting with him and Michael Heffernan at Lisburn Road to keep them sweet. This time the gang were running short of luminal sodium. So, on Richard McGee's advice, the phenobarbitone was to be mixed with bromide contained in a physic ball which was meant to open when the horse swallowed it and dissolve in its bloodstream. Ted Smith prepared it and Darkie Steward collected it and took it up to Lawler in Newmarket.

On the morning of the race, Bill, Jackie and Joe conferred together in London before going on to Ascot where the going was good, an autumnal breeze blowing across the heath. The race was run on the round course over the

Old Mile and the betting in the ring was fierce. St Paddy eventually went off as one of three 11-4 co-favourites. The other two were Goose Creek, owned by the multi-millionaire American philanthropist Paul Mellon,[9] and Jet Stream, a Glorious Goodwood winner, owned by another rich American, Paul Widener, and trained by Murless's Newmarket neighbour, Captain Cecil Boyd-Rochfort. There was significant support for both Goose Creek, who had opened up at 4-1, and Jet Stream who, according to *The Sporting Life*'s betting man, Geoffrey Hamlyn, was heavily backed at 100-30, 3-1 and 11-4 at the off.

Bill would sometimes attempt to spread disinformation in advance of a coup. For example, he would tell rival bookies that one of his biggest clients, a regular winning punter, had assured him that such and such a horse was a good thing. He was usually tipping favourites that he was secretly planning to lay but, at Ascot that September Friday, the plotting backfired. For both the legitimate operators following the market and the dopers and their friends trying to fix the result, the 1959 Royal Lodge Stakes was a disaster. Jet Stream, who looked well and was positively ridden, made the running but Lester Piggott, oozing confidence on the supposedly nobbled St Paddy, was never far away. Second at the turn into the home straight, he took it up with over a furlong to run and came away effortlessly to win by five lengths. Goose Creek ran on to be second with Jet Stream a head away third.

---

9 Paul Mellon went on to own the 1971 Derby and Arc winner, Mill Reef, one of the greatest racehorses of the 20th century.

All of the gang were hit hard, especially Bill Roper and Jackie Dyer who were at the forefront of the racecourse trading. Ascot was a Rich Charlie's track and the Members' Enclosure was packed with old-money punters, Knightsbridge and Mayfair gentlemen, who had backed the winner with Maxie, Cyril, Jackie and Bill.

Darkie Steward, who had been in charge of the doping and had assured various faces that St Paddy wouldn't win, had some serious explaining to do and there were angry scenes in London as Albert Dimes and his friends demanded their money back. When an embarrassed Joe Lowry tracked down Snuffy Lawler, the stable lad insisted that he'd given St Paddy the physic ball but that it might have broken before the horse swallowed it. He said there was no way he could communicate with Joe on the day of the race without alerting Noel Murless and arousing suspicion. But was it really just a cock-up – perhaps the bromide sedative had failed to take effect – or was Snuffy Lawler lying? Later he claimed to police that he threw the drug away.

Suspicion also fell on Ted Smith. Maybe he'd stitched them up and the doses of luminal sodium he'd been selling them were not as strong as they'd thought?

It was a bitter and recriminatory moment but if it was uncomfortable losing money – and losing face – with Max Parker at least the bookmaker confined his disdain to expletive ridden abuse. Fronting up to Charlie Mitchell was another matter. Mitchell was Jackie Dyer's nephew, although there was only a four-year age difference between them, and he was about to play a major part in Jackie and Joe and Bill's activities.

Charles Edward Mitchell, who was born in 1928, was a Fulham boy whose father and stepmother had a stall in the market on the North End Road. Young Charlie left school at 14 and embarked on a career trajectory not dissimilar to Dirk Bogarde's young hoodlum in *The Blue Lamp* although, as far as we know, it didn't end with him shooting any uniformed policemen.

In 1946 he was making a living among the spivs and bomb sites of post-war London when he was arrested for receiving stolen goods, almost a national occupation at the time. He had enlisted in the army as a private in 1945 but was discharged after a couple of months as medically unfit. He joined up again when he was released from Borstal in 1947 but he went AWOL within days and then, a few years later, appeared at the Old Bailey on a charge of shop breaking with intent. This time he was sentenced to two years' adult imprisonment and, when he came out in 1953, he went to work for his family on their costermonger's stall in Fulham.

In the years that followed he had a spell as a fitter with Austin Motors and 15 months as a driver with a scrap metal business in Shepherd's Bush. He also worked as a part-time tic-tac man around various London dog tracks and, along with fellow greyhound racing faces, Peter Hubbard and Johnny Coulson, he became versed in dog doping at the same time as Dandy McGreevy and Bernie Howard were beginning to stop horses. Some of the phenobarbitone used to nobble the dogs was probably supplied by Ted Smith who knew a couple of kennel-maids at Sunbury

Kennels and was a regular at Wandsworth Stadium and Park Royal.

By the late 1950s, Mitchell, who lived on Rannoch Road in Fulham, had become a wealthy man with interests in haulage, property and a garage and car sales business. He was also collecting modern art. An inveterate punter, he owned a legal credit bookmaking firm and an illegal street bookmaking firm and he liked to bet big on both horses and dogs, preferably when he knew the result in advance. His combined losses on St Paddy's Ascot race were believed to be in the region of £20,000 (or over £350,000 in modern money) and Charlie wasn't about to write them off.

Six foot three and broad shouldered with short, close-cropped hair, Mitchell was tailor-made for the Bill Sikes role. He was angry with Bill, Jackie and Joe and he was positively incensed when another racecourse face mocked his misfortune in an Ascot bar after racing. Tommy Lawrence, a bookmaker's clerk and tic-tac operative, was there and saw what happened. 'Mitchell, who was a big man and always something of a bully, finally picked up his beer glass and smashed the other fellow in the face with it. The other man went down and there was blood everywhere but nobody did anything and Mitchell just walked away. Everyone was frightened of him.'

The bar brawl wasn't the end of Charlie's anger. He held Darkie Steward especially responsible for what had happened. Steward fancied himself. Steward was overly familiar. Steward had been boasting about his contacts and his inside information and Charlie reckoned it was time to teach him a lesson. What he had in mind wasn't the sort of thing you'd read about in an Enid Blyton story. When he caught up with the unfortunate Darkie, he took off his belt and beat him with it repeatedly and that was only the beginning. He also kicked him in the balls and threatened him with the sharp edge of a chopper which seems to have been a favourite tactic with psychotic villains of the period. 'Mad' Frankie Fraser, the agreeable coffee-time companion of Albert Dimes, once went to work on fellow gangster Eric Mason with an axe, thoughtfully dropping him off at Accident and Emergency when it was all over. There's no way of knowing whether Charlie Mitchell offered a similar service but all those who witnessed his rages testified they were a thing to fear.

It's probable that Snuffy Lawler trembled too at the thought of retribution for his St Paddy blunder. But, once again, Joe Lowry played the role of forgiving parent with the proviso that Snuffy, who had been paid £75 up front, had to do better next time and there had to be a next time soon. The races chosen for payback were at Newmarket in October and, once again, Noel Murless was the target. The fixture began on hard ground on Wednesday 14 October and Laminate, a two-year-old filly owned by Sir Victor Sassoon, trained by Murless and ridden by Lester Piggott, started 11-10 favourite for the five-furlong Prendergast Stakes. She was beaten six lengths and the winner, ridden by Scobie Breasley, was the 11-4 second favourite.

The following day, the three-year-old filly Collyria, owned by Sir Victor Sassoon, trained by Noel Murless and ridden by Lester Piggott, started the 13-8 favourite for the Newmarket Oaks. She was beaten a head by the heavily backed second favourite, Water Wings.

Then on Friday 16 October, the two-year-old Whisk, owned by Sir Victor Sassoon, trained by Noel Murless and ridden by Lester Piggott, finished an easy-to-back second in the Rowley Mile Nursery. The winner, Apostle, ridden by Scobie Breasley, was a major gamble and returned at 7-4 from 9-4 and 3-1 first show.

All three Murless horses had been successfully got at with fresh drugs supplied by Ted Smith and administered by Darkie Steward and Snuffy Lawler, and the winnings on the three races went some way to repairing the damage done at Ascot the month before.

Bill Roper sat in his penthouse flat that Saturday night, nursing a Cutty Sark and reviewing his options. The days were getting shorter and before long the clocks would go back and the smell of coal smoke return to the London streets. The racing seasons would change too with the jumpers replacing the flat. Traditionally the winter game was less lucrative than the summer sport and many of Bill's big clients packed up in November and didn't get back in touch until spring.

As Bill waited for Micheline to join him after work, he could see only one possible course of action. He had completed the purchase of an office for his new business in Monmouth Street near Seven Dials. He hoped to take a significant number of his old Max Parker punters with him though there was an understanding that he would continue to mark the older man's card in return for a remuneration.

But Bill's proposed partner, Alex Willmore, had let him down and had decided to go in with Dickie Gaskell at Ladbrokes instead. Bill was planning to invest about £190,000 worth of his own money to float the book at the new firm and he needed to get some of it back quickly as he also had to complete the financing of Micheline's business. She had her eyes on a possible site in Knightsbridge and, in readiness, she was planning to move from Marylebone to a new flat at Malvern Court near South Kensington tube station.

Before then Bill wanted to take Micheline away on a winter holiday. Monte Carlo, maybe, or Cannes or the Bahamas where Lester Piggott went as a guest of Sir Victor Sassoon. But first he would have to sort things out. There was one obvious, lucrative, if risky, way to raise all the finance he needed. This doping business. It could be a car crash when they got it wrong. But it could be the answer to all his problems and a proper high-stakes earner if they got it right. What it needed was someone with a real business brain, someone like himself, to take hold of it and organise it. Joe Lowry and Jackie Dyer would be his lieutenants. Joe the Newmarket correspondent, Jackie laying the horses on course. He'd keep Darkie Steward on too, in his personal employ at Monmouth Street. He was a fly boy, and a little too confident for his own good, but the beating he'd received from Charlie Mitchell should have taught him a lesson and his experience with horses would be invaluable when they moved up a level as Bill intended to. And then there was Mitchell who badly wanted his money back. His methods were distasteful but in the treacherous seas up ahead, his aura and reputation might be necessary to protect Bill from the depredations of rivals, criminal and legitimate, in the West End and elsewhere.

Roper didn't stop to worry about the Metropolitan Police who, when they came anywhere near gambling, had always been easy to bribe. And as for the Jockey Club and racecourse security . . . what security?

Bill was crossing the line and it was a conscious choice. He could feel a tightening in his chest and a patch of sweat forming on his upper lip. But he convinced himself it would be just the next step. To go from profiting from betting on races he believed to be fixed, to fixing the races himself. It was what it was in racing and always had been. From Snouty Parker's time to Maxie and Cyril and from the crooked jockeys to the Frenchies doping to win. Besides, with his contacts, charm and skills how could Mr Roper, the human comptometer, possibly lose?

7

ROPER THE DOPER

NOT EVEN grey skies and the hint of a downpour could depress the atmosphere at Number 51 Beauchamp Place, the new premises of Michelle de Paris, Cosmetics and Beautician. It was mid-June 1960 and barely five years since arriving from Geneva, the now 23-year-old Micheline Lugeon had her own business, albeit with a little help from Bill Roper and a loan from the National Provincial Bank. The smart, ground-floor shop with an attractive bow window was in a prime site in Knightsbridge with Harrods only a short stroll around the corner.

Today the shop is occupied by Hamilton & Inches, a silversmith and clock specialist by appointment to the Queen, and there's an estate agent next door and the offices of Relais Chateaux opposite. Other shops in the street feel a bit cheaper and tattier than during its 1980s heyday and the nearby houses less exclusive than they would have done 50 years ago. But just a few doors down from Number 51 there's Fifi, a Paris lingerie boutique – which both Micheline and

Bill might have enjoyed – and that old paparazzi standby, San Lorenzo, is still there across the road.

Micheline had hired a PR woman called June Downie who lived in Beaconsfield and commuted to London every day. The two women became good friends and Downie's job was to promote the new business and get some local advertising and newspaper and magazine coverage. A smart gathering of clients, old and new, enjoyed drinks in the shop in the early evening of 13 June, the eve of Royal Ascot, after which Bill took the hostess out to dinner at the Coq d'Or (later Langans) on Stratton Street and then on to the Bagatelle, a new gaming club run by the Uruguayan-born Ricky Dajou, the so-called King Of Clubs. All the talk was of the gentleman cat burglar Peter Scott, a sometime client of Roper's, who had stolen £200,000 worth of jewellery and a selection of underwear from Sophia Loren's hotel room near Elstree Studios where she was filming *The Millionairess* with Peter Sellers. Legend has it that Scott had then gone to a gay nightclub, Dorothy's, in Knightsbridge and boasted to friends that he was wearing a pair of Loren's black silk knickers.

Micheline Lugeon felt more sympathy for Loren than admiration for Scott and would have loved to have the actress as a client. She was already thinking beyond a narrowly British context and the week after Ascot, traditionally one of the quietest of the racing year, she and Bill took a business trip to Paris. They travelled in the first-class carriages on the Golden Arrow, the Pullman express train that left Victoria at 11 a.m. every morning. At Dover

Marine they boarded the ferry *Invicta* for the run across to Calais and then a big, black French Pacific class locomotive pulled the Flèche d'Or the remaining 180 miles to Paris, arriving in the cavernous, steam-filled Gare du Nord just after half past five. Bill, following the custom of a number of his well-heeled punters when they attended the Arc or the Grand Prix de Paris, had booked a room at the George V under the name of Mr and Mrs Roper. The pristine sheets were crisp and cool, the colognes plentiful and the bath towels vast and there were enough cushions, chaise longues and faux Louis XIV writing tables, not to mention vintage champagnes available on room service, to satisfy the fantasies of any corrupt bookmaker and his mistress.

The next day the couple went to Galeries Lafayette on the Boulevard Haussmann where Michelle de Paris now had a stand next to the other make-up, or maquillages, brands like Arden, Rubinstein and L'Oréal and a full-time sales assistant too, like Micheline at Fortnums a few years before.

Travelling back to London it must have seemed to Mlle Lugeon that Roper was an even cannier and more successful gambler than when she had met him again the pevious year. So was that the real basis of their attraction? Bill's luck and deep pockets? Or was there something more? Later, when the pair achieved notoriety, there was much speculation as to what the lovely young Swiss girl could possibly have seen in the almost ancient South Londoner. Well, he was generous and fun and, reportedly, a considerate lover – which was by no means true of all Englishmen at that time – who had known many women, some long before he met Doris during the war. Maybe too, Micheline saw him as a father figure and protector in a strange land. As dependable as the one back in Geneva but more tolerant and easy-going. Then there was his investment in her business. A lot of men had promised to help her in an attempt to get her into bed with them but, so far, only Bill had been as good as his word and placed his money at her disposal.

What must have been baffling to Micheline was the precise nature of Bill's relationship with the mother of his children. His new telephone credit bookmaking business was up and running on the first floor at Number 71 Monmouth Street and the remarkable Doris, whose two boys were now at prep school, was installed there as licence holder and office manager. She had a secretary and clerk to help her and Bill often popped in himself to see how things were going. Whatever the truth of the arrangement, it all amounted to a significant monthly outlay which was why most afternoons, and evenings in summer, Bill and his new assistant Darkie Steward, who had been given a retainer of £15 a week, were busy on the racecourse. And some nights in the early hours, Darkie and a few other members of the gang were busy in some top racing stables too.

Bill had decided that if he was going to become 'Roper The Doper', as he would be known, he should go at it hard before the authorities had time to work him out. That winter, plans were laid and at the beginning of February, Bill went down to Surbiton and met Ted Smith at his flat. Balaclava Road runs parallel to the main Waterloo to Portsmouth and Southampton railway line on the western edges of the town. Number 38 was a tall, three-storey Edwardian villa, redbrick with white-painted window frames and a pebble-dash finish on the top floor. There was a porch on the left-hand side of the house and a wooden front door with a stained glass window. Buses and lorries trundled past the tiny front garden with its gravel lawn and dilapidated wooden fence and there was a small development of post-war council houses on the other side of the road. At the end of the street was a bleak, 1930s Baptist church and beyond the Brighton Road was the Black Lion, a draughty Youngs pub and one of Ted Smith's locals.

Number 38, like the houses adjoining it, was almost always in the shade and on a foggy February afternoon it had a gloomy feel. The entrance to Ted and May Kibble's flat was up a flight of outside stairs on the right-hand side of the building. From the outset, Roper let the Witch Doctor know he meant business. He arrived with three chemist's dictionaries he'd been studying. He'd been thinking of doping to win as well as to lose and he told Smith that he was interested in cocaine but Ted wasn't sure he could get any. So Bill said he'd also like to get hold of some amphetamines like methyl amphetamine hydrochloride. He understood that it would stimulate a horse for a while but, as the effects wore off, the horse would be listless and lacking in energy and safe for a bookmaker to oppose. Smith said that he'd see what he could do.

After his visitor had gone, Ted rang McGee at home in Newcastle and asked him if he could find out for sure what effect methyl amphetamine hydrochloride might have on racehorses. An unhappy McGee warned that it wouldn't be easy to obtain despite his trusted position and he asked for more time to look into it. Smith reminded him of the money they would make if he could deliver. A week later McGee rang back, calling Ted's number, Elmbridge 4784, on the Winthrop office line. He said it could be done but he'd prefer Smith to come up to Newcastle in person to collect as he was nervous about sending it in the post.

Roper provided the funds for the drugs and gave Ted Smith £40 for his role in acquiring them along with a return train ticket from King's Cross to Newcastle. When Ted returned he had the gear and instructions about using it too. McGee said that it was soluble in water but could also be given as a bolus, using between 22 and 26 grains at least 14 hours before a race. If that didn't work they should give it more like 18 hours in advance. If it worked properly, the horse would be awake and buzzed up in its box all night and by the time it got to the racecourse the next day, sleep deprived and groggy, it would be in no position to show its true form.

Roper had new instructions for Joe Lowry and Jackie Dyer too. He was no longer just acting for himself. He was also giving tips to Charlie Mitchell and putting money on for him and Max Parker and, with the stakes significantly higher, he wasn't prepared to leave the doping in the hands of unreliable stable lads. From now on the stable staff would be paid for identifying the boxes of specific horses in a number of yards and then Darkie Steward and the others would take care of the rest.

Bill would never go near a doping himself. As Jackie Dyer recalls it, 'Bill's job was to find the horses' but before he could pinpoint them geographically he had to spend long hours going through the entries in the *Racing Calendar* and *The Sporting Life*, trying to find potential favourites in contests with small fields where good money could be made from opposing the 'jolly' and where there was a better than average chance of the second or third favourite scooping the prize. There would then be planning sessions in London cafés like the Lyons Corner House at Marble Arch, Bill taking care of the teas and coffees, the doughnuts and the sausage rolls.

As the start of the new flat-racing season drew near, Roper asked Joe and Jackie to get their stable lads to come up with maps of a number of Newmarket yards, including Noel Murless's stable, Warren Place. By this point Uncle Joe had recruited a couple more Newmarket lads to assist the gang with locating their targets. Jack Stiles was a good-looking Teddy Boy and punter who wore a black leather jacket and spent a lot of time on his hair. Jack liked cash in hand and, like Darkie Steward and Dandy McGreevy, he didn't much mind who put it there. He had been friends with Darkie since 1959 when the pair were working at Captain Ryan Price's yard at Findon in West Sussex. Neither of them much cared for the piratical Captain who wore his trilby at a jaunty angle like Captain Hook and whose skill at training racehorses to peak on a given day, often in big betting handicaps, was hailed as genius by some and rascality by others. Price once claimed that he never had a bet which makes the old bookmakers laugh who say they've still got the scars to prove otherwise.[10]

The Captain may have comported himself like an officer and gentleman but, like Bill Roper, he mixed with all sorts. Jackie Dyer remembers rumours about one of his owners in the 1950s, a mysterious Hungarian called Baron Hatvany who was an art collector as well as a racing man. The Baron had an equally shady associate, Dr Reuter, and the two of them were meant to accompany Price on trips to the Imperial Hotel in Torquay at the start of the jumping season in August. There they would allegedly plot up which of the Baron's horses would be given a little chemical assistance, à la the French, when the money was down in the coming months.

The Captain's approach to industrial relations was robust to say the least which was probably at the root of his testy relationship with Darkie Steward and Jack Stiles. On one occasion a group of Findon stable lads threatened to go on strike. Price confronted them in the tack room and enquired which one was their spokesman. When one of the lads stepped forward the Captain, who had been a commando in the war, promptly knocked him out. He then asked who wished to take the representative's place? Not surprisingly the lads all declined the offer and that was the end of the dispute.

By the end of 1959 Jack Stiles, glad to be free from the

---

10 Tommy Lawrence reckons the Captain had 'up to a hundred punters putting money on for him at times'.

Captain's iron rule, was back in Newmarket and living in a second-floor flat in the Carlton Hotel on the High Street. One night in the Milk Bar, a cheap and routine attraction for Newmarket stable lads, he met an old mate called Kenny Santus who had worked with him at a small jumping yard in Ludlow two years before. Santus had gone on from there to various other stables and was now employed by Fergie Sutherland who was also Michael Heffernan's boss. Little Santus, who was married and had a baby, had three convictions for dishonesty, dating back to 1956 and he had the nervous manner and slightly startled expression of the A6 murderer, James Hanratty.

Jack Stiles had already decided to join Darkie Steward's firm and he persuaded the weaker and more passive Santus to meet his new friends and see what he thought of them. If Kenny had expected the encounter to take place over a sociable pint in the Waggon and Horses, he was sorely disappointed. Joe Lowry and Jackie Dyer came up from London a few nights later in Jackie's red and cream two-tone Ford Zodiac. They picked Santus and Stiles up at midnight and drove them out to a deserted lay-by on the Cambridge Road. It was a moonless night and the country all around was silent and dark.

Jack Stiles explained that Kenny was 'a good boy' who could be trusted to keep his mouth shut and just wanted to earn a few bob for his family. Joe told him that good boys were looked after and that he would be paid £20 for meeting them, a further £20 for finding out where certain horses were stabled and a further £50 if they were successfully doped.

Santus, who later claimed to be scared stiff but too scared to back out, agreed to help. But his nerves didn't improve when he got back to town and Jack Stiles reminded him that the gang knew where his wife lived and he would be wise to keep that in mind.

A fortnight later flat racing resumed at Lincoln's Carholme racecourse and all the big bookmakers, including Bill Roper, Max Parker and the Ladbrokes representatives, were there as usual. The skies were grey and the facilities spartan including a 19th century brick grandstand that was open to the elements. But the Lincoln remained one of the most popular betting races of the year and on Wednesday 23 March the stands were packed, not just with northern racegoers but scores of London punters who had travelled up on one of the three race specials from King's Cross.

The big race was off at 3.15 but, 40 minutes earlier, all eyes were on the two-year-olds in the five-furlong Lincoln Plate which went to the heavily backed favourite Treasure Hunt, who was owned by the Honourable Major Broughton, trained in Newmarket by Jack Waugh and ridden by Eph Smith. Described in *The Sporting Life* as 'a compact and neatly made colt', Treasure Hunt was reportedly 'well forward' and the market knew all about him. He opened up at 7-4 and was backed in to 10-11 at the off. His supporters never had a moment's worry as he scooted home by six lengths and assorted bookies, punters and racing correspondents marked him down as one to be on again next time out.

Jack Waugh, keen to make the most of his smart early season juvenile before the better horses came out, entered

Treasure Hunt in a similar event, the Cannon Yard Plate at Windsor on 1 April. But the night before the race, the little black colt with the white mark on his forehead was doped in his box by the Bill Roper gang and Kenny Santus was one of the participants.

Santus lived in Market Street in Newmarket. The terraced houses were knocked down long ago but, in 1960, they were no more salubrious or gentrified than Michael Heffernan's place on Lisburn Road. Around 11 p.m. on the night of 31 March, Kenny left his sleeping wife and baby and set off for Jack Stiles's flat in the Carlton Hotel. There was a cold wind blowing across Newmarket Heath. Not the kind of icy blast that blows in from Siberia on a mid-winter morning but enough of a breeze to rattle an empty beer bottle lying in the gutter outside the Waggon and Horses. It made Santus shiver and wish that he'd worn a windcheater beneath his thin nylon jacket. A black cat scurried across his path but the little stable lad didn't feel lucky.

Shortly after midnight the two-tone Ford Zodiac arrived, Joe Lowry having telephoned Stiles from a call box to tell him they were on their way. There were four of them in the car this time: Lowry, Jackie Dyer, Darkie Steward and another ex-stable lad called Jimmy Cronin who was nicknamed Taffy. The two Newmarket lads piled into the back with the others and they drove slowly up the High Street to the clock tower and then turned right on to Moulton Road.

There were no late night lap-dancing clubs in Newmarket in 1960 and no pub licence extensions either, at least not on a Thursday night. By 1 a.m. it seemed as if the whole town was peacefully asleep, its hundreds of equine residents bedded down along with their trainers and lads. At Jack Waugh's Heath House stables, 50 yards along Moulton Road, the front gates had been locked at 7 p.m. but, other than that, security was almost non-existent. Today the grand old Victorian house and stable yard is home to Sir Mark Prescott. The cigar-smoking baronet has been known to enjoy a punt and a plot and is spiritually more akin to the trainers of the old days than most of his Newmarket counterparts, but what happened at Heath House on that March night 50 years ago would have disgusted him.

Santus and Stiles got out of the car with Darkie Steward and 'Taffy' and the Ford Zodiac drove on 'nice and steady' up Warren Hill. Cronin's job was to keep watch on the pavement outside but first he helped the others climb over the seven-foot wall. Fortunately for them there were no shards of glass on the top to deter intruders as there are today. Just as he'd promised, Kenny Santus – tiptoeing exaggeratedly like a burglar in a silent film – led Steward and Stiles to Treasure Hunt's box which was the sixth one along on the left overlooking a manicured lawn. There was no padlock to pick. All they had to do was slide back the bolt and walk in.

Jack Stiles had told Santus that 'Darkie did the horses by pulling their tongues out and sticking the stuff down its throat'. But as Santus now discovered, the innocuous accounts of doping that Stiles and Joe Lowry had furnished were a sham. The unsuspecting Treasure Hunt had first to be woken and then forcibly restrained. Steward, who was wearing rubber gloves, used the doper's standard implement, a twitch, which was a stick with a hole in the end through which they'd looped a length of twine in the shape of a tourniquet. Using a head collar to restrain the horse, the loop was then applied to its upper lip and twisted cruelly until the little colt's head was in the air. Darkie Steward then took hold of the tongue with his left hand and twisted that too while slipping the dope, which was in a silver packet, in with his other hand. He pushed the bolus, which was bound with elastic bands, right down into the horse's mouth and then gave it a drink of milky water to make it swallow.

Within 20 minutes it was all over and within half an hour of scaling the wall, they were all back outside on the street. The Ford Zodiac came slowly down the Moulton Road from the direction of Warren Hill and picked them up. At the junction of Old Station Road and Rous Road, Stiles and Santus got out. But then a few minutes later, as they were walking back towards the Carlton Hotel, they saw a policeman.

PC Charles Pickin was on his regular nocturnal round, strolling along the deserted Newmarket streets, hands behind his back, like PC George Dixon in *Dixon Of Dock Green*. Unbeknown to the gang, he'd seen the red and white Ford Zodiac driving up the High Street earlier and had noticed there were six men in it. He was still in the vicinity of the clock tower when he heard a car door slam and then moments later the Ford Zodiac reappeared. This time he noticed there were only four men in it. The constable flagged it down, shone his torch inside and asked the driver to identify himself. Genial Joe Lowry said that they'd met up with some fellows in the

Carlton and had made a bit of a night of it. Pickin let them go – there were no breathalyser tests in 1960 – but, as they drove away, he noted down the make and number plate of the car in his notebook. XGH557.

As he started to walk back down the High Street, the policeman saw the other two hiding in the shadows on Rous Road. He challenged them to step forward and, when they did, he recognised Kenny Santus but not Jack Stiles who gave his name as John Stiles of Flat 35, the Carlton Hotel. When Pickin asked them why they were out so late, they said they'd been having a few beers with some mates. Pickin jotted the details down in his notebook and then wished them goodnight. But he didn't forget them and nor did he forget the driver of the two-tone car.

Jack Stiles was bullish afterwards. The local coppers. What clowns! They couldn't catch a fucking bus. But Santus's heart was pounding as he hurried back to his family on Market Street.

April Fool's Day dawned showery and bright. At Heath House, Jack Waugh and his staff were up early as usual and by 6.30 a.m. Treasure Hunt had been loaded into a horsebox for the drive to Windsor.

If the stable lads saw anything odd in the colt's demeanour, they didn't say so. The Cannon Yard Plate, due off at 2.30 p.m., had drawn a field of 18 but the only horse the punters wanted to back was Treasure Hunt. *The Times* racing correspondent spoke for many when he said 'Jack Waugh's runner was so impressive at Lincoln last week, winning in a fast time, that I have no intention of opposing him.'

There were plenty of punters at the Thames-side track, even on an early season Friday, and betting was brisk. Once again Bill, Joe and Jackie conferred on the morning of the race and, when trading began on the Cannon Yard Plate, they laid Treasure Hunt whose odds contracted from 5-4 to even money to 10-11. But, as *The Sporting Life* reported the next day, he 'did not appear to start too well, was soon crowded out and had to be taken to the outside in an endeavour to get a run'. It was all to no avail. The hot favourite could finish no nearer than tenth.[11]

The result was a highly profitable one for the doping gang. As well as taking on Treasure Hunt in the ring at Windsor, Bill's Monmouth Street office and the off-course offices of Charlie Mitchell, Max Parker – and, so the police later believed, Albert Dimes - all laid the horse too. There had been no cock-ups with misfiring drugs or bungling stable lads. The methyl amphetamine provided by Ted Smith and Richard McGee had done its job and left Treasure Hunt only half a horse by post-time.

At least on this occasion there was no long-term damage. Jack Waugh, initially mystified that his colt could run so badly, agreed that horses, like humans, can have an off-day. Treasure Hunt was reportedly 'as right as rain' 48 hours later and came out and won his next two races at Wolverhampton

---

11 The winner was a 20-1 outsider called Welsh Prince, trained by Willie Stephenson. The runner-up, Para Queen, trained at Epsom by Ron Smyth and ridden by Geoff Lewis, was backed in from 14-1 to 6-1. 'Faces', who had been told that Treasure Hunt wouldn't win, backed Para Queen.

and Nottingham, where he was well backed by his dopers who could confidently expect an improved performance. But there was no official dope test after Windsor and no stewards' inquiry into the contrasting results. It was exactly the kind of supine response by officialdom that Roper had been expecting and Bill and the gang were laughing.

Heath House wasn't the only Newmarket stable they infiltrated that spring. On the night of 28 March they had broken into Major Dick Hern's yard, La Grange, and doped another two-year-old called Gravitation who ran in the Robin Hood Maiden Plate at Nottingham the following afternoon. The gelding, owned by Hern's landlord, Major Lionel B. Holliday, opened up at 11-4 on course but drifted out to 100-8 and finished third, beaten a total of three-and-a-half lengths.

Then, on the night of Tuesday 10 May they broke into Henri Jellis's yard on the Exeter Road and got at Guitarist, a consistent five-year-old who was due to run in the Meldreth Handicap at Newmarket the next day. But this time Michael Heffernan overdid the dose. When the lads awoke Guitarist he was dull and listless and was found to be running a temperature of 103. Jellis promptly withdrew him from the Newmarket contest. The new favourite, Small Slam, who would've been the second favourite with Guitarist in the field, was 'all the rage' in the ring and won easily by four lengths but at odds of 4-6 which were too short for Bill Roper's liking.

In between mornings in Monmouth Street, days at the races and nights poring over the entries and the formbook, Bill made frequent visits to Beauchamp Place. Business was going well and Micheline had received lots of compliments from satisfied customers, but overheads were high and to survive, let alone expand, she needed to persuade other, bigger shops to stock some of her goods. Bill sometimes drove her around London in his Ford Zephyr, visiting her old stamping grounds like Selfridges and Fortnum & Mason, Micheline hawking a selection of lipsticks, eyeliners and blushers with varying degrees of success.

Bill was interested in hiring out his products and services too. Three times during the 1960 flat-racing season the gang tried to bribe Noel Murless's stable lad, Snuffy Lawler, to help them dope St Paddy. But each time Lawler, who co-operated in stopping up to a dozen other Murless-trained horses between 1959 and 1961, refused. St Paddy, the gang's nemesis at Ascot the previous year, was the stable star, their top three-year-old and classic prospect and it was Lawler himself who looked after him every day. His Liverpudlian face was the first thing St Paddy saw each morning and the last he saw as he was shut up in his box at night.

On 18 May the bay colt, with Lester Piggott in the saddle, was the impressive winner of the Dante Stakes, a recognised Derby trial at York. Just before the race, he was heavily supported for the Derby itself at 10-1 with the big credit bookmaking offices. Only two other horses, one trained in France and one in Ireland, were trading at shorter odds.[12] Minutes after the Dante he was backed again on the rails at York and he ended the day as the new 5-1 Derby second favourite. These were thick bets from high-rolling punters,

12 The French colt, Angers, and Vincent O'Brien's Die Hard.

including the kind of Rich Charlies who had backed him in the Royal Lodge Stakes and were regular clients of Bill Roper, Max Parker and Ladbrokes. Whether they were struck at 5-1 or 10-1 or at 20-1 the previous August, they were all 'ante-post' bets, which means that if St Paddy won the Derby and his SP on the day was, say, 7-2, his ante-post backers would be paid out at the much bigger price they'd obtained weeks and even months before. But there was a downside too and if, for some reason – lameness, ill-health or loss of form – St Paddy didn't run in the Derby, the ante-post punters would lose their money and the bookmakers would keep the lot.

It was a situation ripe for a doping gang who already laid horses every day of their working lives and who had connections to bigger bookmaking firms who had substantial ante-post liabilities. Bill Roper, Jackie Dyer and Joe Lowry came up with the idea of persuading Snuffy Lawler to give St Paddy a physic ball containing a purgative that would cause such violent diarrhoea and so weaken the poor horse that it would have to miss Epsom altogether. The big credit bookmaking concerns, like Max Parker's, would not only profit directly from such an outcome. They'd pay the gang handsomely for doing their dirty work for them.

So, on the eve of the Dante, Snuffy Lawler was offered £200 (about £3,600 in today's money) to dope St Paddy with the physic ball but he declined. He was then offered £300 to dope the horse the weekend before the Derby but, once again, he refused.

Wednesday 1 June was a hot summer's day and the Epsom enclosures were overflowing. Alfred Hitchcock was in the crowd along with an evangelist carrying a sandwich board proclaiming that 'if you believe in the Lord Jesus Christ, thou art saved'. The punters believed in Lester Piggott and, given a copybook ride by the Long Fellow, St Paddy was never out of the first four. He hit the front two furlongs from home and, running on strongly, won the race by three lengths just as he had done at York. It was Lester's third and easiest Derby victory, Noel Murless's second and Sir Victor Sassoon's fourth.

There were celebrations all round at Warren Place and anticipation of further triumphs to come. The Epsom hero's end of season target was to be the St Leger, the last of the five classic races, run over a mile and three quarters at Doncaster on 10 September. The opposition appeared to be competing for second place and, by the Saturday before the event, St Paddy was trading at odds-on across the board. Once again the Roper gang dangled the apple of temptation in front of Snuffy Lawler's eyes, offering him £500 (£9,000 in modern money and their biggest stable lad bribe yet) to give St Paddy a physic ball the night before the race. But, for a third time, Lawler – who was on a good cash tip from Sir Victor Sassoon every time the horse won – declined. St Paddy was in total command of the Leger field with a quarter of a mile to run and won in a canter.

Bill Roper, Joe Lowry, Jackie Dyer and their cohorts had failed to make money out of the best English three-year-old of 1960. But the thought of getting at a big ante-post classic favourite, a Noel Murless-trained favourite, didn't go away and would return, infamously, the following year.

8

RICH PICKINGS

THE SUMMER of 1960 was played out to the sound of 'Apache' by The Shadows, 'Running Bear' by Johnnie Preston and 'Itsy Bitsy Teeny Weeny Yellow Polka Dot Bikini' by Brian Hyland which reached number eight in the UK charts. The song may have been ringing in Micheline Lugeon's ears as she and Bill went to a friend's poolside party at a house in North London. Maybe Micheline wore a bikini – which was still a sensational new fashion item at the time – or maybe she opted for a Gina Lollobrigida black one piece which nowadays would be the height of retro glamour.

Bill Roper, the former military policeman who kept himself fit, probably looked better in his trunks than many men half his age. Bill would've been gallant around his girlfriend as he was to all women, whether they were aristocratic old ladies wanting a shilling each way at Royal Ascot or the Diana Dors and Jayne Mansfield peroxide blondes who habitually flirted with the bookies at tracks like Epsom and Alexandra Park.

It wasn't difficult for a well-dressed bookmaker with money in his pocket to go further than flirting if he wanted. But, that summer, Bill only had eyes for Mickey. Her education in horseracing and betting was continuing although, in truth, her favourite sport was not racing but tennis at Wimbledon and, when she wasn't busy in the shop, she watched on television as the lovely Brazilian, Maria Bueno, won the ladies singles. Bill rarely watched tennis. He was a Spurs fan and he liked cricket but, other than the pools and the weekly fixed odds football coupons, there wasn't much betting on other sports back then. It was all racing and dogs and Bill was making money at the racecourse almost every day.

Friday 15 July 1960, was the first day of the King George VI and Queen Elizabeth Stakes meeting at Ascot, one of the most prestigious of the season. It was also the beginning of a dramatic seven-day spree during which the Roper gang struck with impunity. The Duke of Norfolk, Her Majesty's Ascot representative, owned the favourite for the Granville Stakes, a six-furlong race for two-year-olds. Skymaster, trained at Arundel by Willie Smyth and ridden by Scobie Breasley, had already won three times, including the Windsor Castle Stakes at the royal meeting in June. He had only two opponents that Friday afternoon and he was sent off the even money favourite. But he finished a well-beaten runner-up, trailing in five lengths behind the second favourite Good Old Days, who was owned by the

American ambassador to London, Jock Whitney, and made all the running.[13]

Tommy Lawrence, the bookmaker's clerk who saw the Charlie Mitchell bar fight at Ascot in 1959, was there that day too and he remembers the race well. 'All the bookies in the ring could see the money coming for Good Old Days and we could see who was backing it, Jackie Dyer for one, and we could see how happy the big firms were to lay Skymaster and we all guessed something was up.'

The Skymaster race was the first in a series of three dopings in eight days. The fix was in and on each occasion Bill, Joe, Jackie and the rejuvenated Bernie Howard laid the favourite, backed the second or third favourite and sold their information to a few other select bookmakers and punters.

On Wednesday 20 July they picked the Duke of Norfolk's pocket once again. Red Letter was Willie Smyth's runner in the mile and a quarter Charles Greenwood Handicap at Kempton's evening meeting. Just like Skymaster, the six-year-old was owned by the Duke and ridden by Scobie Breasley and he was sent off the 7-4 favourite to beat four opponents. But the race was won by the 5-2 second favourite, William F, ridden by the Epsom lightweight jockey, Tommy Carter, who took up the running five furlongs out. Red Letter finished a distant fourth, beaten a thumping 18-and-a-half lengths.

---

13 Skymaster eased from odds-on to even money while Good Old Days came in from 2-1 to 11-10.

On Saturday 23 July the London racing circuit moved on to Hurst Park, barely a mile away from Kempton on the other side of the river. There was thundery rain as the Grinling Gibbons Handicap, for three-year-olds over five furlongs, closed the show at 4.30 p.m. The Lambourn trainer Bob Read supplied the even money favourite, Silver Kumar, ridden by no less a man than Lester Piggott. He had only five others to beat but, according to the formbook, he 'began to drop back a furlong and a half out' and he ended up plumb last, beaten over twenty-three lengths. The winner was the 5-1 third favourite, Selly Oak.

There was no steward's inquiry afterwards any more than there had been at Ascot and Kempton Park and the victims of the July dopings all recovered quickly and ran well again later in the season. For the ordinary Hurst Park punters, once-a-week racegoers throwing away their losing betting slips and their pages of form and queuing, skint, for the buses back to Hampton Court and the trains to Waterloo, the result must have been mystifying. But for Bill, Joe, Jackie and the boys there were celebrations up west that Saturday night. The three results represented another major extension of their activities with stable staff in Sussex and Lambourn now brought into the fold. No paper trails or audited accounts survive to tell the story but the odds on both Selly Oak and William F had been successfully knocked out on course and in the following weeks, there was a noticeable injection of funds into Bill's Monmouth Street business. Along with more dinners at Chez Victor and the Coq d'Or, more nights out at Pigalle and the Astor

Club and more bottles of scent and bunches of flowers for Doris Curd and sweet Micheline Lugeon.

Snuffy Lawler chipped in too. Noel Murless's top lad may have refused to dope St Paddy but, in the early hours of 25 June, the eve of the Northumberland Plate at Newcastle, a valuable handicap like Redcar's William Hill Gold Cup, he helped Darkie Steward nobble a Murless-trained colt called Sleepner. The next day the supposedly improving three-year-old was backed in from 7-2 to 11-4 for the Plate on course. But he finished only tenth.

Then on the night before Variety Club Day at Sandown in August, Snuffy helped them get at a four-year-old filly of Murless's called Saucy Queen who started 9-4 favourite for the Prince Philip Handicap but 'weakened a long way from home', according to the formbook, and finished a distant seventh.

But the summer of 1960 wasn't quite an unbroken success story for the gang. Saturday 2 July was the date of the July Cup, the historic six-furlong sprint at Newmarket, and the favourite was the lightning fast Sing Sing, owned by the fearless gambler Colonel Bill Stirling and trained by Jack Watts. Unbeaten as a juvenile and reckoned to be even better at three, Sing Sing was due to face just one solitary opponent, Tin Whistle, trained up in Malton by Pat Rohan.

On the Friday night, Sing Sing was doped at Watts's yard, Fairway House on Newmarket's Bury Road. But this time Darkie Steward and his assistants Jack Stiles and Kenny Santus overdid things, like Michael Heffernan with Guitarist, and when Watts went to look at his horse the following morning he found him dazed and in no condition to race. He was promptly withdrawn, leaving Tin Whistle to 'walk over' which meant he only had to be saddled up and canter down to the start and back to collect the £2,000 first prize. In a match with a nobbled Sing Sing he'd have been on offer at around 5-2 which, for the dopers, would have been money in the bank.

The overdose may have seemed a small mistake at the time but it had consequences and, in the weeks that followed, there were the first faint but discernible signs that the Jockey Club, the slumbering custodians of racing's integrity, were beginning to wake up. Jack Watts, who had as little faith in the stewards as Bill Roper, conducted a private urine test on Sing Sing which confirmed his suspicions that his horse had been got at. Then, in defiance of the existing Jockey Club rule, he disclosed his findings to the Newmarket correspondent of *The Sporting Life* who in turn wrote an article referring to 'reports of similar cases, not yet confirmed' and warned that Newmarket trainers felt the problem had reached a critical stage and that there 'must be immediate and drastic action'.

When the Duke of Norfolk himself confirmed that private tests on Skymaster and Red Letter showed that they too had been doped and then when Bob Read followed suit regarding Silver Kumar, the Jockey Club – who never did anything in a hurry – were compelled to revise their position. On 18 August a statement appeared in the *Racing Calendar*, a kind of *Pravda* of the Turf and the only publication in which the Jockey Club would disclose, even elliptically, their views, that henceforth 'it would be helpful to the stewards if trainers who are in a position to give any information as a result of their own enquiries would communicate immediately with the secretary to the Jockey Club.' Four months later the Club announced, again through a statement in the *Racing Calendar*, that a three-man team had been set up under the chairmanship of the Duke of Norfolk charged with reviewing the efficiency of dope detecting methods and the efficacy of the Club's rules.

It wasn't exactly the sound of alarm bells ringing or the tyres of a police Humber Hawk screeching to a halt outside Bill Roper's door but, before the end of the flat-racing season, Jockey Club justice did catch up, albeit fortuitously, with one of Joe Lowry's stable lads. On 2 July, the same day as the July Cup, a two-year-old filly called Sweet Solera won the Princess Stakes at Newmarket by three lengths. The 6-4 favourite was trained in the town by Reg Day and a couple of days before the race Michael Heffernan had bumped into her stable lad, Harry Ellis, on Newmarket High Street. Heffernan had worked with Ellis in the past and he tried to recruit him into the doping gang with the promise of ready money if he helped to insure that Sweet Solera didn't win. Ellis not only spurned Heffernan's offer but reported the encounter to Day, who in turn informed the secretary to the Jockey Club.

An enquiry was set up by their security director, Colonel Neville Blair, who always seemed to be otherwise engaged when races were being fixed. Michael Heffernan was summoned to appear before the stewards, which was an intimidating experience, and thanks to Ellis's testimony he was warned off. It was a bitter blow for the 35-year-old Heffernan who had not only lost his livelihood but was now out of reach of Joe Lowry's bounty. He didn't grass up any of the doping gang, not then, but his career in racing was over. Joe, Jackie and Bill stuck him some money to help him pay the rent at Lisburn Road but they decided there could be no more meetings at the terraced house as Heffernan was now a marked man and the other lads like Snuffy Lawler, Jimmy Hilliard and Kenny Santus were reluctant to be seen with him. Bill Roper concluded that the gang needed a new base of operations from which to plan dopings and pool information and that, with the temperature hotting up in Newmarket, they would have to find a metropolitan HQ.

In November 1960 Bill and Micheline had a big night out in London. It was the opening of the film director Joseph Losey's noirish black and white thriller, *The Criminal*, which starred Stanley Baker and came out in the same week as *Saturday Night Sunday Morning* starring Baker's friend and fellow working-class actor, Albert Finney. There was a party after the premiere in the Latin Quarter Club and a lot of racecourse and underworld 'faces' were in attendance.

The Criminal was the first British movie of Losey's distinguished career which included such classics as *The Servant*, *Accident* and *The Go Between* – and there was plenty in the story to interest a betting and racing man as Baker was himself. His character, Johnny Bannion, gets out of jail and pulls off a £40,000 heist in the Tote offices at Hurst Park but is then double crossed by his partner, Mike 'The Snake'

Carter', played by a suave Sam Wanamaker complete with sheepskin jacket, cigarette holder and murderer's driving gloves. The technical adviser on the film was Baker's good pal, Albert Dimes, who was able to verify the authenticity of the brutally realistic prison scenes, dominated by Patrick Magee as a sadistic warder, as well as the wild party that Baker's fellow villains throw for him on his release.

Losey was apparently fascinated by Italian Albert, describing him as a 'huge, staggeringly handsome man who drove around in a smashing big white convertible with black leather upholstery'. Losey used the self same car in the movie and, if the jail scenes made even hardened old lags shudder, they could enjoy the atmospheric party where Johnny's past and present lovers, played by Jill Bennett and Margit Saad (shades of Doris and Micheline), fought for his attentions. Saad wore black stockings and smoked Gauloise. There was a modern jazz soundtrack and Bannion's flat had black satin sheets on the bed and a painting of a female nude on the wall. There were no sniggering teenage hoodlums around like Dirk Bogarde's character in *The Blue Lamp*. Only hard men, who were neither wholly good nor wholly bad, and hot, bouffant women. But while Bill Roper may have been seduced by Baker's portrait of a professional criminal, and a racecourse racketeer at that, he should have remembered that in screenwriter Alan Owen's scenario there was no honour among thieves.

Amidst the champagne bubbles and the gossip, there was something else for the racing fraternity to celebrate that night. The historic Betting and Gaming Act had been passed by the

House of Commons on 1 September. All those long hours of negotiation between the bookmakers and the Home Office had resulted in the legalisation of off-course cash bookmaking. Betting shops were to be permitted from the following May and the application process for licences, and the hunt for sites for the new shops, was already under way.

For bookies, punters and dopers like Mr Racing, the game was changing and the stakes were getting higher. 1960 had been a good year . . . but for all of them, Micheline Lugeon included, 1961 would be the big one.

9

PINT O'SHERRY

NEWMARKET IS a garrison town. The trainers are the officer class and the jockeys and stable lads are the rough and licentious soldiery. It's a community beset with rumour, gossip, intrigue, gambling, drinking and sex. If there's one thing that sustains the population through the boredom of their long working days it's the possibility of being associated with a really good horse. They may train it or ride it or muck out its box or they may just have been tipped off about its potential and be planning to back it with their hard-earned wages next time out.

The best time to catch that tide of optimism is in early spring. That's when the Classic prospects for a new season are just beginning to emerge from winter quarters and all the hopes and expectations that have been invested in them have yet to be dashed. The spectacle of thoroughbred horses at work at dawn on Newmarket Heath is a thing of timeless, mesmerising beauty and, in late March and early April 1961, the heath was crowded each morning with work watchers and touts. It had been the mildest winter in the south since the war and the trainers reported that their aspirant 2,000 Guineas and Derby contenders were well forward in condition. In the houses of the big, ugly stables on the Bury Road and in the stable lads' hostels and pubs, the talk was of what trainers such as Captain Boyd-Rochfort and Major Hern, Jack Jarvis and Harry Wragg might have to go to war with in the coming months. But most of all the talk was of the number one man, Noel Murless, and of the, as yet, unraced colt, an equine *Tirpitz* or *Bismarck* if the rumours were to be believed, he was about to launch. The best horse, they said, that Murless had ever trained. Better than St Paddy. Better than the 1957 Derby and 2,000 Guineas winner Crepello. Better than Royal Forest or the sprinter Abernant and better even than the great filly Petite Etoile. The horse's name was Pinturischio.

A tall, rich bay, owned and bred by Sir Victor Sassoon, Pinturischio was by the 1953 Derby winner Pinza out of an Italian mare. Pinza had gone to stud six years before and big things were expected from him as a sire. Pinturischio – or 'Pint O' Sherry' as the bookmakers called him – was a powerfully built horse who didn't race at two and took after his father in many ways. Murless had hoped to get a race into him in the autumn of 1960 but exceptionally heavy ground, which he felt would take too much out of the colt first time out, followed by an outbreak of coughing at Warren Place, forced him to draw stumps until the following year.

There's a remote landmark in Newmarket known as the Poor Boy's Grave. It's situated besides a crossroads about a mile outside Kentford and allegedly commemorates a shepherd boy who committed suicide there in 1861 after losing his master's sheep. The small roadside memorial is tended by local gypsies and superstition has it that when flowers appear on the Poor Boy's Grave, a Newmarket-trained horse is going to win the Derby.

On Saturday 8 April 1961 flowers were seen on the Poor Boy's Grave. Earlier that day, Pinturischio took part in a special mile gallop on a stretch of land known as Racecourse Side. He was accompanied by three stable companions, including Aurelius, ridden by Lester Piggott. The gallop was meant to be private but the work watchers were never far away. Pinturischio was held up about a length behind his stablemates who were galloping line abreast. Then with about half a furlong to go, his rider let out a reef and asked him to quicken. Pinto responded instantaneously and shot past the others only to be steadied again by his pilot. According to one of the Newmarket correspondents for *The Sporting Life*, 'the manner in which he accelerated when given the office was that of a high-class horse and reminiscent of what we used to see St Paddy do at this time last year.'

Pinturischio's first run was to be in the Wood Ditton Stakes which takes place at Newmarket's Craven meeting in April. The mile contest, over the same course and distance as the 2,000 Guineas, is for unraced three-year-olds and gives late-developing horses an opportunity to compete against other similarly untried types before taking on more experienced opposition.

The principal Guineas trial at the meeting is the Craven Stakes which is also over a mile and usually attracts horses with good form as two year olds. On Tuesday 11 April, Pint O' Sherry's galloping companion Aurelius, with Lester on board, won the Craven by two lengths. The result had an electrifying effect on the ante-post betting markets. Aurelius was said to be over a stone behind Pinto on the gallops, which meant he would've had to receive at least 14lbs of weight from his stablemate to have any chance of beating him. Yet Aurelius had just come out and dismissed a bunch of genuine Guineas prospects with proven form. What might the son of Pinza do to them?

On the night of 11 April there was a call-over on the 2,000 Guineas and Derby at the Victoria Club in London. The Victoria Club, founded in 1864 and situated on Wellington Street in Covent Garden, was exclusively for high-stakes bookmakers and commission agents. Albert Dimes had an office on the ground floor and Bill Roper, Max Parker, William Hill and Joe Coral were all members. Coral, who had a withered arm and used to play snooker there one handed, was chairman for a while. The atmosphere was sociable, if exclusively male, and old members testify that you could eat and drink very well and enjoy the finest Havana cigars in the leather-upholstered smoking room.[14]

Victoria Club call-overs, which took place at regular intervals in the run-up to big betting races like the Lincoln, the Grand National, the Guineas and the Derby, enabled members to level up their ante-post book by

---

14 Gerry Parker used to go the club for dinner, acting as minder for the East End-born, but Brighton-based, bookmaker, Jackie Cohen.

hedging money on horses they had substantial liabilities for and backing horses they fancied at odds offered by rival layers. It was a kind of person to person version, albeit one confined to club members, of the futures trading that takes place nowadays on internet betting exchanges like Betfair. The call-over was presided over by a small, silver-haired man called Arthur Cassani who was at least 70 in 1961 but still as sharp as a whip. The members stood on either side of the billiard table in the smoking room, the air thick with cigar and cigarette fumes. Mr Cassani then went through the list of runners in alphabetical order and after each horse's name, members would call out what odds they were prepared to offer and to what amounts and others would take the price or call out the odds they were hoping to do business at. Arthur Cassani kept a record of all the transactions struck, which became debts of honour, and apparently he never missed a trick.

By the end of the call-over on 11 April, Pinturischio – who had yet to set foot on a racecourse – was no bigger than 4-1 for the 2,000 Guineas and 5-1 for the Derby. William Hill's spokesman said that the volume of betting on the horse was 'quite fantastic'. Hills had already laid one client a bet of £1,000 to win £10,000 on Pinto for the Derby over the winter and another £2,000 to win £10,000 in the 2,000 Guineas and, as the smoke cleared in Wellington Street, the word was that other high rollers, like Max Parker and Ladbrokes, were similarly 'full up' with bets on the favourite.

On Thursday 13 April the whole cast of owners, trainers, jockeys, bookmakers, punters and racing correspondents reassembled on Newmarket's Rowley Mile racecourse. Bill Roper was there, naturally, and Jackie and Joe and Darkie Steward. Maybe Bill, indulging in a little pillow talk, had told Micheline about the supposed wonder horse who was about to grace the stage. 'Mickey' was dutifully following the racing every day now in *The Sporting Life*.

Doris, the official proprietress at 71 Monmouth Street, would have been eager for news over the blower. The Roper firm already had a big ante-post book running on the Guineas and the Derby and she would've been as interested in how Pinto got on as her erstwhile husband and his confederates.

The Wood Ditton, which was worth £500 to the winner, was off at 3 p.m. and a huge crowd of spectators gathered by the saddling boxes to see Pinturischio enter the pre-parade ring. First impressions were favourable. Frank Byrne of *The Times* described the bay colt as 'a sensible gentlemanly type' with strong quarters and a long stride. It was noticeable that he carried 'his head rather high when at rest', but in the race he was faultless.

There were other fancied debutants, other Guineas and Derby entries with illustrious pedigrees, but Pinturischio was much too good for them. Piggott tracked the others in the early stages but then moved Pinto up to challenge at the Bushes two furlongs from home.[15] Passing his rivals 'quickly and easily on the bit' he won by a length with plenty in hand and no hint of greenness.

---

15 The Bushes are a famous landmark on the Rowley Mile, about two furlongs from the winning post.

It was typical of Lester to keep it tight. He rarely indulged in Frankel style demolitions of the opposition but still everybody expected Pinturischio to improve for the race. 'He couldn't have done it better,' said Murless and the bookies and punters agreed with him. There was another flurry of ante-post betting on the rails straight afterwards and by the end of the day, Pinto had contracted to 5-2 for the 2,000 Guineas and 3-1 for the Derby.

The going at Newmarket a fortnight later was somewhere between good and hard with a strong drying wind. Noel Murless, looking up anxiously at the skies and hoping for a downpour, warned that Pinturischio was more of a Derby horse than a miler and might not appreciate the firm track. But Pint O'Sherry had put in another conspicuously good performance in a gallop on Saturday 22 April, giving weight and a beating to two older stable companions and he was backed down to 7-4 favourite on the course.

There were 22 runners for the first classic of the season and, as well as Pinto, there were fancied challengers from Ireland and France, but the result was a shock for the punters and a skinner for the books. Rockavon, a 66-1 outsider from Scotland, triumphed by two lengths from another 66-1 shot, with Pinturischio a couple of heads away in fourth. Piggott's mount was going strongly, just behind the leaders, at the Bushes and he momentarily hit the front. But he couldn't accelerate running down the hill and was passed by the fast-finishing Rockavon in the final furlong.[16]

16 Rockavon was trained in Dunbar by George Boyd and ridden by Norman Stirk. Prior to the Guineas, he had finished fourth in the Northern Free Handicap at Newcastle.

Racing historians have concluded that the 1961 2,000 Guineas was one of the worst ever run but that wasn't the view at the time. Even in defeat nothing could dispel the excitement about Pint O'Sherry and the old cliché that 'losses are only lent' was heard widely afterwards in the press room and bars. Pinturischio was, after all, a stayer by breeding not a miler, as Murless had stressed, and his supporters felt he had done well to finish fourth. St Paddy had been equally inexperienced when coming sixth in the previous year's Guineas and he had gone on to win the Derby. Why shouldn't history repeat itself?

At the Victoria Club call-over on Monday 1 May, Pinto was eased to 8-1 for Epsom, challenged at the head of the market by an upstart French colt called Moutiers. But he was expected to reaffirm his potential next time out in the Dante Stakes at York, following the same path that St Paddy had taken 12 months before. On May 5 Murless showed just how highly he rated the horse by entering him – along with St Paddy and Petite Etoile – in the King George VI and Queen Elizabeth Stakes at Ascot, the midsummer showpiece of British racing. But tragically for Pinturischio and his owner, trainer and supporters, there was to be no next time. The bay son of Pinza had already run his last race.

On the same day that Pinto's Derby odds were eased at the Victoria Club, Britain's regular cash punters, excluded from high-stakes credit trading, were finally emancipated by law. Off-course betting shops opened nationwide on 1 May and most commentators, taking their cue from the general public, welcomed the innovation. *The Times*, setting a precedent still followed by broadsheet newspapers to this day, took the story away from their racing columnists and got a leader writer to pen a fruity encomium predicting that 'betting shops will rapidly find a place in daily life and provide as rich a seam for the study of English character as the rest of racing'.

Other correspondents opined that the new shops would 'soon find their own social level' with 'some being as clean and scrubbed as a kitchen or front parlour' and others 'seedy, litter-strewn rooms inhabited by listless youths and old men sucking pencils'. Home Office regulations prohibiting what it called 'spectacular advertising' made things difficult for the shop owners. Some of the offices were not easy to find and amounted to little more than a hole in the wall but some of the new London shops were in prime locations like Jack Swift's first floor emporium on Dover Street just across from the Ritz. Men like Swift had formerly deployed a fleet of illegal runners, collecting up to 2,000 bets a day but costing them around £400 a year in fines. Now the runners were redeployed as clerks in the shops and 'Chuckles' calculated that as long as the volume of business was high, and it was, it didn't matter if some of the stakes were small.

By September 1961 there were 8,780 shops in Britain. By September 1962 that number had shot up to nearly 20,000 thanks to a licensing regime that was about as watertight as the Jockey Club's security policy. Jackie Dyer had been one of the first racecourse bookmakers to apply for a licence in

London and he reckons he owned the first legal office in Hammersmith. His nephew Charlie Mitchell successfully applied for a licence in Fulham and Albert Dimes applied for a licence to open a shop on the ground floor of his Frith Street credit office. The Westminster magistrates were initially reluctant to embrace Italian Albert as a reputable person but he got round them by applying for it in the name of Al Burnett, owner of the Pigalle Club and another of his good showbiz friends. Racecourse faces joked that, in most cases, an appearance before the magistrates was such a formality that, provided they owned a jacket and tie, Noddy and Big Ears would be classed as fit and proper persons if they applied.

'Are you a good chap of sound moral character?'

'Absolutely, your honour.'

'And do you have the necessary readies to pay out your customers should the blighted little perishers get lucky?'

'Definitely, your honour.'

'Very well then. You are now officially a turf accountant and the legal proprietor of an off-course betting shop. Good luck to you.'

'Thank you, your honour.'

William Hill, the biggest racecourse bookmaker of them all, was initially against the new shops, warning – not inaccurately – that they were a licence to pick the pocket of the working man. His colleague Alf Cope, who had a grandiose credit office on Ludgate Hill complete with liveried footmen at the entrance, was also opposed on the grounds that the new shops might lead to a rise in protection rackets and gangsterism. But there was also a feeling that high-stakes credit bookmakers like Cope and Hill thought the shops and their customers would be rather depressing places that would lower the tone.

Max Parker and Cyril Stein were initially in the sceptics' camp too. But by the summer of 1962 Cyril, who was determined to keep transforming the old Ladbrokes business and wanted to challenge William Hill at every turn, realised that a fundamental shift was taking place. He began buying out small chains in places like the Isle of Wight and then gradually started moving into London. Meanwhile his uncle applied for planning permission to turn a disused bank by the clock tower in Brighton into the biggest betting office in the town, putting some dozens of other smaller shops out of business.

It wasn't just Maxie and Cyril who were getting into property. Micheline Lugeon was worried that the rates and overheads at Beauchamp Place were too high and she was seriously considering selling the shop and looking for a more economical outlet. She was also on the lookout for flats to buy, do up and sell, recognising that whole chunks of unreconstructed post-war London were ripe for development. Her lover was looking at London properties too but he had no plans to renovate or improve. In fact for Bill's purposes, the seedier the locale and the accommodation, the better.

10

TOUGH BOYS

WHEN ROPER chose 24 Colville Terrace as the new London headquarters of the doping gang he could hardly have picked a more inflammatory address. But then it was precisely the neighbourhood's louche reputation that attracted him. If Notting Hill was indeed a haven of 'jukebox parties, pimps and prostitutes' making life unbearable 'for decent honest folk', as the *Kensington News* maintained, it might deter those self same decent folk, including stewards and Jockey Club officials, from nosing around in Bill's business.

The nastiest business in the neighbourhood in the late 1950s and early '60s was Peter Rachman's slum housing racket. The Polish-born property developer, who came to Britain after the war, made his fortune buying up run-down old houses and mansion blocks in North Kensington. He evicted the existing tenants and then divided the houses up into abject, unfurnished flats and rented them out for extortionate sums to Caribbean immigrant families who had no rent tribunal to protect them. Rachman wasn't the only slum landlord in the area. A pair of ex-Guards officers also did well from buying up and letting out unfurnished slum properties but it was Rachman who employed a coterie of strong-arm men, black and white, to act as rent collectors. Men like Michael de Freitas, who went on to call himself Michael X and later Michael Abdul Malik,[17] and an ex-wrestler called Norbert Rondel, alias the Polish Eagle. Alsatian dogs were sometimes deployed as a persuader.

It wasn't just John Aspinall who was running private gaming parties. Rachman had illegal gaming clubs, including one in a basement on Inverness Terrace in Bayswater which, according to a breathless report in the *News of the World* in November 1961, was populated by 'wealthy young layabouts, ponces, queers, spivs, gangsters and girls, dozens of them, all drinking champagne'. Rachman rarely showed up at the club in person. He kept an office on Westbourne Park Road but, if you wanted to discuss business with him by day, the best place to find him was in the Kenco coffee bar on Queensway.

In August 1958 the toxic cocktail of Rachmanism, race and crime contributed to the Notting Hill riots. For a fortnight, the area was assailed by nightly violence as gangs of white youths fought with West Indians and attacked their homes and businesses. The following year Sir Oswald Mosley, the old daemon king of British fascism, stood as the

---

17 In 1975 Michael de Freitas was hanged in Trinidad for the murder of Gale Benson, the sister-in-law of the racing correspondent Charles Benson.

candidate for the British Union Movement – a forerunner of the National Front and the BNP – in the North Kensington by-election. He only polled 3,000 votes, some eight per cent of the electorate, but even without his racist rhetoric to inflame things, the conjunction of Portobello Road with Talbot Road, Powis Square, Ledbury Road and Colville Terrace continued to be a flashpoint. The *Kensington News* lamented that on Friday, Saturday and Sunday nights the area was 'taken over by flashy cars, loud women, men, fights and arguments'.

Not everyone disapproved of the new cultural mix and, if the newspapers sensationalised Notting Hill, the cinema loved it for its seedy exoticism. In 1962 a bedsit in St Luke's Road, near All Saints Road, was the setting for the Bryan Forbes film *The L-Shaped Room*, which starred Leslie Caron as a pregnant French girl and Tom Bell as a struggling writer. The building's other tenants included a black jazz musician, a lesbian actress and a couple of prostitutes in the basement.

There was exoticism of a sort about Number 24 Colville Terrace where some of the new tenants were seedy, disreputable and dangerous in equal measure. The building belonged to Rachman's fellow property developer Robert Jacobs who was also an associate of Charlie Mitchell who was beginning to get into the property racket in a big way himself. Jacobs had bought the Hedgegate Court slum in Powis Terrace for £95,000 and was buying out the nominee landlords and tenants to convert the building into flats for white tenants. He had similar plans for Colville Terrace.

When he first acquired it, there was a brothel in the basement and Michael de Freitas was living on the top floor.

De Freitas moved out and the crumbling old mansion, with black railings around the front and steps down to the basement, was converted into 11 flats on four different floors. In April 1961 Jacobs sold it for a nominal sum to the Honourable Mrs Barbara Robson. She didn't live there herself but she was the acting landlord and, from June to September 1961, one Major Haines, a retired army officer and friend of Mrs Robson's, lived on the top floor. Haines and Mrs Robson became fascinated by the Major's fellow tenants, especially the three young men who lived on the floor below.

In February 1961 Darkie Steward, now calling himself Leonard Bland, moved into flat number five although the name on the board outside was Roper. The following month, Darkie's old pal Brian Perry, who had moved up to London from Surrey and had been living in a more expensive bedsit on Castletown Road, moved into flat number seven. Then a few weeks later Jack Stiles, who seemed to be doing particularly well from race fixing and was now driving a Mercedes, moved into number six. The three men became friendly with Elaine Donaldson, a sexy Liverpudlian stripper whose stage name was Elaine Grande and who lived on the top floor across the landing from Major Haines. She often had her boyfriend in tow, Alex Field, who was known as Harry, and Darkie, Brian and Jack became friends with him too. Harry Field, who was born in Islington in 1924, had a string of convictions from approved school and Borstal on up. His speciality was safe breaking and he was an expert locksmith.

Mrs Robson and the Major noted that 'Bland', Perry and Stiles seemed to spend a lot of time in bed with their girlfriends, especially Darkie and his lover Sylvia Cross. They also noticed that they regularly watched the racing on their new Rediffusion television set acquired on HP. The unmistakable tones of Peter O'Sullevan and his BBC and *Daily Express* colleague Clive Graham, and the friendly chatter of their ITV counterparts John Rickman and Tony Cook, boomed out of flat number five every Saturday afternoon and on numerous weekday afternoons too.

When they weren't watching the racing or entertaining female company, Darkie, Brian and Jack spent their time in the pubs, clubs and cafés of North Kensington and from 1 May they were often round the corner in the betting shop on Golbourne Road. They drank in the Warwick Castle on Portobello Road, they went to hear Chris Barber and Ken Colyer play in Joe Cannon's Jazz Club on Westbourne Park Road, they ate breakfast, lunch and tea in the Continental Café in Blenheim Crescent or in Wraggs Café on All Saints Road, they played cards for money and sometimes they put on a suit and tie and went to the Contessa, Rachman's 'chemmy' (chemin de fer) club in Inverness Terrace. It was all a lot more fun than spending night after night in the same old racing pubs in Newmarket and Epsom.

From time to time the trio had an older, male visitor, the polite and smartly dressed Mr Roper who had first looked over the building with Robert Jacobs and Charlie Mitchell in February and who often paid Darkie's rent – £22 a month – in cash up front. It wasn't the only financial matter that Mr Roper took care of. Mrs Robson also saw him settle a debt with the representative of a finance company who had sold Brian Perry a car on hire purchase and came calling for an overdue payment.

Bill had decided that it was too risky to continue holding meetings in cafés or in his Monmouth Street office. Unbeknown to the others, he suspected that his phone was being tapped by either rival bookmakers or gangsters, like Albert Dimes, or both. So instead he conducted planning sessions in Darkie's room at Colville Terrace which was at the back of the building and looked out over the rooftops and lock-ups of Lonsdale Mews. The gatherings must have resembled a cross between Pinkie Brown's gang in *Brighton Rock* and Alec Guinness and his fellow 'musicians' in *The Ladykillers*. When Bill arrived, Mrs Robson often heard the cry 'Girls out . . . it's business' and on one occasion, when Bill disturbed Darkie and Sylvia in bed together, Darkie hastily pulled on a pair of trousers and went outside to talk to the boss in his car.

Sometimes, said Mrs Robson, Roper brought his 'brother' with him (Joe Lowry) and sometimes he arrived with 'a tall, powerfully built man who drove a black Jaguar' (Charlie Mitchell). Mr Roper and his friends occasionally left the building in the late evening in a convoy of cars. 'We'll take the M1,' Mrs Robson heard them say one night. The younger men – Bland, Perry, Stiles and Field – often arrived back at breakfast time and then slept for the rest of the day. One such Saturday morning in July, Major Haines noticed that young Bland appeared to have a cut on his hand which Sylvia was bandaging ineffectually. What the gang didn't know was that the Major had been at the army veterinary college in Poona in India and he recognised the teeth marks on Darkie's skin.

One person Mrs Robson never saw was Micheline Lugeon. It would have been anathema for Bill to bring his well-spoken and well-groomed young girlfriend to Notting Hill. The Stafford Court penthouse was only a mile away but there was a huge gulf in tastes and standards between the two residences. Colville Terrace meant overflowing ash trays and unmade beds whereas Bill wanted Micheline to associate him with clean, well-laundered sheets, the smell of furniture polish where his cleaning lady had been in and fresh flowers left in a vase in the window.

On Friday 12 May Bill went racing at Lingfield Park near Edenbridge. The leafy Surrey track staged its annual Derby trial which was won by a promising colt trained by Cecil Boyd-Rochfort called Pardao who booked his ticket to Epsom. But the following morning Bill was in Newmarket where there was a much more significant trial involving Pinturischio, who worked brilliantly on the gallops, leaving Aurelius and another stable companion for dead. Everyone associated with the horse, from Sir Victor Sassoon and Noel Murless and Lester Piggott to the legion of ante-post punters, including all those wealthy and well-bred Ladbrokes punters, who had backed him for the Derby and in some cases combined him in doubles with the favourite for the Oaks,[18] was now looking forward to his appearance at York the following Tuesday.

18 The Oaks is the classic race at Epsom for three-year-old fillies, run over the same course and distance as the Derby.

But on Monday 15 May the news slipped out of Newmarket that Pinto was unwell and running a temperature which had first been detected the previous day. Some kind of stomach upset was apparently responsible and, although his temperature was only just above normal in the evening, come Tuesday morning Noel Murless withdrew him from the Dante Stakes. There were no other trials on the horizon and there was a palpable air of disappointment as *The Sporting Life* reflected that punters would have no more chances to assess the favourite's ability before Derby Day on 31 May.

On the evening of 15 May there had been another Derby call-over at the Victoria Club but, following the news that Pinturischio was 'indisposed' and with few people expecting him to run at York, he was deposed as favourite. The Frenchie, Moutiers, closed as the new 8-1 market leader with Pint O'Sherry out to 9-1 at which odds Arthur Cassani reported there was 'no business'. Of course there wasn't. Racecourse rumours were already spreading fast and certain wily Victoria Club members would've known exactly what was going on and what would happen next.

On Thursday 18 May the mood picked up a bit as Murless reported that 'Pinturischio seems to be improving. He did light work yesterday and he will canter today.' There were still 13 days to go and the master trainer had not yet given up hope of saddling his new star at Epsom. But then, on Saturday 20 May the telephones rang early on the newspaper sports desks and in the offices of the big credit bookmaking firms like Hills and Ladbrokes.

Pinturischio was not out on Newmarket Heath with the rest of Noel Murless's string. It appeared that there had been a recurrence of the colt's 'internal trouble' and when Murless got back to Warren Place after Sandown races on the Saturday evening, he issued a statement saying that Pinturischio would not run in the Derby.

The sensational development was front and back page news on Monday 22 May. 'Pinto Riddle,' exclaimed the *Daily Express*. 'Was he got at?' The scout, Clive Graham, reminded *Express* readers that 'the big Pinza colt's mystery illness first became evident a week before, 24 hours after a hugely impressive gallop against two stable companions.' Graham emphasised that Pint O'Sherry had been 'the subject of a huge ante-post gamble and coupled in doubles and accumulators to win many thousands of pounds with starting price bookmakers'. He then quoted Noel Murless directly who said that 'there's no doubt that during the past week he [Pinturischio] has been suffering from the effects of some form of poisoning. I can't entirely rule out foul play.'

In the *News of the World* the following Sunday, Quintin Gilbey described the Derby favourite's defection as 'a classic bombshell. Big backers, some of whom stood to win thousands, have been dealt a body blow by the recurrence of Pinturischio's mysterious stomach trouble.'

With exquisite irony the Norfolk Committee's report on Jockey Club doping policy had been published a few weeks before. From now on there would be routine and random dope testing at racecourses on a daily basis. No medication was to be permitted to be given to a horse within 72 hours of a race and, most importantly for the trainers, where a drug or stimulant was detected, no one would lose their licence provided the stewards were satisfied that the trainer concerned had taken all possible steps to protect the horse in his care.

The report was hailed as a victory for common sense though, as many journalists observed, it was too late to rebuild the careers of Clive Chapman and the many other innocent men whose lives had been wrecked under the old regime.

Noel Murless could now reasonably have gone to the Jockey Club without fear of repercussions, shared with them his suspicions about Pinturischio and called in the police. But the trainer was loath to accept that he had been the victim of an inside job and, to begin with, he continued to try and find other explanations. When Murless had been called to Pinto's box on the morning of Monday 15 May he'd found him to be in agony. He had been suffering from violent diarrhoea during the night and Murless summoned Fred Day, a leading Newmarket veterinary surgeon, who reported that the horse had a temperature of 103 and thought at first that he might have a twisted gut. Day took samples of the colt's prodigious droppings and a blood test and sent them to be analysed at Newmarket's Equine Research Station. The colt was still distressed and the symptoms didn't abate until his temperature dropped to normal on the Tuesday.

On the Friday morning Pinturischio was well enough to canter five furlongs with Aurelius but, on the Saturday morning 'the symptoms had re-appeared', as Clive Graham put it. What that really meant was that the poor horse was in agony once again and purging himself profusely. When he still wasn't any better that night, Murless decided there and then that he wouldn't be going to Epsom. Surprisingly, on Sunday morning Pinto was one of the hungriest horses at Warren Place but the mini recovery was too late for the Derby. He wasn't actually scratched until 27 May, four days before the race and after Lester Piggott had teamed up with him for one final, futile gallop. Even then Noel Murless found it hard to believe he'd been doped. 'Why would they have got at him before he'd proved his Derby credentials in the Dante?' he asked. He wondered if Pinturischio could have gobbled up sump oil while picking grass on the heath after his brilliant gallop on the 13th.

But it wasn't sump oil that poisoned him. It was a disgusting, foul smelling liquid called Croton Oil which was one of the most powerful purgatives known to man. The viscous, yellowish brown substance comes from the seeds of a shrub, *Croton tiglium*, that grows in India and Malaysia and was used as a laxative in ancient Chinese medicine. Taken orally it causes intense stomach pains and diarrhoea and if you get it on your skin it can cause blisters, swelling and discoloration.

In the first half of the 20th century Croton Oil was used in zoos to cure large mammals like elephants of what was politely termed 'obstinate constipation' and, in the 1920s, Chicago bootleggers sometimes poured it into whiskey bottles to catch out light-fingered rivals tempted to steal their goods. In the Second World War the US Navy even added it to their torpedo fuel in an attempt to deter alcoholic sailors from trying to siphon off and drink the grain alcohol that was the main fuel component in the tubes.

The two doses of Croton Oil that were used to dope Pinturischio almost killed him. They were recommended by Richard McGee, supplied by Ted Smith and administered by the colt's own stable lad Philip 'Snuffy' Lawler with the assistance of Darkie Steward, Jack Stiles and Alex Field who picked the lock on his box once Lawler had shown them a way in. When the horse showed signs of recovering the Colville Terrace gang went back – or rather they were sent back – and did it again. This time Murless had a nightwatchman sitting beside a brazier in the yard but Darkie Steward later boasted that he threw a brick on to a nearby roof and that drew the nightwatchman's attention away while the others did the business. 'They really finished him off,' reflected Murless in 1980 in conversation with his biographer, Tim Fitzgeorge-Parker. 'In fact, from their point of view, they did such a good job that he was never able to run again.' The rich bay with the kind intelligent eye and the 'sensible gentlemanly manner' remained engaged in races like the King George and the St Leger and there was talk of him staying in training as a four-year-old but he never came right. He had little success as a stallion either although he did slightly better when exported to Germany where he died in 1976.

Doping the Derby favourite was a shocking act. The racing equivalent of assassinating a president or a prime minister.

It was only made possible through the collusion of Snuffy Lawler who, having turned down numerous offers to dope St Paddy the previous year, finally gave in, accepting a cash bribe believed to be in the region of £600, or £10,800 in modern money.

Noel Murless had had his suspicions for some time as so many other horses Snuffy looked after had been beaten when expected to run well. He found it hard to believe that one of his best lads, St Paddy's lad, an employee he had liked and trusted, could have betrayed him and harmed the horses in his care. But other voices – including jockeys, racing correspondents and friendly bookmakers like William Hill – kept telling him that the word in Newmarket was that Snuffy was bent and had to have been involved. Nothing was said openly in the press but a painful meeting followed and Lawler left the yard. He would never work in racing again and initially he went back to his native Merseyside but it was not the last that either the sport or Bill Roper's gang would hear of him.

The nobbling of Pinturischio was unlike any other crime the gang carried out. This wasn't about getting at a favourite the night before, befuddling it with amphetamines or barbiturates and then backing the second or third favourite the following day. This was a job done to order and specifically designed to ensure that Noel Murless's horse would never run at Epsom. The gang supplied the drugs, the personnel and the 'expertise' and, as Clive Graham was quick to point out, their efforts saved the big credit and SP bookmaking firms thousands of pounds' worth of ante-post liabilities. Bookies like Max Parker who had got the Big Loser they were always looking for. Bookies like Alf Cope, Jack Swift and Bernie Howard not to mention such sterling independent operators as Charlie Mitchell and Albert Dimes.

Scotland Yard investigators were eventually involved, and they concluded that some £200,000, or £3.6million in 2013 currency, was won by the bookies as a result of the doping. But no one was ever charged with ordering it or carrying it out. The police believed that 'a knot of not inconsiderable bookmakers were involved' but found it well-nigh impossible to obtain sufficient evidence for a prosecution. William Hill admitted that he had benefited financially but he had tried to alert Murless a week before the Dante to the possibility that the horse would be got at. Over the next two years the police and the Jockey Club frequently appealed to the big bookmakers to come forward and share what they knew but only two of them, Hill and Archie Scott, were prepared to co-operate fully and disclose the details of their ante-post trading. The rest stayed away, many of them losing or discarding their ledgers and accounts on the 1961 Derby, even as the betting ring bush telegraph buzzed with rumours of what had happened. When the finger was pointed specifically at Max Parker and Cyril Stein, the crafty old operator and his nephew maintained a discreet silence.

Jackie Dyer, who had been in Newmarket with Joe Lowry the night Treasure Hunt was doped the year before, remembers: 'Maxie would often have all of the gang back to his flat for dinner on a Saturday night. He lived in Montagu Square not far from Marble Arch and he loved to cook. That was one of his main pleasures.' The bookie, who was 61 years old in 1961 but looked older, could afford to bring out the best silver and get in the finest wines and beef sirloin from Smithfield after the running of the 174th Derby.

May 31 was a cloudless, blue sky summer's day. A day of huge crowds on Epsom Downs. Of crushed grass and cigar smoke. Of escapologists and three-card-trick merchants. Of Rollers and Bentleys and gypsy caravans. Of open-topped buses and all the fun of the fair. Prince Monolulu was there and the Pearly Kings and Queens and Lord Rosebery accompanying Queen Elizabeth and the Queen Mother. Bill Roper was there too but not Micheline. She was officially working that Wednesday but Bill had put £50 each way on Pardao for her and she popped out to see the race on television at her Malvern Court flat.

With Pinturischio sidelined and Aurelius not ready, there was no mount for Lester Piggott. At the Press Club lunch the Monday before, Sir Francis Cassel said that he'd dreamed that his horse, Fontana di Trevi, won the race. Sir Gordon Richards fancied Nicomedus. The jockey Harry Carr thought Pardao would win with luck in running and the glamorous French owner Madame Suzy Volterra was backing her runner, Dicta Drake. His fellow countryman, Moutiers, went off favourite, backed down from 8-1 to 5-1 on the day. But he didn't win. Following on from Rockavon's 66-1 triumph in the 2,000 Guineas, the race went to another 66-1 outsider, Psidium, who was last of all coming round Tattenham Corner but took off in the home straight and passed everything on the wide outside. Dicta Drake finished second and the Lingfield trial winner, Pardao, was third. Psidium's owner, Etti Plesch, the wife of a Hungarian financier, led him in afterwards. His jockey, the Frenchman Roger Poincelet, was winning his first Derby. His handler Harry Wragg, who had won it three times as a jockey, was winning his first Derby as a trainer – and the Poor Boy's prophecy was right, a Newmarket horse had won the big race.[19]

Punters had queued in their thousands to get into Epsom and they'd queued in their hundreds to get into the new betting shops and they had left hundreds and thousands of pounds behind them, both in the offices and on the racecourse.

That summer the doping gang seemed invincible and Bill and Micheline's fortunes on an ever-upward curve. As for the bookmakers, whose old illegal street businesses had only recently been legitimised, they could truly echo the words of the Prime Minister Harold Macmillan that they 'had never had it so good'.

19 Psidium, who had been 18th in Rockavon's 2,000 Guineas, injured a tendon not long after the Derby and never raced again. His owner, an Austro-Hungarian countess who married six times, also won the Derby in 1980.

11

FOUL PLAY

AN ENTHUSIASM for cafés and coffee bars by day, or diners in the US, wasn't the only thing that united British and American gangsters in the 1950s and '60s. The mobsters, and their bookmaker associates, also loved their nights out. Clubs and cabarets like the Astor and the Pigalle in London and the Copacabana in New York, were their kind of places and taking a table the visible evidence of their prosperity and success. Just like the sartorial etiquette on the racecourse, it was vital to look the part. The men sometimes wore a tuxedo, otherwise their best whistle and flute along with crisp white shirts, thin ties and a top pocket handkerchief. Their women, be they wives or mistresses, were expected to be made-up adornments. Bouffant, bee-hived and smiling. Everyone had a cigarette in their hand and another bottle of champagne was never far away.

On Saturday 10 June Roper took Micheline Lugeon to the Pigalle Club for a special benefit concert for the Astor Club's owner, Solomon 'Sulky' Gowers. A sometime bookmaker, dog doper and pub singer, Sulky was recovering from a leg amputation and Shirley Bassey, Max Bygraves and Tommy Steele all performed on his behalf. Sulky had his own moment in the spotlight, treating the audience to a special number he'd written about the royal family.

'Princess Margaret's gone and married
That Anthony Armstrong-Jones
When will they give a Jewish boy a chance?'

The following week the good Jewish bookmaking boys and their Gentile cousins were all at Royal Ascot where the self-same Anthony Armstrong-Jones made his debut in the royal procession. The Duke of Norfolk was there at 6.55 a.m. on the first day, ordering the lawns to be swept for 'the umpteenth time'. The big story was the opening of the new £1million stand, the Duke's 'dream project' which had two floors of private boxes, many of them housing past and present clients of Max Parker and Bill Roper. The Maharanee of Baroda was in attendance, as were Lord Cornwallis and Lew Grade and Sir Charles Clore and the band-leader Jack Hylton who brought his own wine. The City man, and Rich Charlie, John Topliss-Smith, came with a laundry hamper containing a crab, a present for his host. 'Everyone seems to have lobster,' he said. 'But really crab is much nicer and it's the done thing to carry food about in a hamper, isn't it?'

If you weren't bringing your own lobster or crab, the racecourse caterer's menu featured melon, smoked salmon, a cold collation, or a 'cold coalition' as one waitress described it, and strawberries and cream.

Racegoers were buoyed by a victory for the Queen's filly, Aiming High, in Wednesday's Coronation Stakes and that evening Her Majesty took a party of guests to Windsor's Theatre Royal, booking the front two rows of the balcony. They had come to see a musical version of *Jane Eyre* – which only ran for three weeks – and, during the interval, the monarch was heard to ask: 'Please tell me, someone, has this got a happy or a sad ending? I quite forget.'

Bill Roper was at Ascot every day, popping in and out of the boxes along with the butlers and waitresses, laying bets and accepting commissions. Bill was adept at flattering clients whose judgement he doubted but whose business he was determined to keep. 'Snuff Box, your Lordship? Five hundred pound to one, on the nose? Very bold. I couldn't have him myself but then what do I know?' Alternatively, if trade was slow, he was not above encouraging some rich, foolish and currently 'resting' punter to step back into the ring. Usually with disastrous consequences for the punter's wealth. 'How about Trelawney, Mr Topliss-Smith? Nine thousand pounds to one and a monkey each way? You've got that, sir. You've got that with me.'

But Bill didn't win every time and if Micheline still believed that all his income came from his regular bookmaking business, she may have noticed that the 1961 royal meeting was a disaster for the layers. Doris, who knew a thing or two about betting, would have definitely felt the impact in the Covent Garden office. Noel Murless had four winners, including Pinturischio's galloping companion Aurelius, who landed the King Edward VII Stakes or 'Ascot Derby', and on the Friday all six favourites went in, among them the heavily backed Irish challenger Moss Bank, who romped home by eight lengths in the Queen Alexandra Stakes.

There were a number of plain clothes detectives hanging around conspicuously in the betting ring but they weren't after Bill. They were trying to catch a gang of card sharps who had been fleecing mug punters on the race trains from Waterloo to Ascot and Windsor. There were also rumours going around that two horses, Noel Murless's Favorita and the Aga Khan's filly Opaline II, would be doped. But the stories were baseless and had nothing to do with Bill's crew. It felt too soon after Pinturischio for them to be going back to work though other interested parties were impatient for a resumption.

One of the few profitable results for the ring at the meeting was in the big race, the Ascot Gold Cup, which had a field of ten, six of them trained in France. The favourite was the 1960 Prix de l'Arc de Triomphe winner Puissant Chef, who was backed in from 11-10 to even money and odds-on. But the supposed Gallic certainty could finish only seventh as English horses filled the first four places and, for once, the bookmakers were cheering Lester Piggott who rode the 100-8 winner, Pandofell. The four-year-old, who had been thought to be nothing more than a useful handicapper, landed the prize by five lengths and was clearly still improving. He had been a bargain buy for his owner, Mr Warwick Daw of Henley, who had paid just £600 to acquire him and had now won £16,500 of prize money.

'Pando', as he was nicknamed, was estimated to be worth £50,000 as a stallion prospect and his trainer, Farnham Maxwell, was planning to run him in more of the top staying races like the Goodwood and Doncaster Cups. But before then he was scheduled to have another run at Ascot in the Sunninghill Park Stakes, the last race of the day on Friday 15 July, the day before the King George VI and Queen Elizabeth Stakes.[20] The two-mile contest attracted just four runners and the morning papers predicted that Pandofell would go off 5-4 favourite with Prolific, who had finished third in the Gold Cup, beaten five lengths and a head, rated a 5-2 chance and the only realistic danger.

It was a perfect target for the dopers. Stop the favourite in a four-horse race, lay it on and off course and back the second favourite. It had worked before and it would surely work again. Especially as Darkie Steward had broken into 'Freddie' Maxwell's yard in 1959, getting at Accompanist before his Brighton race, and he still had a contact among the stable lads.

Thursday 14 July was a hot summer night, precisely the kind of night when the society osteopath Stephen Ward was taking his friend Christine Keeler on sex tours around Notting Hill, looking out for prostitutes on the corner of Colville Terrace and Powis Court and photographing pimps and dope dealers in Fiesta One and the Rio on Westbourne Park Road. If Ward was being particularly observant that week, he may even have noticed Jack Stiles's Mercedes pulling out of Colville Terrace around 10 p.m.

There was no M4 in 1961 and, to get to Lambourn, the gang had to take the old A4 out through Maidenhead and

20 It was the same day's racing on which the gang had doped Skymaster the previous year.

Reading and on to Newbury before heading north across the Downs. It should have been a straightforward job but Steward and Stiles were over-confident and clumsy and when they got into Pandofell's box they frightened him. The horse attempted to defend himself and bit Darkie, who had forgotten his rubber gloves, on the hand. Angry and hurting, the ex-apprentice responded by sticking more than the usual dose of drugs down Pando's throat. 'To pacify him,' he claimed to the others later.

When he got back to Colville Terrace that Friday morning, Darkie was still bleeding and in pain. Sylvie Cross attempted to patch him up and their neighbour across the landing, Major Haines, who was always an early riser, came out to investigate the commotion. The Major not only recognised the signs of a horse bite on Steward's hand, he and Mrs Robson also saw what appeared to be a map of a racing stable on Brian Perry's bed.

Later that day Bill went to Ascot as normal, all set to back Prolific in the last and lay Pandofell. Jackie Dyer was going to lay it too along with Bernie Howard, Charlie Mitchell and the Max Parker firm, not to mention Albert Dimes, as Darkie always kept the big man in the picture. But when Bill got to the races at lunchtime, the first thing he heard was that Pandofell had been withdrawn from the Sunninghill Park Stakes and, a few urgent telephone calls later, he discovered why.

When Farnham Maxwell and his wife went to Pandofell's box that morning they found him to be 'shockingly dazed and ill, so ill he could hardly stand'. The overdose of barbiturates had taken a horrible toll on the Gold Cup winner who was staggering and bleeding from cuts around the eyes, probably caused from falling against the walls. Maxwell's wife was in tears when a *Sporting Life* reporter caught up with her. 'It was no accident,' she said and her husband, angry and distressed, concurred: 'The whole thing is in the hands of the police now.' Like every other trainer in the land, Maxwell had heard about Pinturischio and some of the other nobbled horses, and now it seemed that Pinto had been followed by Pando. A Derby favourite and then an Ascot Gold Cup winner both got at viciously within the space of two months.

Happily for the Maxwells and owner Warwick Daw, Pandofell did recover from his doping and although he was last of four on his next run at Newbury in August, he ended his career on a high, winning the Doncaster Cup by three lengths and then retiring to stud as arranged. But in the high summer weeks, the doping story was on the front and back pages as both the racing community and the wider public began to come to terms with the scale of the problem. 'FOUL PLAY SUSPECTED' said a banner headline in *The Times*, going on to warn that 'if it turns out that, like Sing Sing last year, this was an attempt which went wrong to slow the horse in his race by administering a drug, it will cause an outcry on the racecourse such has not been heard before.' In a rider that might have worried Bill Roper if he read it, *The Times* added that 'the Jockey Club and Scotland Yard came to an agreement that this type of investigation is police business when they met a month ago.'

The tone was suitably severe and some local police forces were making random enquiries but Scotland Yard could not take over an investigation unless they were specifically asked to by a local force or unless the Jockey Club requested their involvement and, as of July 1961, no such request had been made. There was still no official police enquiry into the Pinturischio case and the Jockey Club's response was in the hands of the aforementioned Colonel Blair, the amateur sleuth of Cavendish Square. But the Colonel had little knowledge of police work and even less of the betting ring and, in the view of the bookmakers, Bill Roper included, he couldn't run an errand let alone a criminal investigation department.[21]

In fairness to the Colonel, he did supplement his team by recruiting a couple of private investigators, including ex-Metropolitan Police Detective Sergeant Robert Hill who was forever referred to by the press as 'portly Bob Hill'. The private eyes began sniffing around in Newmarket and Epsom and talking to stable lads, much as Joe Lowry used to do, but it would be November before their efforts bore any fruit, and even then the gang were several steps ahead of them.

Roper, who realised that the authorities must bestir themselves eventually but didn't believe they'd ever catch up with him, decided to press on. But then, if Bill was honest, he didn't really have a choice. The repercussions over the Pandofell blunder were not quite as bad as the St Paddy race at Ascot in 1959. The horse had been withdrawn before proper trading could begin but if there were no heavy losses, there were no profits either. Prolific won the race but at odds of 8-13, which

---

21 'He was a complete waste of time,' reckons Gerry Parker. 'He'd drop in to the office for a nice cup of tea and a chat and then he'd go home again.'

meant you would have had to invest £13 to win £8 – not the sort of price the gang did business at. Charlie Mitchell was furious, especially with Darkie Steward who got a second and final warning for incompetence. It was a bad time for Darkie. On 6 June he'd appeared at Marylebone Magistrates Court and been fined £20 for receiving a stolen camera. He claimed he'd bought it off a fellow he met in Kingston market and, in court, he gave his occupation as 'professional gambler' and said that he was employed by the 'respected bookmaker' Mr William Roper of Monmouth Street W1. It wasn't the sort of publicity that Bill wanted. Throughout his career Roper was notoriously camera shy having been taught by Max Parker that their business worked best out of sight of prying eyes.

Roper was still putting money on for Mitchell, who in turn was giving tips to Rachman and Robert Jacobs, and although he was beginning to find the younger man's company intimidating, he felt he needed him. He'd made good money from the Pinturischio job but the story of the doping was now common knowledge in the underworld and Roper was more convinced than ever that he was being tagged by other gangs who wanted to find out what he was going to do next. There was one West London racket run by a character called The Professor who specialised in extorting money from small betting shop owners. Then there was Mr Albert Dimes who was always asking after Bill's health and keen to know all his latest news. In the circumstances, Charlie Mitchell was Bill's insurance policy. But the only way to keep him happy was to pay him money and that meant fixing more races.

Roper had other overheads as well. The gang's foot soldiers – the stable lads and the Colville Terrace crowd – all had to be paid and so did Ted Smith and Richard McGee. Then there was Monmouth Street and Doris and the boys, and then there was Micheline Lugeon. The Beauchamp Place shop hadn't lasted. The rates there were indeed too high, even before she'd paid June Downie and a part-time assistant. So Micheline had sold the lease and was temporarily working from her Malvern Court apartment, inviting clients, some of whom were wives and girlfriends of Bill's punters, to see her there on a one-to-one basis.

It should have been the perfect arrangement, Micheline bringing out her wares like a pop-up shop or trunk show. But to her intense frustration, especially after she had expended time and effort trying to charm them, the landlords in South Kensington were unhappy about the flat being used as business premises and a new site was urgently required. Micheline had a possible shop in mind on Crawford Street, equidistant from Marylebone High Street and the Edgware Road. It was not quite as upmarket as Knightsbridge and a step back in the direction of Selfridges and the beauty school where she had started out from. But the brand had many admirers and so did Micheline, none more ardent than Bill who was still madly in love with her and couldn't abandon his pledges of support now. With the right kind of bravura and cunning, Mr Racing was convinced he could still pull it off.

The week after the Pandofell race, Roper and Charlie Mitchell went to see Ted Smith at his Surbiton residence. Bill was unhappy with the methyl amphetamine hydrochloride and wanted Smithie to get them some more luminal sodium which he thought was more reliable. He assured Ted that there'd be 'plenty of money' for him if the results were good.

Mitchell, who wasn't there to pour the tea, was less friendly. He had his suspicions about Smith and felt that all this Witch Doctor business was going to his head. He wanted to make it absolutely clear that Ted shouldn't get any ideas about holding out on them or diluting the gear. Charlie was closer to the truth than he may have realised but, that July afternoon, Ted was unstoppable, handing round the digestives and the custard creams like a rich man. Anything they required, he'd fix it. One day, not far off maybe, he was thinking of retiring from his current line of work and moving May and the kids to the country. But until then it was a pleasure, an honour even, to do business with them. May, who was in the kitchen, overheard Ted's boasting and winced. It was the first time that she had met Charlie Mitchell. She said afterwards that she found him terrifying and, that, as soon as she could, she took her youngest daughter into the bedroom and locked the door behind them.

Smith promised to ring up Richard McGee in Newcastle and then liaise with Darkie Steward. A few days later the message came through that McGee could get what they wanted but that Smith would have to go up north to collect it. Bill arranged to meet Smith on the Metropolitan Line concourse at Baker Street Station. He gave him an envelope containing £50 cash for himself, £50 for McGee and a return train ticket, first class this time, from King's Cross to Newcastle.

The following morning the Witch Doctor headed north.

12

A DIFFERENT PLAN

TED SMITH had never had it so good. Putting on the dog in his first-class compartment. Just the three seats on either side. Soft cushions, head rest, arm rest, all decked out in British Rail blue. Some snooty business type in the corner and an old maid and her teenage daughter – not a bad looker either – sitting opposite. On their way to Scotland, so she said. To visit family. Ted nodding pleasantly. Ted in his leather windcheater jacket and his winklepicker shoes. Puffing on a fag and flicking through his copies of *Parade* and *The Sporting Life*. The miles of flat green country racing past outside.

Shortly after Peterborough the ticket inspector came round. Eyeing Ted up suspiciously. As if to say 'I know your type and you don't belong here.' Examining Ted's ticket several times but unable to find any fault with it. An unnecessarily loud 'Thank you sir' as he handed it back. Ted grinning. Thinking, 'You don't know who you're dealing with, mate. I've got friends who'd sort you out. Proper men.'

The train accelerating through Newark and Grantham and then on into sunlit south Yorkshire. Smoke stacks and mine shafts. A quick stop at Doncaster. Ted taking his seat in the dining car. Sipping Brown Windsor soup and a light ale. The steward in his navy blue jacket with the red epaulettes. Some old Scots git. With a toupee by the look of it. 'Roast beef for sir?' 'Not half.' 'Horseradish for sir?' 'Pour it on, squire.' The steward bending over the table opposite. His too tight jacket riding up at the back and one of the buttons on his braces coming loose.

Ted skipping coffee and dessert. Lighting a panatella and making his way along to the buffet car. Getting some beers in while he could. It was the beginning of the school holidays and the second-class carriages were packed with families and luggage. No restaurant car lunches for them. No first-class compartments with arm rests, head rests and cushions. No money, no room. But room for Ted Smith on Mr Roper's private business.

More stops at York and Darlington and then they were gathering speed again, the lines multiplying and spreading out, sidings, coaches, goods vans, points and then the train was slowing down and coming over the big bridge across the Tyne. Ted knew a bit about Newcastle. It was full of Geordies with their incomprehensible accents. But Ted couldn't wait to see his old mate and best pal, Dick McGee.

The Witch Doctor took a cab out to Fawdon. He'd been told to wait in a café in the city centre. McGee would meet him there after work. But Ted wasn't having any of that. Wasn't hanging around for an hour in some Geordie caff listening to whining Geordies. So he told the taxi driver to take him to the laboratory front door and told security right out. He was Mr Edward Smith from Surbiton, Surrey come up first class on the train from London and come to see his friend, Mr Richard McGee.

McGee said later it was an excruciating moment. Ted, pissed up and boastful and demanding to be shown around. The security guard sending for McGee and the secretary, Mary Cross, smiling but looking surprised. McGee trying to smile too and be delighted. Introducing Ted to his office manager, John Eversley. An old friend, he said. An old friend from the West Molesey days who just happened to be passing through. Eversley looking surprised but keeping it very civil and encouraging Dick to leave work early and take his friend out and show him the sights. McGee and Ted walking out together under the eyes of the security guard. Two bottles' worth of luminal sodium burning a hole in McGee's inside jacket pocket.

They had their night on the town. Drinking Newkie Brown until the early hours. Ted catching a few hours' kip on Dick's sofa. A fry-up in the morning and a hug before he left. Taking the train back down to London still full of it. Another bloody ticket collector trying to catch him out. But Ted was somewhere else. He nearly said it out loud. 'I bet you don't know what I've got in my pocket! Enough dope to stop every fucking horse running in England today.'

When the Witch Doctor got back to London he passed on a quantity of the goods to Darkie Steward on Baker Street station and when Bill Roper and Charlie Mitchell had inspected them, Bill sent Darkie back to Ted with further remuneration. Bill had lots of thoughts about horses and trainers they might target before the end of the season and there was talk of them launching operations in Ireland.[22] But Charlie had a different plan and, instead of just being Bill Roper's partner in crime, he had decided that from now on Bill should work for him.

Mitchell broke the news one evening at the Monmouth Street office, Doris and her secretary, Lizzie Barnes, having been sent home early. Bill sat behind his desk, a telephone on either side of him, and Charlie made himself comfortable in the chair opposite. Tobacco smoke swirled around the room and through the open window they could hear the sound of the traffic on Charing Cross Road and Shaftesbury Avenue. It was a mild September evening and the working day was almost over. Couples would soon be meeting in pubs and coffee bars and hurrying to the cinema and the theatre.

Mitchell studied the racing calendar on the wall and the old prints of horses and prize-fighters. Bill had a small safe in the corner and on top of the safe was a tray with gin and whisky bottles, a soda siphon and some glasses. Charlie helped himself to a drink and then began to tell Bill a story. It was all about this fella he knew, another speculative character not

22 Bill Roper, Charlie Mitchell, Darkie Steward and Alex Field went on a reconnaissance mission to Dublin in September 1961, staying at the Gesham Hotel. They planned to bribe a stable lad who worked at Paddy Prendergast's yard on the Curragh but their contact was rumbled by Prendergast's head lad and the Englishmen flew home before the Gardai could talk to them.

unlike Roper. His name was Charles Da Silva, a Sri Lankan-born conman and gent who was said to resemble 'Omar Sharif's better looking brother'. Bill Roper, who knew a bit about Da Silva, laughed politely. The smooth-talking grifter, explained Charlie, had managed to sell a fleet of Grimsby fishing trawlers, sight unseen, to a Yorkshire fur farmer he met in the dining car on a train from Hull to King's Cross. Da Silva convinced the farmer that he owned the trawlers and that the Ceylonese government would pay handsomely for them.

Da Silva was the master of both the long and the short con and he liked to put himself about when things were going well. But then assorted villains came round demanding a share of the spoils. Or else. At which point Charlie had stepped in and generously offered Da Silva his protection in return for 75 per cent of his profits. He now had a similar arrangement in mind for Bill.

As Roper sat there in silence, his mind whirring, Mitchell outlined his strategy. His bookmaking and moneylending business was doing well and he'd decided he'd like to open a club in Fulham. The doping racket would be the ideal way to raise the necessary funds. Roper was an acknowledged genius at finding the horses and deciding which ones they should get at and when. Well, now it was time to branch out. If the flat was getting dicey they should move on to jump-racing stables and not just in the south of England. They should go into the Midlands. They should try the North East. They should go anywhere where there were favourites who could be laid and underpaid stable lads who could be bribed. Bill was the big brain. He could work it out. Charlie would pay his expenses up front and provide security for the gang's activities. Bill didn't want Albert Dimes and the West End boys getting their hooks into him or that dodgepot Ted Smith. But what Charlie needed, couldn't do without to be honest, was ready cash for his club. Say, £100,000 by Christmas? If Bill did all right, there would still be some left over for that sweet little Swiss girlfriend of his. The young one that was half Bill's age and that plenty of other chaps, younger men, hard men, would love to get their leg over.

When Mitchell had gone, patting Bill on the back as he left, the human comptometer poured himself a Scotch and, hand shaking, tried desperately to think of a way out. But there was no way out. The doping gang had become a victim of its own success. Bill realised that what Mitchell was proposing was extortion, pure and simple and he had no illusions about the menace beneath the bonhomie. There was a shark in the harbour and if Bill shut up shop and tried to hide away, Charlie would find him and kill him or at least hurt him, or hurt Micheline or Doris and the kids, and then throw him to Dimes or the police or both. No matter how he looked at it, there was no alternative other than to do as he was asked. But doping steeplechasers would be hazardous and not just for the horse and jockey. If a chaser or hurdler were to fall under the influence of barbiturates and the rider were to be killed, the men who planned it and carried it out could end up with a rope around their neck.

The gang had tried it a few times the previous winter. Most notoriously they got at a horse called Blessington

Esquire who was owned by Lord Carnarvon and trained at Compton in Berkshire by 'Atty' Corbett. The six-year-old was regarded as one of the most promising young steeplechasers in the country and on Saturday 11 March 1961 he lined up in the four-runner George Williamson Chase at Hurst Park. His main rival was an equally exciting young Irish horse, Scottish Memories, who was sent off the 11-8 favourite and had Bobby Beasley in the saddle. David 'Duke' Nicholson took the mount on Blessington Esquire who was on offer at 6-4 with the racecourse bookies.

Nicholson was one of the hard men of the weighing room but he later described that March ride as a nightmarish experience and believed he was lucky not to be killed. Blessington Esquire, 'normally a superb jumper', acted 'as if he was drunk' and 'didn't take a single fence cleanly', even hitting some of the fences with his head. Pure class and his jockey's tenacity enabled him to complete the course in second place, but well beaten, and although he recovered after a fashion and won more races he was never as good again. There was no official dope test afterwards and no stewards' inquiry but Nicholson's view was that dopers should be 'strung up' and Bill Roper would have known that many other jockeys and trainers agreed with him.

Whichever way the racket went, jumping or flat, many more stables, stables outside the Newmarket/Epsom/Lambourn axis, would have to be reconnoitred. New horses would have to be identified. New locks picked. New lads bribed. What Bill really needed was a spy. A secret agent, like in the war, who could go into a yard unannounced and charm the necessary intelligence out of the staff. A bookmaker like himself wouldn't do and an ex-stable lad like Darkie or Jack Stiles would never cut it. Neither would Jackie Dyer or Uncle Joe Lowry. It would have to be someone not yet connected to the gang. Someone smart, well spoken and well dressed who could maybe pass themselves off as a rich owner. Someone who loved Bill . . . very much . . . and would willingly help him in return for all the help that he had given her.

The previous March, Max Parker had talked to Bill about the Grand National contender Nicolaus Silver. The grey chaser, trained at Kinnersley in Worcestershire by Fred Rimell, had been well backed ante-post and Maxie sensed the possibility of a coup much like the result they eventually obtained in the Derby with Pinturischio. But neither Roper nor anyone in his gang had any knowledge of Rimell's yard or any contacts there. So one morning, while they were on a racing trip in the Midlands, Bill persuaded Micheline to call in at the stable, 'act French and high falutin' and say that she was interested in having a couple of horses trained there. Persuaded that it would be 'fun' and 'a dare' she did as she was told and returned with as much information about the lay-out as she could remember.

A few nights later, Darkie Steward, Jack Stiles and Alex Field broke into the Kinnersley yard and doped Nicolaus Silver or, rather, they doped the horse they thought was Nicolaus Silver. But Fred Rimell, a tough and resourceful character, had seen the 'charming young Frenchwoman' at Stratford races in the company of men he recognised (probably Roper and Joe Lowry) to be professional gamblers. He had also been warned by a betting owner that Nicolaus Silver might be a target. So he cunningly moved the National favourite out of his box and into another part of the yard and put a different grey horse, High Spot, in there in his place. It was the unfortunate High Spot who the gang unwittingly doped, and whose hair fell out as a result, leaving Nicolaus Silver to win the big race unharmed.[23]

Roper was extremely reluctant to involve Micheline in his activities again, not least because he'd have to confess to her about the racket he'd been running and the jam he was in. But, while she may not have realised it, his lover was as much at risk from Charlie Mitchell as he was and maybe getting her to play an active role was the best way to protect her? If Bill was careful there was no reason why anything she did could be actively construed as breaking the law.

But she couldn't be plain Micheline Lugeon. For safety's sake she'd need an alias and a good cover story and, of course, she'd need a chauffeur to drive her around.

23 Nicolaus Silver was returned at a generous 28-1 on course amidst the unfounded rumours that he had been got at and couldn't win.

13

MICHELINE'S JOURNEY

MADEMOISELLE ROSEMARIE Laumaine took to the stage in Shropshire on Wednesday 4 October 1961. The previous day Bill and Micheline had checked in to Shrewsbury's Lion Hotel, which was one of the best in the county. It had a comfortable panelled lounge where 'Mr and Mrs Roper' were served afternoon tea before being shown up to their room, number 62, which had a bathroom en suite and a view over some of the town's attractive half-timbered buildings and narrow, cobbled streets.

Dickens, Disraeli and Paganini were previous guests at the Lion but Roper was not overawed by the comparison. Smartly dressed in a tailored suit and tie, he slipped easily into the role of the Big Man up from London. The menu in the hotel restaurant, where the local Conservatives and the Rotarians dined regularly, was tame compared to Chez Victor and the Coq d'Or. But Bill ordered a good bottle of wine, tipping the waiter well but not too ostentatiously, and after dinner Mr and Mrs Roper were happy to have an early night. The official pretext for their visit was that Bill's 'French wife' was planning to open a branch of her beautician's business in the North West so they'd decided to come up to Shrewsbury and take a look around. Provincial life, in fact, held little interest for Bill but Shropshire's sleepy tempo suited his purposes ideally. It wasn't on the way to anywhere much but that made it just fine for prospective fraud and horse doping and Roper wasn't planning to spend any more time there than was strictly necessary once his business was done.

The following morning, the couple browsed around some estate agents and antique shops and had coffee in the town. Then, shortly after mid-day, they set off in Bill's black Ford Zephyr saloon to drive about 13 miles north-east towards the Cheshire border. A few miles outside the village of Hodnet, near Market Drayton, Bill pulled into a side road and Micheline got into the back seat, leaving Roper up front as her chauffeur. The first stable they were planning to visit was the Wollerton yard of Roy Whiston, a good and consistent jumps trainer who never won a Grand National or a Cheltenham Gold Cup but whose horses were always competitive at tracks in the Midlands and the North West.

Beech House – which is now a care home – was nowhere near as grand as Peter Cazalet's yard, Fairlawne, or one of the top Newmarket stables. Nor were Whiston's owners as rich or as socially smart. But for Bill's strategy to work, Micheline still needed to make the right impression, conveying the aura of a woman of wealth and quality and she had chosen her clothes with care. She had the fur coat that Bill had bought her the previous winter but it was a mild, early autumn day and she decided to leave it off. She still looked extremely smart in a 25-guinea grey worsted skirt and jacket by Marcus from Derry and Toms, worn with a silk scarf around her neck, Golden Lady stockings from Hayfords in Sloane Street and black high-heeled shoes. Her dark brown hair was cut short at the back but was soft and full at the sides and she had on Michelle de Paris eyeliner and red lipstick.

As they drew closer to Wollerton, Micheline sat quietly in the back of the car, smoking a cigarette. There was a still beauty about the Shropshire countryside. A landscape of stubble fields and woods, of warm, red-brick farm buildings and black and white half-timbered cottages and occasional bigger houses with names like The Hall and The Grange, glimpsed through the trees.

When they got to the stable, the racehorses had all finished morning exercise and were back in their boxes though a couple of hunters were grazing peacefully in a paddock beside the drive. Micheline waited in the car as Bill, smartly turned out as always, walked into the yard to find the head lad. He explained that his passenger was Mademoiselle Rosemarie Laumaine from Paris who had recently met Lady Broughton at Ludlow races. Mademoiselle was planning to open a shop in Shrewsbury and would like to have a few steeplechasers in training in the area. She was thinking of bringing three horses over from France and Lady Broughton had recommended Roy Whiston and suggested Mademoiselle drop in and see his set-up next time she was passing. Mademoiselle was on her way to Holyhead to take the ferry to Dun Laoghaire to stay with some old racing friends in Ireland and this had seemed like the perfect opportunity. Bill had rehearsed his lines and it was, basically, the same speech that he and the other chauffeurs spun at all the stables they were to visit, including Fairlawne.

The head lad, lost for words at first and unsure of the correct response, began to explain that Mr Whiston was away and wouldn't be back until the following evening. Maybe they'd like to come back then? Roper, who knew very well that Whiston was away, feigned disappointment. Mademoiselle had such a busy schedule, he said. She'd be flying back to Paris after her Irish trip and might not be back in the Shropshire region for several months. Bill turned his head towards his waiting passenger and, on cue, the rear door of the Ford Zephyr opened and out got the smiling, charming and stunningly attractive Rosemarie Laumaine. As she walked towards the two men, hips swinging in her grey worsted skirt, the head lad could feel his reservations melting faster than butter in a chip fryer. Mademoiselle held out her hand, head on one side and, in her best accented English, said how sorry she was for the inconvenience but how delighted she was to be in such a charming stable that she had heard so much about. Would the head lad care for a cigarette? He'd love one. Bill Roper lit them both with a silver cigarette lighter. And would it be possible to see some of the horses in their boxes, just out of interest? Of course it would. As they started to move towards the red-brick stable block, the head lad hardly noticed that the chauffeur was following behind them, a pen and paper in his hand, and taking notes as he went.

Mademoiselle Laumaine, showing she knew her English racing, remarked how impressed she'd been by Mr Whiston's good chaser Fresh Winds, who she and Lady Broughton had seen win at Ludlow the previous week. The head lad explained that Fresh Winds was in the trainer's second, or overflow, yard at his brother Alec Whiston's farm a mile back down the road but that he was sure they'd be welcome to drop in there too later on. The visit ended half an hour later with Mademoiselle waving from the back seat of the car and the star-struck head lad waving back enthusiastically.

Back in the hotel that evening, in the quiet hour before dinner, Roper ordered a bottle of champagne on room service. Bill was lying on the bed and totting up his winnings from a credit bet he'd placed by telephone during the afternoon. He'd had a £200 double on Ryan Price's horse, Sky Pink, in a handicap on the flat at Lingfield and Lester Piggott's mount, Flower Drum, in the big race at York. Both had won and Roper was looking at a profit of over £2,000 which he was planning to add to the bank he was trying to build up to pay off Charlie Mitchell.

Micheline was running a bath and, as Bill watched, she started to undress. First kicking off her shoes and hanging up her jacket and then stepping out of her skirt and petticoat and peeling off her stockings. When she was completely naked, she looked across at Roper, arched one eyebrow and smiled.

'My, my, Mademoiselle,' said Bill, tenderly. 'What a lucky man I am.'

'Yes,' she replied. 'And don't forget . . . you're my servant.'

'At your service . . . Madam,' he replied.

He was too. At her service and in her debt. But why did an intelligent and well brought-up young Swiss girl allow herself to become emeshed in Bill's fraudulent enterprise? Mr Racing was charming. Mr Racing was confident. He was also manipulative and a liar but he seems to have had little difficulty persuading her to assist him in his criminal schemes. Some say she was a lot tougher than she looked and, being determined to make the most of her cosmetics business, needed her sugar daddy to stay in business too. But others believed she felt guilty about Doris and the boys and was horrified to think they might be in danger from Charlie Mitchell. Anything she could do to help Bill raise the money to avert that outcome was worth it.

Thursday 5 October was a busy day. The couple checked out of the Lion after breakfast and, dressed once again for their respective roles, drove first to Whiston's second yard at Hodnet where neither Roy nor his brother Alec were present. Then they carried on a few miles north-west to Betton House near Market Drayton, a handsome Georgian pile with outbuildings and stables that had been Oswald Mosley's birthplace in 1896. The house was now lived in by Bill Tellwright, a sporting amateur who kept a few horses as a permit trainer and had ridden Nicolaus Silver to victory in an amateur riders' race at Cheltenham in March. Tellwright had already left for Woore races, as Roper had anticipated, and Mademoiselle and her chauffeur were given a brief tour in his absence.

Woore was Roper's next stop. The pretty North Shropshire jumps course, which closed in 1963, had only the most basic facilities and an atmosphere more akin to a point-to-point than a metropolitan racetrack. There were three winning favourites there that Thursday afternoon and a double, as trainer and jockey, for Bill Tellwright, including French Cottage, a useful handicapper who won the three-mile Arbour Chase by ten lengths at even money.

Leaving Woore about three, the black Ford Zephyr continued north by north-west into Cheshire to George Owen's stable, Ferney Lees, at Tiverton near Tarporley. The 53-year-old Owen, a former jockey turned trainer, was another sound and traditional jump-racing man like Roy Whiston and his horses competed at much the same tracks. His landlord was the Unilever heir Viscount Leverhulme, a Jockey Club member and steward at Liverpool where Owen saddled the 1949 Grand National winner, Russian Hero. Owen was a good tutor of jockeys as well as horses and Dick Francis had been one of his best pupils in the years after the war.

After a quick tour of Owen's yard – the trainer was still at Woore – Roper drove on another three miles through rolling countryside to Sandy Brow stables, the Cheshire base of the very shrewd Eric Cousins who trained both over jumps and on the flat and was renowned for landing betting coups in big handicaps. One of his owners was Robert Sangster for whom he'd won the 1961 Great Jubilee Handicap at Kempton with Chalk Stream, bought by Sangster as a present for his first wife. Another patron was the high-rolling punter Ian Murray, who was one of Bill Roper's biggest clients.

Mademoiselle's chauffeur went through his story once again, explaining this time that his employer was considering opening a business in Chester and would like to have a few horses to race there. After being conducted round Cousins' yard, the chauffeur following dutifully behind and taking more notes as he went, charming Mademoiselle said how much she looked forward to coming back soon.

As soon as they were out of sight, Roper turned tail and drove them back the way they'd come. They passed Tarporley and Market Drayton and continued south to the Shropshire town of Wellington about ten miles east of Shrewsbury. Their destination was Buckatree Hall, a black and white half-timbered country house hotel in the midst of orchards and farmland at the foot of the Wrekin. The couple checked in again as Mr and Mrs Roper and ate dinner in the restaurant after which the staff noted salaciously that 'they went upstairs together for about an hour' returning later for a drink.

They stayed at Buckatree Hall until the weekend. The new steeplechasing season had yet to hit top gear and on Saturday 7 October the two biggest meetings were on the flat at Ascot and Manchester. Bill Roper phoned through a string of bets to his London office, including a £400 wager on Pellegrino, a Noel Murless-trained two-year-old who made a winning debut in Ascot's Sandwich Stakes having been backed in from 6-1 to 7-2 on course.

That same afternoon, Mademoiselle Rosemarie Laumaine called in at the Leicestershire stables of the Irishman Tim

Molony, a former top-class jump jockey who rode the winner of the Champion Hurdle four times between 1951 and 1954.[24] There was a distressing subtext to the visit. Molony and his wife Stella were old friends of Bill's and had often given him tips and information, especially about Irish runners at Cheltenham and Liverpool. But Roper was now in a place where anyone, old friends or not, had to be used and exploited if there might be a profit in it. Molony only had about 15 horses in training, mostly flat racers, and was financially dependent on them all staying fit and well but, for Bill's purposes, if one of them turned out to be a short-priced favourite in a small field, they'd be fair game.

Not that Roper could risk playing the 'chauffeur' at The Manor Stables, Wymondham, near Melton Mowbray. He'd have been instantly recognised so Alex Field had been fetched up from London and entrusted with the job, which he did very adequately, returning Mademoiselle, and such information as they'd been able to acquire, to Roper who was waiting at the hotel. It seems that as well as his telephone wagers, Bill had been betting heavily – and unsuccessfully – in a nearby betting shop and staff at Buckatree Hall discovered a waste-paper basket full of losing betting slips when he and Micheline left early the next morning.

They weren't heading back to London though, not yet. Mr and Mrs Roper were going north and this time Micheline was sporting a blonde wig and a black Cossack fur hat.

---

24 Molony rode the triple champion hurdler Sir Ken, trained by Willie Stephenson, and also won the 1953 Cheltenham Gold Cup on Vincent O'Brien's Knock Hard.

WA, or plain Arthur Stephenson, was one of the most statistically successful jumps trainers in the country. His stable, Crawleas, was in Leasingthorne, a Durham mining village a few miles east of Bishop Auckland. A flat cap man and a Wearsider to his roots, Arthur Stephenson spurned the soft southern meetings, like Sandown and Kempton Park, and stuck to his local tracks, regularly clocking up 50 winners a season which was a notable achievement in the early 1960s. If Arthur was mystified by the young French female – Mademoiselle Brouillon rather than Rosemarie Laumaine – who turned up unexpectedly on the Sunday morning, so were some of his staff, though Bill Roper seems not to have noticed at the time. But at the two stables where the black Ford Zephyr called next, Mademoiselle made an excellent impression.

Middleham in the Yorkshire Dales, roughly 20 miles south of Bishop Auckland, was the Newmarket of the North. There were over 20 racing stables in the town and Colonel Lyde, who trained flat racers at Spigot Lodge, was enough of a ladies man to be charmed by his surprise guest and assure petite Mademoiselle Brouillon of his best attention at all times. He would be delighted to welcome her three horses from France and should she wish him to buy her another at the sales, he said, as they toured the boxes, chauffeur in tow, he'd be delighted to oblige. Mademoiselle Brouillon assured him she'd be delighted too.

The third stable visit of that October Sunday was the one Roper imagined would be the toughest yet and the most challenging for Micheline. Captain Neville Crump, ex-Marlborough, Balliol and the 4th Hussars, was a robust hunting and steeplechasing man. Fifty years old in 1961, Crump had a bluff, military edge as befitted a former cavalry officer who'd served in Egypt in the Second World War. He'd established Warwick House Stables as a top-class jumping yard and had won the Grand National three times, including the 1960 running with Merryman II. His owners included large county ladies who stood no nonsense with horses, dogs or humans and wealthy landowners such as Hugh Joicey and his wife Joan, whose fortune was in coal and who owned a couple of exciting young prospects called Springbok and Hoodwinked.

The Crump manner was gruff, not to say bloody rude, to non-racing strangers like the car-driving Japanese tourists who stopped him one day in Middleham and asked the way to Leyburn. 'You found your fucking way to Pearl Harbor,' the Captain is alleged to have replied. 'You can find your own fucking way to Leyburn.' In similar vein he was once asked for his opinion of an elderly Yorkshire toff who was being considered for the role of a local racecourse steward. 'He'll be perfect,' replied Crump. 'He's deaf, blind and he knows fuck all about racing.'

To beard the Captain in his lair of a Sunday tea-time, Micheline had dressed with particular care, favouring a girdle by Lejaby of Paris designed to 'coax your figure firmly but gently into the required shape' and worn under her petticoat and her Hardy Amies wool short coat and matching skirt. She had also abandoned the blonde wig and the black hat and gone back to being Rosemarie Laumaine.

When Bill Roper, who was back in the chauffeur's role, went into the yard ahead of her he was expecting a frosty reception. But as Jackie Dyer said of Micheline, 'she could charm the birds right out of the trees' and Neville Crump, who had been relaxing after a good lunch, was captivated by her presence.

Micheline played her part to perfection. She explained that she was planning to open a branch of her beautician's business in York and that she had some horses in France, running at Auteuil and Enghien les Bains, which she wanted to send over to be trained in the UK. The Captain, who later admitted that he wasn't used to attractive young female visitors at the best of times, but envisaged more winners at Aintree and Cheltenham, said that he would have room for three and would be delighted to take them.

Mademoiselle, affecting almost girlish excitement, wondered if she could see a few of the horses in their boxes like the famous Merryman II? Crump, one hand brushing over Mademoiselle's shapely bottom, escorted her into the yard where she duly saw 'a horse or two, Merryman among them, and her chauffeur took a few notes'. Before she left, the Captain wanted to know how to get in touch with her in future and Mademoiselle gave him an address in Paris that sounded very smart: 15 Avenue de la Roche in the fashionable 16th arrondissement.

The next day, Monday the 9th, Bill and Micheline returned to London, Micheline to check up on her Crawford Street business and Bill to see his family in Mill Hill. It's hard to believe there was much of a welcome for Bill by this stage. Yet friends said that he and Doris always remained touchingly close. They had never been formally married, so there was no need of a formal divorce, and while Doris wasn't about to leave Uphill Drive she didn't bar the door to Bill who wasn't going to renege on his promise to provide for her. Doris understood racing and bookmaking and she knew what kind of a man Bill Roper was and what kind of company he was keeping. There were probably some questions she didn't ask and some things she didn't want to know but that didn't mean she wasn't fond of him. She had decided to settle for what she had and she may even have continued to launder his shirts and send his suits to the cleaners and make sure his suitcase was packed and ready for his next trip on the road.

Bill and Micheline stayed in town until the end of the week. But Saturday the 14th found them back in the North East, Micheline wearing the blonde wig, and calling on Major Calverley Bewicke at his Shawdon House stable at Glanton near Alnwick. The Major was away at Ayr races, as Bill had expected him to be, saddling a young horse called Half Change who started at 6-4 on for a two-mile novice chase and won by four lengths. With the master away, the couple were given a thorough tour by his guileless staff and, as well as horses' names and box numbers, were able to get a good picture of the rudimentary security arrangements.

Leaving Bewicke's in mid-afternoon, they carried on across the border to Hawick and the Midshiels stable of Harry Bell where they experienced one of the few rebuffs of their grand tour. Bell said the horses had already bedded down for the night and that if they wanted to see inside the yard, they'd have to come back another day. Speaking on his employer's behalf, Roper said he was sure that Mademoiselle would be delighted to come back another day.

On the Sunday they drove all the way back to London arriving late at the Stafford Court flat. Bill would normally have spent the previous few days at Newmarket's Cesarewitch meeting where the former Derby winner St Paddy suffered a shock defeat, beaten by a French horse in the Champion Stakes.[25] This year Bill had been a conspicuous absentee, flu keeping him 'tucked up in bed' according to the ever helpful Joe Lowry. But 'Roper the Doper' still made a profit on the meeting.

The target was the Newmarket Oaks for three-year-old fillies which was run on the Thursday afternoon. The night before the race, Darkie Steward, Jack Stiles and Brian Perry drove down to Epsom with Uncle Joe, broke into Dermot 'Boggy' Whelan's stable, Lavandou, on Chalk Lane and doped Indian Melody with luminal sodium. The filly had finished third behind Sweet Solera in the 1,000 Guineas and sixth in the Oaks at Epsom. Her trainer, a Kerryman by birth and much liked locally, was more associated with training handicappers than classic horses and Indian Melody was the best horse in his string.

Darkie Steward, who had a contact among Whelan's stable lads, like his other old friends at Harold Wallington's

25 Bobar II, ridden by Max Garcia, beat St Paddy – the odds-on favourite – by three-quarters of a length.

and Peter Thrale's yards, gave her just the right dose of barbiturates to ruin her chances while still ensuring she'd line up. There were only four runners in the Newmarket Oaks and Indian Melody was sent off at 5-2 behind the well-backed 11-8 favourite Aphelandra, who was ridden by Doug Smith. The favourite won easily by five lengths while Indian Melody finished last, beaten 13 lengths. 'Made no show', as the formbook reported later. Indian Melody had been laid by Bill Roper through his Monmouth Street office and through representatives on course including Jackie Dyer and Bernie Howard and had also been laid by Charlie Mitchell and Albert Dimes. The gang had all backed Aphelandra heavily and had laid further bets against Indian Melody for the forecast. Mitchell was delighted with his winnings. Bill was doing well and all the gang were more than satisfied by the result. But for the genial Boggy Whelan it was a tragedy. Indian Melody never recovered and was ruined both as a racehorse and as a potential broodmare.

On Monday 16 October, Bill was back in the world he loved best. It was the beginning of a three-day meeting, jumping and flat, at Hurst Park and Roper was there on the rails in his brown trilby hat and his sheepskin coat, surrounded by fellow bookies and punters like Jackie Dyer and Joe Lowry. Conferring with the earwiggers and the putters-on, the old cockney and Jewish faces. Revelling in the noise and patter of the tic-tac men and the boards bookmakers. Popping round to the dilapidated Tote building, where Stanley Baker's gang pulled off the heist in *The Criminal*, and drinking whisky and soda in the Owners and Trainers Bar, no problem about admittance for Mr Racing.

The old military types in black bowler hats and British Warm overcoats were all muttering about doping and race fixing but they still had little clear idea who to blame. But Bill's fellow faces would have known what was going on by now. They would have been aware of the apparent health and wealth of Bill's business and they would have heard rumours about Max Parker and the Witch Doctor and known that Charlie Mitchell was in the background and Albert Dimes too. Not that any of them were about to turn Bill in. Not even when a reward was offered. It just wasn't part of their culture.

To watch the first race, the Mayflower Novices Hurdle, Division One, Roper climbed up into the stands. Twenty-eight runners and one very hot favourite, Morland Jack, with Bobby Beasley on board, making his English debut and a big tip for Bill from his informants in Ireland. Backed in from 5-2 to 5-4, Bill heavily involved both for himself – and Charlie Mitchell – and the firm.

Peter O'Sullevan was surely there among the crowd, in a trenchcoat and trilby, a cigarette holder balanced elegantly between his lips.[26] He was surely on too. As Morland Jack coasted home by four lengths in a course record time. Roper delighted as he came down off the stand. Making a mental note to target Morland Jack next time out and

---

26 Peter was a consummate punter as well as a great broadcaster and journalist and his selections appeared Monday to Saturday in the *Daily Express*. He was knighted in 1997.

thinking, tonight, he'd take Micheline out to dinner in the West End. He owed her something special for the superb job she'd been doing. Maybe Au Jardin des Gourmets for a change, or Le Boulestin, and then on to one of Ricky Dajou's clubs, the Casablanca or the Bagatelle, and then back to Stafford Court . . .

Roper couldn't say yet that they were safe but he thought he was doing all right, so far. The betting bank was growing and plans had been laid. But as he drove away through the big racecourse gates at the end of the afternoon, autumn mist drifting across the river, he knew that the real business of Micheline's journey, the dirty business, was still to come.

14

THE MYSTERIOUS MADEMOISELLE

THROUGHOUT THEIR travels, Roper and Lugeon only ever stayed in the best hotels. Bill clearly believed that doping and fraud, like sex and seduction, worked better in comfortable surroundings. In Newcastle in 1961, the Royal Station Hotel offered the best accomodation in the city and, on the evening of Friday 20 October, Mr and Mrs Roper checked in and were allocated room 59. They had driven all the way up from London that day and Micheline's suitcase contained several changes of costume including the blonde wig.

The couple ate dinner in the restaurant and later that night they were joined by Alex Field and Darkie Steward who had arrived off the last train from King's Cross. They were booked into single rooms and in the early hours they left the hotel, Field driving Roper's Ford Zephyr and headed up to Verley Bewicke's stable, Shawdon House, to dope two horses, Bronze Warrior and Irish Honour, who were due to run at Kelso that afternoon. It was about an hour's drive to Glanton and the dopers got back at 5 a.m., checked out and took an early train back to London.

Mr and Mrs Roper enjoyed breakfast in bed after which Bill had an hour-long meeting in the lounge with the representative of a Manchester bookmaker who was the top credit bookie in the North and had pitches, or nominees, at most of the northern and border tracks. Roper was now selling information to the Mancunian firm, as well as his existing customers, and they could ensure that any doped favourites were laid on course at Kelso or Newcastle or Catterick, just as Jackie Dyer and Bernie Howard were laying them in the South.

The 68-mile journey to the races took Bill and Micheline up the A68 through the Northumberland countryside, crossing the border into Scotland and then on through Walter Scott country to Jedburgh and Kelso. On a crisp October afternoon, there was no better place to be than the pretty borders track with its 19th century grandstand and stiff, uphill finish. There was a decent crowd to watch the six-race card but, from a doping and race-fixing perspective, it got off to a false start. Irish Honour, who would have started favourite for the two-mile Kalewater Handicap Chase at 2.30 was a non-runner. The horse had been found to be 'not himself' at Verley Bewicke's yard that morning and had been withdrawn. As Roper quickly realised, Darkie Steward had overdone the dose once again.

Bronze Warrior was due to run in the three-mile Berwickshire Handicap Chase which was due off an hour later and an anxious Roper went down to the racecourse stables to see if he'd turned up. Micheline, who was dressed as Rosemarie Laumaine, went with him which was risky as several of the trainers she'd already met, including Captain Neville Crump, were on the racecourse. The couple spent about ten minutes hanging around the saddling boxes and trying to get a glimpse of Bronze Warrior. When he was finally led into the paddock, outwardly calm and ready to race, Roper hurried off to a telephone box and rang Manchester and London and told them to lay him as planned.

How his unfortunate jockey, Johnny Lehane, would have loved to know what the gang knew about Bronze Warrior's chances. The six-year-old went off the 6-4 favourite but 'slipped up on the flat' and failed to complete the course. Lehane survived unscathed but he was lucky. He said afterwards that his mount had galloped through the first few fences 'as if he was drunk or blind' which was similar to David Nicholson's description of riding the doped Blessington Esquire at Hurst Park the previous March.

As well as laying Bronze Warrior, the gang had also backed Neville Crump's runner Napfield, a 5-1 chance ridden by Pat Buckley, but he let them down and could only finish second, beaten two lengths by an 8-1 shot, Duplicator.

Roper and Micheline left well before the last and drove back down to Denholm, near Hawick, to call in at Hassendean Bank Stables, home of the rubicund Ken Oliver whose nickname was The Benign Bishop. His Grace had yet to return from Kelso and, in his absence, Mademoiselle Brouillon, wearing the blonde wig, was shown a number of good horses. Two of them, Happy Arthur and Punch Bowl Hotel, were entered up at Perth the following week.

From Oliver's it was only a short drive to Harry Bell's yard at Midshiels where they made good their promise to return the week before. Bell, like Ken Oliver, was still not back from Kelso and they got a good half-hour stable tour, clocking the names and box numbers of half a dozen horses as well as the security details. It was dusk by the time they left.

On the Sunday morning, Mr and Mrs Roper checked out of the Station Hotel and, for the second weekend running, drove back to London, arriving in Kensington that evening. But Darkie Steward and Alex Field returned to the North East, armed with some of the drawings and jottings that Bill had made on his travels and handed over to them in Colville Terrace, and, in the early hours of 25 October they broke into Ken Oliver's stable and doped Punch Bowl Hotel. Later that day the nine-year-old gelding, a Perth course winner the previous month, returned to the small racecourse in the grounds of Scone Palace for the Dan Flynn Handicap Chase over two miles. He was the second favourite in a field of five, trading at 3-1 from 7-2 and 9-4 first show. Harry East was his unsuspecting jockey and, like Nicholson and Lehane, he had a nightmare ride, pulling his mount up at halfway and reporting afterwards that it 'came down on its head at halfway and was leaning against me all the way back to the paddock as if it could hardly stand'.

With Punch Bowl Hotel out of the reckoning, the Perth race was easy pickings for the 2-1 favourite Loch Sloy, who won by five lengths and, like Alephandra in the

Newmarket Oaks, was well backed by the gang who also laid Punch Bowl Hotel through their credit offices and sold information about the race in advance to interested parties in London, Manchester and Newcastle.

Three weeks into Micheline's journey, 11 yards had been visited between Shropshire and the Scottish borders and so far three horses – not counting Indian Melody at Newmarket – had been doped. Now Bill turned his attention back to the Midlands and, on the afternoon of 25 October, even as Harry East's life was imperilled on a drugged horse at Perth, the black Ford Zephyr beat a path to Guy's Cliffe Stables near Warwick. At the time the Victorian stableyard housed one of the best, if most controversial, strings of steeplechasers and hurdlers in the land.

The official licence holder was Arthur Thomas, a Black Country native and trainer of moderate talent. But in reality, the horses were trained at Grange Con in County Wicklow by Paddy Sleator who was one of the canniest jumps trainers Ireland has ever produced. Sleator had latched on to an anomaly in the way horses were handicapped in England. In so-called 'conditions races' the weight they were allotted depended on the amount of prize money they had won. The majority of bread-and-butter races in Ireland then were worth a good deal less than their English counterparts and it was possible to enter a horse with good Irish form in an English contest and see it run off a far more lenient handicap mark than its ability merited.

Sleator hit on the ingenious idea of having what was in effect a satellite yard in the UK. To satisfy officialdom, the horses were nominally in the care of Thomas but he was just a front. They were really conditioned in Ireland before being shipped over to Guy's Cliffe where Sleator kept a few of his own lads and work riders led by head lad John Leigh. The trainer and his owners were gamblers, counting on the fact that even in the early 1960s, a decade or more after Vincent O'Brien had started pillaging the Cheltenham Festival, many run-of-the-mill English bookmakers were ignorant of Irish form and too lazy to study it in detail. Top horses like Scottish Memories – the conqueror of Blessington Esquire at Hurst Park – Rupununi, Forgotten Dreams and the 1960 Champion Hurdler, Another Flash, were making the English pay for that ignorance.

But when Paddy and the boys were about to have a punt, only John Leigh and the stable jockey, Bobby Beasley, another Irishman and exemplary horseman who had ridden Nicolaus Silver in the Grand National, were told about it. Beasley was cautioned on no account to share the information with the inquisitive Arthur Thomas who was forever wanting to know, in a shrill Brummie accent, when one of 'his' horses was 'off'.

Thomas wasn't at home when Bill and Micheline reconnoitred Guy's Cliffe Stables and neither was John Leigh or Bobby Beasley or any of the Irish staff. They were all at Ludlow races for the first day of a two-day meeting, as the ever diligent Roper had expected. In their absence, the visit was a complete success. It was cold in Warwickshire in the last week of October and Micheline was now sporting the sealskin fur coat that Bill had given her the previous winter, along with the black Cossack hat of the type that became fashionable when *From Russia With Love* hit the screens a few years later. She was also wearing the blonde wig, easy to come by for a coiffeur and beauty specialist, and very fetching it looked too with her pink jersey dress.

When Arthur Thomas got home that evening, having stopped off on his way back from Ludlow for some liquid refreshment, the stable lads told him all about the glamorous visitor, Mademoiselle Brouillon, the French beautician from Neuilly-sur-Seine. She had said that she had some steeplechasers in training at Maisons Laffitte and would like to have them based in Warwick while she was expanding her business in England over the winter. If Paddy Sleator had been there, his antenna would have warned him to be suspicious. But Thomas seems to have been flattered by the enquiry and he said nothing about Mademoiselle to Sleator or Beasley before Morland Jack ran again at Ludlow the next day. The Irish trainer and the gelding's owner, J.J. Fitzpatrick, had landed some big bets when Morland Jack won at Hurst Park and they were hoping to land a few more in similarly small races before stepping up in class.

By now the word was out that the five-year-old had been working impressively with Another Flash and before the Halford Novices Hurdle, Division Two, he was backed in to 4-9 on course with Sleator and Fitzpatrick's money having gone on early with the London offices. Only some of whom, the ones out of the loop, sent those bets back to the course. The knowledgeable Ludlow crowd had already witnessed one very good horse the previous afternoon when the future Gold

Cup winner Mandarin made his seasonal debut.[27] Morland Jack was expected to win every bit as easily but, in a ten-runner field, he made mistakes throughout and finished a distant fourth, beaten 23 lengths. That was because on the eve of the race, while Arthur Thomas was having a nightcap and the staff were all asleep in their beds, Jack Stiles and Darkie Steward broke in to Guy's Cliffe, armed with the directions Bill Roper had given them in Notting Hill that afternoon, and doped Morland Jack with luminal sodium.

On the day, Roper's London office laid Morland Jack and so did Max Parker, Jackie Dyer, Charlie Mitchell and assorted other of their bookmaking associates. They never had a moment's worry. Some of the gang also backed the second favourite, Terry Biddlecombe's mount, Lowe II, who shortened from 6-1 to 7-2 but second was the best he could manage. Roper's crew may have got the result wrong but the successful nobbling of Morland Jack, stinging a couple of big Irish punters like Sleator and Fitzpatrick, was both profitable and satisfying. The big loser was the horse. According to Bobby Beasley, Morland Jack 'had his tongue hanging out the whole way and smashed every hurdle on the track'. He never raced again.

Bill's kitty was growing, the threat of Charlie Mitchell still very real but perhaps manageable if he and Micheline could carry on spying together for another few months. At

---

27 Mandarin won the 1957 and 1961 Hennessy Gold Cup, the 1962 Cheltenham Gold Cup and, most famously, the 1962 Grand Steeplechase de Paris despite his bit breaking in the early stages, leaving his jockey, Fred Winter, without brakes or steering.

the end of the week, Bill went up to Liverpool to resume work, albeit briefly, as a normal bookmaker/gambler. It was Aintree's three-day mixed meeting, the highlight of which was the Grand Sefton Chase, run over a circuit of the Grand National course on the Saturday afternoon. Micheline stayed in London but Roper spent a couple of nights at the Adelphi Hotel mixing, on the best of terms, with the usual champagne-quaffing racing crowd – owners, trainers, jockeys, bookmakers and punters, including professional gamblers like the old reprobate Monty Cosky who habitually supplied cavalier jockeys with girls in return for information.

It was almost two years now since Roper had taken charge of the doping gang and, just like at Hurst Park, the bookies at the Adelphi knew all about it. The racket – and its backers – was the main topic of conversation in the betting ring and tension was mounting about where they'd strike next. With the exception of William Hill, Bill's fellow layers weren't talking. But in the non-gambling world beyond the racecourse, doping was becoming an increasingly emotive issue and, although Bill didn't realise it yet, small details, sightings and clues were beginning to mount up. Details that would enable the police, the press and the Jockey Club's security department to gradually build up a picture of Mr Racing and his friends . . . and also of the mysterious Mademoiselle.

15

A CALCULATED RISK

THE WEEK after Indian Melody was doped at Epsom the editor of *The Sporting Life*, Ossie Fletcher, received an anonymous phone call from a man who claimed to have information about the doping gang and who said he just wanted 'to see justice done'. He told Fletcher that 'Billy Roper and Max Parker' were behind it and advised him to 'try and find Roper's French girlfriend' too. Fletcher immediately passed on the information to the Jockey Club and Colonel Blair passed it on to Scotland Yard even though their official interest in the case had still gone no further than 'surveillance'. The police would return to the tip-off in time, trying to establish whether the source was a genuinely impartial witness or another bookmaker, one who had been stung by the gang perhaps, out to settle scores. But for the moment the *Life* was warned that, with investigations pending, they should be careful not to publish anything that might prejudice a future prosecution. So the racing paper sat on its story.

There were more dopings at the end of October and the beginning of November. At the next Kelso meeting on Saturday 28 October, two Harry Bell-trained runners, Raes Gill and Lively Spirit, lined up for the Caverton Handicap Hurdle over three miles. Unusually, the stable companions went off as the 4-1 joint favourites in a field of 14. But Raes Gill, ridden by Johnny Leech and an easy winner at Carlisle on his previous start, finished a well-beaten seventh while Lively Spirit, with Tommy Barnes on board, slipped up on the flat and failed to complete. Both horses had been got at in Bell's Midshiels yard the night before the race.

In the early hours of Saturday 4 November, the gang returned to Bell's yard and doped the novice chaser Royal William, who was due to run in the Ellerton Novices Chase at Catterick Bridge that afternoon. The eight-year-old was the 5-1 second favourite in a field of 16 but fell heavily halfway round. Once again the unfortunate Tommy Barnes was in the saddle but he escaped with 'just bruises and cuts'. On the same card, Captain Neville Crump's Napfield – backed by the gang at Kelso in October – was the 11-4 second favourite for the Danby Handicap Steeplechase but he was beaten at halfway and trailed home 22 lengths behind the 7-4 favourite, Lady Nenagh.

Back down south the dopers pulled off a really big sting at Fontwell on Monday, 6 November. The Rank Challenge Cup was a two-mile handicap hurdle and the word in the ring was that Scarron, a five-year-old trained by Captain Ryan Price and ridden by Fred Winter, was a 'good thing'. There was nothing in the formbook to inspire such confidence. Scarron had been well beaten in handicaps at Plumpton and Cheltenham but the inference was that he hadn't been 'off' in those races whereas today was the day.

Jack Stiles and Darkie Steward, two of the Captain's less distinguished old boys, still had a good line to the Findon stable and they knew all about Price's plan in advance. On the Sunday night, they broke into the yard and doped Scarron with chlorbutol, another variant on phenobarbitone, judging the dose to perfection. There was nothing in Scarron's manner on the Monday morning to suggest he was in any way unwell and, in a 14-runner race, he was backed in from 6-1 to 11-4 favourite on course. He finished plumb last.

The Captain and his punters had been fleeced. The off-course offices out of the loop had been fleeced. But Bill Roper, Max Parker, Jackie Dyer, Charlie Mitchell and those bookies to whom they sold the information, cleaned up. They had kept accepting bets on Scarron at a point or two over the odds without laying off and they had also backed the second and third favourites, one of whom, Lerins ridden by Terry Biddlecombe, was the 11-2 winner. Jack Stiles and Darkie Steward, who had nothing but unpleasant memories of the hard grind of Findon life, boasted later that the Scarron job gave them more satisfaction than any other.

That same Monday afternoon, an eight-year-old mare called Caca Dora, trained by Chris Nesfield, won a three-and-a-quarter mile steeplechase at Fontwell by five lengths. She was backed down from 5-2 to 7-4 favourite and looked more than capable of following up in similar company next time out. Nesfield, who had a double on the card, trained at Newlands Stud, a 20-horse yard on the edges of Charing, a pretty Kent village with its own point-to-point course at the foot of the North Downs. Nowadays the stud overlooks the high-speed Eurostar line from St Pancras to the Channel Tunnel but, in 1961, it was surrounded by unspoiled woods and fields.

Just as Caca Dora's horsebox was returning to the stable, Nesfield had a glamorous and unexpected visitor. Mademoiselle Rosemarie Laumaine from Paris, accompanied by her chauffeur – played in this case by Brian Perry. It seemed that Mademoiselle was thinking of opening a branch of her beautician's business in Kent and she would like to have a few of her French chasers and hurdlers trained locally. She had met Lady Rootes recently at Plumpton races and Her Ladyship had recommended Mr Nesfield as the ideal man. As Mademoiselle was on her way down to Folkestone to take the ferry back to Boulogne this had seemed like a good moment to drop in.

Nesfield and his staff were surprised and flattered by the attention and proceeded to show Mademoiselle – and the chauffeur – every horse in the stable, including the victorious Caca Dora as she was fed and led back into her box. The charming French lady left about five o'clock, beaming at one and all and assuring them she'd be back in touch soon.

Chris Nesfield was not one of jump racing's most famous names or highest earners and Bill Roper had never imagined

Micheline and Perry would have any great difficulty getting in and looking around. But to even think of gaining access to Major Peter Cazalet's stable near Tonbridge, some 30 miles west of Charing, was as daunting as it was audacious. But Fairlawne was where the glamorous Mademoiselle was going next.

Peter Cazalet was Establishment through and through. Educated at Eton and Oxford, he was a school and university athlete, playing rackets and cricket to a high standard. In that era of gentlemen and players, it was said that he could have been captain of Kent had he wished. Cazalet's first wife Leonora, a stepdaughter of P. G. Wodehouse, died of a haemorrhage in 1940. His second wife Zara, whom he married in 1949, helped him transform Fairlawne from 'Victorian bachelor accommodation' as one regular visitor described it, into a much more beautiful, grand country house.

Cazalet's grandfather Edward, a rich merchant who did business in Russia in the 19th century, had acquired the house and estate in 1871 and the family owned most of Shipbourne including the church and pub. When Peter Cazalet inherited from his father in 1937 he began to expand the stableyard, encouraged every step of the way by his great friend Anthony, Lord Mildmay, whom he had known since they were at school together. Mildmay was the archetypal Corinthian amateur and forerunner of John Oaksey and he might have won the 1936 Grand National on the Cazalet-trained Davy Jones had the reins not snapped two fences from home when the pair were in the lead.

Cazalet and Mildmay saw wartime service together as officers in the Guards Armoured Division and after the war was over they were determined to establish Fairlawne as a proper racing centre. Fortuitously, Mildmay sat next to the Queen Mother at a post-war dinner at Windsor Castle and managed to persuade her and her eldest daughter to have a horse together. Monaveen, as the resulting chaser was called, gave his owners unbridled pleasure as well as a huge boost to jump racing's image and, in the years that followed, many more good chasers and hurdlers came to sport the Queen Mother's famous blue and buff silks.

Unfortunately for Lord Mildmay he didn't live to see them, drowning while out swimming off the Devon coast in 1950. 'He always valued the race more than the victory and the victory more than the prize,' wrote Ian Fleming's brother Peter in his *Times* obituary. Heartfelt sentiments, no doubt, but the Corinthian amateurs didn't always seem to realise that whereas well-heeled gentlemen could afford to go without the prize, hard-pressed professional jockeys and underpaid stable lads needed something more substantial than just honour and glory to live on.

By 1961 Peter Cazalet was one of the top three steeplechasing trainers in the country. He and the Queen Mother had got over the agonising defeat of Devon Loch in the 1956 Grand National when Dick Francis's mount stopped halfway up the run-in with the race at his mercy. Cazalet enjoyed surprisingly few victories at the Cheltenham Festival, but he sent out regular winners, many of them in the royal colours, at the big metropolitan meetings as well as at the smaller country courses such as Fontwell, Plumpton and Wye.

It was said that the Major 'was respected rather than loved'[28] and he ran his yard on military lines, the horses pulling out for the gallops at 7 a.m. sharp every day. But if Cazalet was a martinet, he was no stick in the mud. His string, who were schooled in Fairlawne's verdant parkland, were kept fit and well through an early version of interval training which enabled most of them to run six or seven times a season and keep on doing it year after year. The Queen Mother's runners were especially popular with the public who responded to her patent enthusiasm whether they won or lost, and when one of them lined up on a busy Saturday afternoon, the BBC or ITV covering the action, they carried not just the hopes but the wagers of countless recreational punters. Small-scale but habitual gamblers whose lives had been changed forever by the legalisation of off-course cash betting.

Bill Roper – a staunch traditionalist in all matters constitutional – noticed that the same royal horses often contested races with no more than seven or eight runners and one or two decidedly useful types starting second or third favourite. So it was that Mr Racing decided that to augment the fundraising that was still necessary to save his and Micheline's skin, Fairlawne would have to be breached. They'd got into Noel Murless's yard in Newmarket and

28 David Mould said that whereas amateurs were always invited to breakfast in the big house after riding out, professional jockeys never were.

they'd infiltrated Paddy Sleator's gambling outpost in the Midlands. But if they were going to case the home of the Queen Mother's horses they would need Mademoiselle Rosemarie Laumaine to give her very best and most confident performance.

If Micheline was intimidated by the thought of going to Fairlawne, she gave no outward sign. Neither did she seem to have registered any serious misgivings about the real purpose of these visits: the subsequent doping of an innocent racehorse and the defrauding of its owner and trainer, not to mention other bookmakers and the general public. But then, perhaps the role playing and illicit, even criminal, nature of their activities had its own seductive allure and was the aphrodisiac that bound her and Bill together.

It was precisely that era described by Philip Larkin as the period 'between the end of the *Chatterley* ban and the Beatles' first LP'. A Conservative MP was thundering about the 'gust of lust' that was blowing in from abroad,[29] the escalators on the London Underground were full of adverts for ladies' underwear and, in the background, the story of John Profumo, Christine Keeler, Mandy Rice-Davies and their circle was rattling on towards the first public revelations. Many British people still lived lives of drab, repressed conformity but in high society and the underworld, sex was in the ozone and

---

29 John Cordle, MP for Bournemouth and Christchurch, whose dire warnings prefigured the salacious reporting of the Duchess of Argyll's divorce case and the photos of the so-called 'Headless Man' that would grip the nation in 1963.

Bill Roper, the top people's bookie, and Micheline Lugeon, his glamorous mistress, were getting lots of it.

Roper had decided it was too risky for him to act as chauffeur on the Fairlawne trip as he had in Shropshire and the North. There was always the possibility that a stable lad or a visiting owner might see him and recognise his face from the betting ring. So, for the second time in two days, he gave the job to Brian Perry who was better looking and more personable than Alex Field and less cocky than Jack Stiles. Bill didn't want to take Micheline to Colville Terrace so he drove the Ford Zephyr over from Kensington to the King's Road and got Perry to meet them in a café, the Fantasie. The ever-thoughtful boss had brought Perry his own chauffeur's hat to complete the image and very smart he looked too.

As the black car progressed slowly through the south London suburbs, Micheline sat in the back, smoking a cigarette and glancing at the headlines in Bill's paper. The Queen's visit to Ghana to meet Kwame Nkrumah was all set to go ahead. At St James's Palace they were doing up the royal nursery in readiness for Princess Margaret's baby and in Downing Street, Harold Macmillan had given an interview, lamenting – somewhat implausibly – that his official duties gave him little time to enjoy Hancock, Maigret and Lennie The Lion like the rest of the TV watching nation.

In the *Express* racing pages, there was a preview of that afternoon's card at Newbury and the Queen Mother was the main story. The royal owner had spent Monday evening at the Royal Variety Show watching Max Bygraves, Sammy

Davis Junior and Kenny Ball and his Jazzmen. At Newbury she was looking forward to watching The Rip who was due to run in the three-mile Streatley Handicap Chase at 1.30 p.m. and Jaipur, a five-year-old French-bred going for the two-mile novices chase at three o'clock. Micheline turned from the newspaper to the copy of the *Sporting Chronicle*'s *Horses In Training* which she and Bill had spent hours leafing through together. She checked again on the names of The Rip's stable companions and especially on those horses owned by the Queen Mother.

Long before Micheline and Perry got to Shipbourne, Bill Roper, who was at Newbury under the pretence of working normally on the rails, had seen The Rip win easily by ten lengths. Jaipur finished third. Bill, who was driving Jack Stiles's Mercedes, left the racecourse before the last and was back in Stafford Court in double quick time. He switched on the soft lamps and the electric fire, filled up the silver cigarette box and got a couple of glasses out of the cocktail cabinet. Around five o'clock he got a phone call from Perry who had stopped at a garage in Bromley. It had gone really well. Micheline was fine and they should be back in Kensington within the hour. Roper put the phone down, breathed a sigh of relief and poured himself a large Scotch.

Saturday 11 November was Mackeson Gold Cup day at Cheltenham, the second year of Whitbread's munificent sponsorship and another boost to the image of National Hunt racing. The big prize was won by Paddy Sleator's Scottish Memories and the main supporting event was won by Blessington Esquire who was having only his second race since being doped at Hurst Park the previous winter. Bill Roper wasn't at Cheltenham. Bill the chauffeur and Mademoiselle Laumaine were back in Yorkshire visiting four stables on the Saturday afternoon while the trainers were at Wetherby races. The couple were planning to stay up in the North for the next week. Roper had plans for some more horses in the Verley Bewicke and Arthur Stephenson yards and he was hoping to profit significantly from the following weekend's meeting at Newcastle.

Then Bill opened *The Sporting Life* on Monday morning and discovered that Fresh Winds, the consistent chaser trained down in Shropshire by Roy Whiston, was entered in a modest handicap at Uttoxeter on Thursday the 16th. It looked like a race that would cut up to a handful of runners and Fresh Winds, whose last run had been against Nicolaus Silver in the Grand Sefton at Aintree, was sure to start favourite. It seemed too good an opportunity to miss but then Roper realised that he didn't have a precise record of where Fresh Winds was stabled. When he and Micheline had asked about the horse on the first day of their grand tour back on 4 October, they'd been told he was in Alec Whiston's overflow yard but when they'd stopped off the next day, Alec Whiston had been out and they'd been unable to look around. If Bill was going to send Darkie Steward and Alex Field down there in a couple of nights' time, he needed to go back and case the yard first.

It was a calculated risk going back to Shropshire in the same guise as before and on the eve of a projected doping but Roper was banking on the continued gullibility of the sleepy provincials. So on the afternoon of Wednesday 15 November, Mr and Mrs Roper checked in again at the Lion Hotel in Shrewsbury and around four o'clock, just as the evening was drawing in, they drove out to Hodnet. They spun the same line as before about the beautician's business and the horses in France and the possibility of opening a shop locally. This time Alec Whiston was at home. He allowed Mademoiselle inside the yard and let her see Fresh Winds in his box but there was something about the visitors that bothered him. In the house next door he had a cine camera that was being used to film a children's party and, just as the couple were about to leave, he surreptitiously filmed the French lady. He also wrote down the registration number of their black car.

In the early hours of Thursday, Steward, Stiles and Field broke in to the Hodnet stable and doped Fresh Winds with a bolus of luminal sodium. But, not for the first or the last time, they overdid the dose. When Roy Whiston arrived to check the horse's box the next morning, a few hours before it was due to leave for Uttoxeter races, he found that the sleek ten-year-old was half asleep and that his hind legs appeared paralysed. He immediately phoned Uttoxeter, withdrew Fresh Winds from the Abbots Bromley Handicap Chase, and ordered a private dope test. He also contacted the local police and gave them the car registration number that his brother had written down. By the morning of Friday 17 November, Superintendent Ernest Smith of Shropshire CID had established that the black Ford Zephyr saloon was the property of a Mr W. J. Roper of Uphill Drive, London

NW7. There was no evidence, as yet, that any crime had been committed but, as a precaution, Superintendent Smith phoned the Jockey Club in London and passed on the information.

When Roper got to Uttoxeter on the morning of the 16th and discovered that Fresh Winds had been scratched, he began to think that the odds were against him. He felt anger towards the increasingly incompetent Darkie Steward and Jack Stiles and, for the first time, a sense of fatality about his chances of accumulating Mitchell's money by Christmas. He'd been undertaking more, and longer, cross-country journeys, and now all his hopes rested on another long drive and an attempt to get more intelligence from stables in the North East.

That evening, Bill and Micheline checked back in to room 59 in the Royal Station Hotel in Newcastle, their third visit in six weeks. On the Friday afternoon, Bill took another big risk and drove them back to Arthur Stephenson's stable near Bishop Auckland. He wanted to try and double check on the stabling arrangements for one of Stephenson's chasers, an eight-year-old stayer called Hiawatha II who had been a running-on third in the Grand Sefton and a winner at Perth before that. He was declared to run at Newcastle on the 18th. Micheline was back in her blonde wig, dark fur coat and black Cossack hat and Mademoiselle Brouillon's story about a possible shop in York and her horses in Chantilly was trotted out once again. Arthur Stephenson was out but his housekeeper, Mrs Audrey Redfern, noticed 'the Frenchwoman snooping about' and became suspicious. She told one of the stable lads to slip out to the front of the house and take down the car registration number. When Stephenson returned, she gave it to him. Big Arthur had by now heard stories about mysterious visitors to northern stables so he phoned the Jockey Club. But he put no added security arrangements in place in the yard and that Friday night, the gang broke in and doped Hiawatha II with luminal sodium. This time they got the dose just right and the gelding set off in the horsebox the following morning, bound for Gosforth Park along with Stephenson's other runners.

It had been another busy night for the dopers. After leaving Leasingthorne, they had driven 30 miles north to Glanton where they broke in – for the third time – to Verley Bewicke's stable, Shawdon House, and nobbled Half Change, the good-looking novice chaser who had won at Catterick on 4 November and been written up in the *Sunday Pictorial* the previous weekend. But, for the second time in three attempts, they bungled it and when Bewicke saw his horse in its stall the next day, it was swaying and half asleep, just like Fresh Winds. The Bewicke horsebox left for Newcastle without Half Change though, ironically, one of the occupants was Bronze Warrior who had been one of two doping victims on the night of 21 October but was now fit enough to race again.

On the Saturday morning, Roper had another hour-long meeting in the lounge of the Station Hotel with the bookie's man from Manchester and another Mancunian who was representing the co-owner of the Cromford

Club, a favourite haunt of jockeys, punters, footballers and boxers when they were partying in the North West. Micheline was not present as the trio, shrouded in cigarette smoke, were served silver pots of coffee with sugar, cream and biscuits. The Londoner – bookmaker, gambler and doper – appraised the Manchester boys of possible developments at Newcastle that afternoon and specifically advised them to lay Half Change, who was expected to start favourite for the Powburn Novices Chase at 2.30 p.m., and Hiawatha II, market leader for the Simonburn Handicap Chase at three o'clock. The three men then left the hotel together and set off for the races. All velvet-collar coats, expensive hair tonic and Monte Cristo cigars, as befitted faces who knew the results in advance.

It was bitterly cold at Newcastle racecourse with sleet coming in off the North Sea. Bill had a hip flask filled with Scotch and he was tempted to down it in one go when he walked into the ring and discovered that Half Change was a non-runner in the second race. But he stuck it out until the fifth, mingling with the North East's finest club owners, property developers and touts. It was worth the wait. Hiawatha II's race panned out exactly as planned. Jimmy Fitzgerald was in the saddle and his mount was backed in to 2-1 favourite in a field of eight. But the hotpot, bidding to continue Arthur Stephenson's good run, finished last, beaten 38 lengths. The 8-1 winner was Duplicator who had landed the fixed race at Kelso on 21 October when Bronze Warrior slipped up. Bronze Warrior, seemingly fully recovered from that misfortune, finished second.

(Extraordinarily, Punch Bowl Hotel, another former victim of the doping gang was also in the race but fell at the ninth.) Favourite backers had been skinned but those bookmakers and their patrons, north and south, who had been in on the scam and laid the 'jolly' were jubilant.

Bill left before the last race, drove back into town and collected Micheline from the Station Hotel. Roper was pushing his luck to the limit now but he reasoned that Arthur Stephenson, who would still be on the racecourse, wouldn't know precisely what had happened to Hiawatha and couldn't know yet that his stable had been broken into. Roper wanted to be absolutely sure about a few more box numbers at Crawleas, horses he wanted stopped before the following weekend's meeting at Doncaster. The Mancunians and the Geordies had assured him that they'd continue to pay well for information about Big Arthur's runners and Bill was convinced that the next big win and the answer to all his problems was only just around the corner.

It was dark when Mademoiselle Brouillon and her chauffeur arrived at the farm. All the fires had been lit in the village and plumes of chimney smoke stood out against the sky. It was the third time that the couple had shown up at Stephenson's yard and it was glamorous Mademoiselle's 19th stable visit in 47 days. It was also to be her last. Mrs Redfern was on guard once again and this time she wasn't having any of it. She turned 'the Frenchwoman in the Cossack hat' and the 'powerfully built chauffeur' away, telling them she wouldn't let them in the yard until Mr

Stephenson had returned. Roper was for trying to push the point but Micheline, sensing danger, executed a gracious withdrawal, saying how sorry she was for any trouble they'd caused and how much she'd like to come back to Crawleas again one day. Mrs Redfern and Stephenson's son, Jonny, watched from the kitchen as the chauffeur opened the door of the black Ford Zephyr, the smart lady got in, turning briefly to smile and wave, and then the car drove away.

Fifteen minutes later, portly Bob Hill and fellow ex-policeman turned shamus, Leslie Davies, arrived in a car they'd hired at Newcastle station. Colonel Blair had passed on the details of Arthur Stephenson's phone call on the Friday afternoon and, when Hill realised the car registration number tallied with the black Ford that had been seen at Hodnet, he'd decided to make a dash up to the North East.

Hill had missed his man – or should it be woman? – this time, but he was beginning to get an idea of who he was looking for.

16

THE YARD STEPS IN

ON SUNDAY 19 November Micheline went back to the flat she had bought at 27 Park Road, near Regent's Park, and which she was planning to do up and sell. Bill went to Mill Hill for another of those strange, outwardly normal encounters with Doris during which presumably certain subjects were never mentioned. Bill wasn't the type to stick around to do the gardening or a spot of DIY and, by late evening, he was back at Stafford Court for a meeting with Charlie Mitchell.

Some of the results had been good. Hiawatha. Indian Melody. Scarron. Especially Scarron. But there had also been blunders and mistakes, too many of them to suit a man like Charlie. If Bill Roper couldn't get Steward and the others to do the job as instructed, Mitchell would sort them out and find others who could. Roper tried to explain that, as far as he could tell, doping was an inexact business, depending on the weight and constitution of the horse. What worked with one might not work with another and the gang was still learning on the job. But Charlie Mitchell didn't want excuses. He wanted to know whose stable they were going to hit next. Only five weeks to Christmas, he reminded Bill, and he was still at least 30 grand shy of his target. It would be a shame if, after so much effort, he missed it. A shame for Bill and an even bigger shame for Miss Micheline Lugeon, or was it Mademoiselle Laumaine or Brouillon?

Roper told Mitchell that the gang were going out again that night to Chris Nesfield's yard at Charing. To dope the Fontwell winner, Caca Dora, who was due to run at Plumpton on Monday, the certain favourite in an eight-horse race. And one day soon they'd get at one of Cazalet's runners, one of the Queen Mother's in a nice televised chase on a Saturday afternoon.

Just do it, Bill, said Mitchell. No more non-runners.

The next day Roper went to Plumpton. He left the black Ford Zephyr in the garage behind Stafford Court and took the train down from Victoria, sharing a first-class compartment with the usual Monday Club collection of bookmakers and faces. It was a fine November day with plenty of sun and a good crowd. The punters always enjoyed Plumpton, drawn back again and again by the sheer excitement of steeplechasing despite the ungilded surroundings and the modest card.

Bill was intent on laying Caca Dora in the three-mile Scaynes Hill Handicap Chase and backing the second favourite, Cameron's Kid, but as soon as he got to the racecourse, he heard that Caca Dora had been withdrawn. His boys had screwed up yet again. But if there was nothing much else of betting interest at Plumpton, Bill discovered that the racing press were buzzing with rumours and stories. Doping stories. Captain Ryan Price was in attendance, Plumpton being one of his local tracks, and he was in a choleric mood. He'd informed the fourth estate that the results of the dope test on Scarron by the Metropolitan Police Forensic Laboratory had been positive. The Captain, still smarting from the loss of his own and his punters' money, wanted hanging, flogging and disembowelling for the dopers, and that was just for starters. He held perfidious, if as yet unidentified, bookmakers responsible for the crime and wanted them driven out of racing.

For their part, some of the perfidious ones present in East Sussex were howling with laughter at the sight of Price blaming his financial woes on the very people who, they believed, he systematically set out to defraud. But the apoplectic Captain wasn't the only trainer talking to the newspapers. Chris Nesfield was there too, explaining that he'd been called before the racecourse stewards to explain why Caca Dora was a non-runner. He'd told them that he'd discovered her 'seriously ill' in her box at Charing that morning and had commissioned his own dope test. When asked by a journalist if he had any idea who might have done it, he kept his counsel, saying only that he had passed on information about unusual stable visitors to the Stewards and the Jockey Club.

The drama was building and, in an increasingly feverish atmosphere, it was unreasonable to expect *The Sporting Life* to sit on their story much longer. On Tuesday 21

November the *Life* ran a teaser, wondering who the woman was, reputedly French, who had visited stables in all parts of Britain recently. It referred to the suspected dopings at Verley Bewicke's and Chris Nesfield's yards and speculated whether they could possibly be the work of a gang associated with the woman. Bill Roper saw the story as he and Micheline settled down to breakfast at Stafford Court, coffee and grapefruit for Micheline, a pot of tea and bacon and eggs for Mr Racing who was still in his dressing gown. Roper had been planning some more trips. First he wanted to go back to the Midlands and have a second look at Arthur Thomas's yard in Warwick and maybe try and get at one of Bill Tellwright's horses at Betton House and then, at the end of the week, he intended to take his mistress on yet another journey up north to check out more Yorkshire stables. But, as he digested the story in the paper, he knew that all further travels would have to be cancelled.

A few hours later, bathed and dressed and sitting in his Monmouth Street office, Bill got a phone call from Joe Lowry who asked him if he'd seen the midday edition of the *Evening Standard*. The paper's racing pages led with the doping saga, and Price's and Nesfield's comments at Plumpton, but it went much further than the *Life*. Peter Bone, the *Standard*'s correspondent, had been briefed by Bob Hill and he described a 'mysterious blonde' wearing a 'Cossack-style hat and a dark coat' who had apparently been seen at a racing stable in the north of England. It described her companion as 'a heavily built man' who drove the car and 'wore a peaked cap as if he were a chauffeur'.

There was a quote from the Secretary to the Jockey Club, Edward Weatherby, who referred to 'a phoney French name and address' that had allegedly been given to one trainer and it was confidently asserted that France was, in some underhand way, at the very heart of the plot.

There was also a public acknowledgement by Peter Cazalet that his Fairlawne yard had been visited by the mysterious Frenchwoman. The Major didn't usually talk to common types from the racing press, only to Bill Curling who was *The Daily Telegraph*'s Hotspur, but here he was confirming that no horse of his had displayed any untoward symptoms. He was taking precautions none the less, locking up his intended runners for 24 hours before a race and he'd asked for extra-vigilant police supervision when the horses were at racecourse stables.

When Bill Roper had finished reading the article he went outside to a call box on Shaftesbury Avenue to arrange an urgent meeting of the gang at Colville Terrace.

On Wednesday and Thursday the racing circus moved on to Kempton Park and doping continued to dominate the headlines. *The Times*' racing correspondent lamented the 'desperate position of trainers while this crime is being practised. They do not know who to trust among their many employees nor where the doper will strike next. The administration of a tiny pill is easy and the chance of catching anyone in the act is small. But if there is to be any sense in the brutality there must be a financial motive which should appear on the surface somehow.'

Captain Ryan Price, who was at Kempton on both days, continued his fusillade against the bookies, saying they were the ones with the financial motive to fix races and that the only way to get rid of doping on British racecourses was to get rid of the old enemy. The men with deep satchels responded angrily to this blanket attack and Archie Scott, the respected independent who had laboured long and hard to secure the legalisation of off-course betting shops, put out a statement on their behalf. 'Does it make sense that a big and carefully built-up profession like ours would risk its future by operations at small meetings like Perth and Fontwell?' he asked. The answer, of course, was 'yes'. In the fraudulent world of Bill Roper and the boys, it made perfect sense if you knew certain high-stakes credit punters, Rich Charlies like John Aspinall's Clermont Club clients, were always backing the short-priced favourites. 'We bookmakers are here to be shot at,' continued Scott. 'But give us fair play. If we are to blame, go for us. Until then, stop these attacks.'[30]

The bookies at Kempton came under attack not just from the press but from Peter Cazalet's super-fit horses. The Major had a double on the Wednesday and then saddled three more winners on the Thursday afternoon, making six winners from his last six runners. Two of the successful horses were odds-on favourites including the Queen Mother's The Rip, who had a police escort as he walked around the paddock before the Cottage Rake Chase.

Newspaper coverage hailed the royal victory, teaming pictures of The Rip with photographs of Princess Margaret and her baby (the future Viscount Linley). There were other

---

30 Archie Scott. (See also p. 37 footnote.)

big news stories competing for attention, like the trial of Adolf Eichmann, the Man In The Glass Booth, who was facing justice in Israel, and the preliminary hearing of the A6 murder case in Bedford in which Valerie Storrie recounted her horrific rape and the shooting of her lover, Michael Gregsten, by the accused, James Hanratty. But the papers had really got their teeth into doping by now and both the tabloids and the broadsheets continued running with it, getting as much inside track from portly Bob Hill as his Jockey Club employers would allow.

On Friday 24 November the *Daily Herald* ran a piece entitled 'The Blonde In The Black Cossack Hat', which claimed that, on Saturday the 18th, Jockey Club investigators had 'failed by five minutes' to catch a 'mystery French woman with a well-known London gambler who drove her to the stables of a leading National Hunt trainer'. The article went on to assert that 'earlier in the day the man had been seen talking to a bookmaker's representative in the lounge of the Royal Station Hotel and, that afternoon, Hiawatha II, a favourite at Newcastle, finished last.'

A Frenchwoman – a blonde Frenchwoman – a well-known London gambler, the rendezvous at the Station Hotel; Bill Roper must have felt as if the net was closing. But then Mr Racing's famed brain went into overdrive and, when he sat down and thought about it, he concluded that there was no suggestion in any of these articles that the Jockey Club, the police, the press or anyone else had a single shred of evidence to place the Frenchwoman and the London punter at an actual doping scene. So why not be brazen about it? Micheline did have a cosmetics business. She was looking to expand. She was French – or rather Swiss – and glamorous. So why not buy her a French racehorse to back up her story and bluff it out?

To assist him, Bill had a word with Max Parker who was still chairman of Ladbrokes. Maxie, who had mentored the early years of Bill's bookmaking career, had a lot of old clients in France and he got in touch with one of them, a gambling Marquise, who in turn knew a horse dealer in Chantilly who could finesse things. Max's man talked to the Lamorlaye trainer Max Bonaventure, and a quick sale was agreed, for £170, of a bay mare called Ganymede II. The three-year-old had run seven times over hurdles without winning but had finished second in a race at Auteuil on 21 November. By the afternoon of the 22nd the deal had been struck and Rosemarie Laumaine's ownership ratified and backdated by the French racing civil service, the Société d'Encouragement. And by the evening of 23 November, Ganymede was in her new box at Bob Kennett's yard in Stockbridge in Hampshire, the stable chosen by Roper as his office secretary's husband, Sid Barnes, used to ride out there.

On 24 November Bill instructed Micheline, or rather Rosemarie, to write to Peter Cazalet at Fairlawne, confirming her recent stable visit and asking, very charmingly, if he would take her horse. That same day Bill's secretary rang the DVLA and the local Mill Hill police station to report that a black Ford Zephyr saloon, registration number WXD575, was missing, believed stolen. The car and its forensic evidence had by then been eviscerated in an automobile graveyard that Charlie Mitchell knew somewhere out where the West London tube lines ended. Bill Roper's last ride in the motor was on the afternoon of the 23rd when Alex Field drove him away from Colville Terrace and dropped him off at Stafford Court. But by the time Roper was upstairs, drinking tea and waiting for Micheline to get home from Crawford Street, Scotland Yard were about to start investigating him.

Peter Cazalet was nothing if not a royalist and if there was one aspect of the doping scandal that disturbed him even more than the threat to his horses, it was its potential to embarrass the royal family. Steeplechasing had never been more popular in Britain, thanks to a combination of increased prize money from sponsors like Whitbread and Hennessy, increased television coverage and the enthusiastic support of the Queen Mother. It was insupportable, in Cazalet's view, for the royal horses to be at risk of being nobbled with the possibility that the Queen Mother herself could be embroiled in an investigation with all the lurid press coverage that would entail. Racing had to take the situation in hand and at the highest level.

Cazalet could initiate action in a way that men like Chris Nesfield and Roy Whiston couldn't. The Major was from the same background as the stewards and knew many of them socially so, as befits a clubland figure in a John Buchan novel, he went straight to the top. A conversation between Cazalet and the Senior Steward of the Jockey Club, Lord Crathorne,[31] led to a meeting in St James's

31 Crathorne was the former Conservative cabinet minister Sir Thomas Dugdale, who resigned over the Crichel Down affair in 1954.

with the Metropolitan Police Commissioner, Sir Ranulf Bacon. The following day, Friday 24 November, Assistant Commissioner Richard Jackson, who was head of the CID, met with other members of the Jockey Club and the National Hunt Committee. The Jockey Club delegation, which included Major General Sir Randle Feilden and Lord Willoughby de Broke, had finally accepted that the scale and severity of the doping menace was beyond their powers to curtail and that they needed to formally ask Scotland Yard to intercede.

The ignorance, incompetence and vacillation that had characterised many of the Jockey Club's actions was like a mirror image of the Macmillan government's stumbling response to assorted emerging sex and espionage scandals. A group of mostly elderly, white, upper-class men, only really at ease with others of their own stamp and circle, were no match for the spies, dopers and wily operators in their midst. Now it was time for the professionals to take charge.

The enquiry set up by Jackson, for which Detective Chief Superintendent George Davis would have overall control, was to have three prongs. The London and Home Counties Squad, comprising two detectives from each of the eight Home Counties – Berkshire, Buckinghamshire, Surrey, Sussex, Wiltshire and so on – would attempt to draw together various strands of evidence uncovered by provincial police forces and then pool their information. This would all be collated by Central Office under Detective Inspector John Bruce. But the main thrust of the investigation, especially in London, would be under the command of Detective Chief

Inspector Ernest Barnett, the head of CID at West End Central.

Portly Bob Hill, who would carry on his own searches in the background, was quick to leak news of the enquiry to the papers. 'Doping: The Yard Steps In', reported the *Herald* in an excited banner headline on Saturday 25 November. It went on to relate how Jackson had issued instructions to a special squad of detectives and of how 'the two French-speaking women' referred to in the paper earlier in the week were thought to be connected.

On Sunday the 26th the *News of the World* gave the story the full treatment, adding a few new, colourful details that appeared to have been provided by Bob Hill. 'Yesterday', it declared, 'detectives were given new information on a smart, attractive blonde, a former West End model and film extra, aged about 36, sporting a phoney French accent and often wearing a dark fur coat.' In a comical boost to the Jockey Club's previous unsuccessful attempts to catch the culprits, the article reported that 'Colonel Neville Blair' and, what it called, his 'hush hush squad' (Portly Bob and Leslie Davies), were 'certain that one of the blonde's escorts is a well-known gambler'. The hunt for the mysterious blonde was underway, the paper reassured its readers, and, if it was a foreign plot, as suspected, Interpol could be involved.

Ernie Barnett didn't think it was a foreign plot. The Detective Chief Inspector had told Jackson and the Home Secretary, R. A. Butler, who had asked to be kept personally informed, that he was pretty sure it originated right there in London town. He believed it was well organised and well financed and he expected to find top professional hard men behind the dopers. Barnett's shoes and those of his number two, Detective Inspector Bob Anderson, crunched over the gravel and wet leaves as they walked through St James's Park on their way back to their offices at the Yard. The Embankment was shrouded in November mist, buses and cars crawling along slowly in the usual rush-hour traffic jams. Somewhere in the city, in Soho, in the West End, or in East or South London, there were men who would know about the gang and maybe provide him with a lead. But first, Barnett decided, he would have to go to the racing towns, to Newmarket and Epsom, and talk to the trainers and the jockeys and the stable lads. Especially the stable lads.

The chase was on.

17

TEARS IN HER EYES

ONE UNINTENDED consequence of the police involvement was to throw Bill Roper a lifeline. Charlie Mitchell saw the coverage in the press and decided it would be a good time to slip out of the country. Mitchell was beginning to mix with other criminals as dangerous as himself, including the Kray Twins, and he didn't want their activities to attract unnecessary attention. He told Bill he'd be back sometime in the New Year, and that as there was no prospect of sending Micheline Lugeon into any more stables posing as a French racehorse owner, he was prepared to let Bill off what remained of his debt. For now. But he left Roper in no doubt that anyone who put Charlie's name in the frame, should Ernie Barnett come calling, would pay a heavy price.

With Mitchell out of the way, Bill was more determined than ever to try and brazen it out and on Tuesday 28 November, he and Micheline put their plan into action. Bill and Doris had already had a visit at Uphill Drive from portly Bob Hill who had turned up unannounced on the Sunday evening. The ex-copper was all cheery bonhomie as he explained to Roper that he was assisting the Jockey Club over this doping business and he just wondered if Bill might be able to help him with his enquiries. Bill responded calmly. He'd heard the rumours, like everyone else. He didn't think there was anything he could do but his Monmouth Street office was the appropriate place to discuss it not Sunday evenings at home. Hill agreed but he happened to have heard, as you do, that Mr Roper's car had recently been stolen. Did Bill have any idea when the theft had occurred? Bill wasn't precisely sure but the disappearance had been reported and he believed the police were looking into it. And the smart black Mercedes parked outside? asked Hill. It had been lent to him by a friend, said Roper, not mentioning that it belonged to Jack Stiles.

As Roper tried to show Hill the door, the former Detective Sergeant asked him very casually if he'd ever been in Shropshire or, for that matter, if he'd been to any stables in the North East recently? Bishop Auckland, for example, last weekend? Bill feigned ignorance of any such visits. Must be someone who looks like me, he said. Don't they always say that all bookmakers look the same? I thought they said that the bookmaker always wins, said Bob. Don't be daft, said Roper. Nobody wins all the time.

The following morning Roper went to see Micheline in Park Road – covering his back all the time – and they met again later that day at Stafford Court. Roper was under no illusions about Bob Hill's best mate's act but he still believed they had nothing concrete to link him and

Micheline to specific acts of doping and, with what seems almost unbelievable insouciance, he convinced her she could talk her way out of it. On Tuesday the 28th, advised and coached by Bill, she rang the Jockey Club and asked to speak to Colonel Blair. She told him she was happy to meet him if it would help to clear up any misunderstandings about her French horses. The Colonel suggested his office in Cavendish Square the following morning and Mademoiselle graciously agreed.

The days leading up to the meeting had been dominated by more dramatic revelations. On Monday the 27th Roy Whiston officially confirmed in *The Sporting Life* that Fresh Winds had been doped at Hodnet on the night of the 16th. 'I am certain that at least two more of my horses were got at too,' he added. On Tuesday the 28th Verley Bewicke's stable confirmed that Bronze Warrior had been doped at Glanton on 20 October and Detective Chief Superintendent Robert Scott of Northumberland CID warned that the crime had represented 'a callous threat not only to the horse's welfare but to human life'. The next day Chris Nesfield confirmed that Caca Dora's dope test had proved positive too, traces of chlorbutol having been found in her sample as they had in Scarron at Findon the week before.

The BPA, or Bookmakers Protection Association, the trade body of the racecourse bookmaking fraternity, responded by offering a £5,000 reward for any information that led to a conviction. There were no takers.

The tales of crime and racecourse skulduggery continued to share top billing in the papers, competing with the news that Eichmann had been sentenced to death in Tel Aviv, and it wasn't just the British media that was obsessed with them. The stories were being picked up overseas including in such unlikely publications as the *Schenectady Gazette* in upstate New York, which reported on 28 November that 'another top class British steeplechaser [Fresh Winds] was drugged before a big race' but assured its readers that 'bobbies and private eyes have today stepped up their hunt for a mystery woman and her gang of dopers'.

Shortly before 10 a.m. on Thursday 30 November, a black cab pulled up outside the Jockey Club headquarters at Number 15 Cavendish Square and the mystery woman got out. A small group of journalists, who had been tipped off by Bob Hill, pressed forward to catch a glimpse of the strikingly attractive young brunette in the dark fur coat. Grimacing in the wind and rain, Micheline ignored the reporters and hurried up the steps into the grand Regency building. A room on the first floor, reached by a Queen Anne staircase with black wrought iron railings, looked out across the square towards Oxford Street and the back of John Lewis. Mighty Jockey Club potentates such as Lord Rosebery, the Duke of Norfolk and Sir Randle Feilden occasionally met in this room to interrogate some delinquent trainer, jockey or even journalist, who had been summoned to explain themselves. But they didn't show Micheline Lugeon up to the first floor. She was escorted in to a smaller side office on the ground floor where Colonel Blair and Edward Weatherby greeted her with studied politeness.

It was an extraordinarily risky option that Roper had put forward, a reflection, no doubt, of his low opinion of the Jockey Club and their powers of detection. Equally extraordinarily, racing's ruling body hadn't bothered to tell the police about the meeting and still seemed to be running their own parallel investigation in which they hoped to sort things out without the need of Scotland Yard.

Micheline hadn't baulked at the challenge and had prepared for the interview every bit as carefully as she had for the trips to racing stables with Bill, selecting her clothes, make-up and handbag to convey exactly the right impression of respectability, credibility and wealth. She wasn't overawed by her inquisitors – but Blair and Weatherby played a good game too. Peter Cazalet had passed them Mademoiselle's letter regarding Ganymede II. She said she hadn't wanted to cause the Major any trouble and that, in fact, the horse was now stabled with Mr Kennett in Stockbridge. 'I believe that owning a successful racehorse or two is the best way to publicise my business,' she said. 'I plan to market my cosmetics and hope to meet many customers in racing.'

Blair and Weatherby explained that she would still have to be officially registered as an owner. To which end, could she give them her former Parisian address as well as her current home, as opposed to business, address and could she give them a few more details about herself and some identification to back them up? Micheline tried to delay, divert and flirt, seeking to give as little specific information as possible. But then the two men left her on her own for about 15 minutes and, for the first time in her whole fantastical and fraudulent journey in Bill Roper's company, the mask began to slip, an anxious look replacing the smile, a hair or two slipping out of place. It was then that Bob Hill, who was in an adjoining room, unobtrusively took a couple of photos of her with his Kodak Instamatic.

Micheline left Cavendish Square shortly before midday, assuring the Colonel that she would be back in touch with the details he required. The reporters were still waiting to meet her in the November cold – even if nobody had bothered to invite Ernie Barnett – but Mademoiselle hurried past them, dodging traffic, jumped into a taxi and was gone. An hour later Bob Hill met the correspondents from the *Daily Mail*, the *Daily Mirror* and the *Sunday Pictorial* in the Fitzroy Tavern on Charlotte Street and fed them a few more tantalising, if not necessarily accurate, details about 'Mademoiselle X'.

The next day the *Mail* reported that the 'young Frenchwoman' was 'more than willing to meet the Jockey Club again and tell them what she knew. If she could help in any way, of course she would.' The paper, which located her cosmetics shop in North London rather than Marylebone, said that when they called there, a woman working in the shop (June Downie), said that Mademoiselle was 'ill and would not be coming in for the next few days'. Alongside their article, the *Mail* posted a £1,000 reward for any information that might lead to a conviction, though their correspondent, J. L. Manning, rightly asked why there wasn't already more professional security in place at racecourses and racing stables.

On 2 December the *Daily Mirror* described the 'attractive dark-haired Michelle Lucerne' who it said ran 'a beauty salon off Baker Street', adding that 'something she overheard in a conversation may prove vital'.

The paper claimed that 'Mademoiselle Lucerne is believed to be in Paris at present. It is not thought that she is in any way connected with the dopers.' Neither statement was true but when Bill Roper saw the front page of *The Sporting Life* that same day, 2 December, Paris was one of several destinations he considered sending Micheline away to. At least the caption beneath Micheline's photograph, one of the less flattering ones taken by Bob Hill during her interview at Cavendish Square, got the name right this time: 'Glamorous West End beautician Micheline Emilienne Lugeon'. There was no mention of horse doping or race fixing. Only a brief story explaining that, like the society hairdresser, Paul 'Teasy Weasy' Raymond, Miss Lugeon had bought a racehorse, a French steeplechaser called Ganymede II, to promote her business. Ganymede was now residing at a stable in Hampshire.

It would have seemed an innocuous enough story to the general reader but the planting of the photograph, the result of collusion between *Life* editor Ossie Fletcher and Bob Hill, was quite deliberate. As assorted racehorse trainers studied the same page that morning, many among them – the Crumps, Bewickes and Stephensons, some vain, some gullible, some naive – realised that the glamorous beautician had been poking around their stable and was very probably the mysterious Frenchwoman alluded to in the tabloids and thought to be involved in the systematic doping of their horses. From that morning on, the trainers started contacting the Jockey Club to tell their stories.

It was a tumultuous weekend and there was more drama to come. 'New Doping Shock', screamed the headline on the West End final edition of that Saturday's *Evening Standard*. Blue Rondo, who had been expected to start favourite for the three o'clock race at Windsor, the Dedworth Manor Steeplechase, had apparently 'been found reeling in his box' that morning at his trainer Ken Bailey's stable near Chelmsford in Essex. The horse had immediately been withdrawn and the police called, said Bailey, who added that 'the lights had been on in my yard all through the night and Blue Rondo's box was padlocked'. The week before, when Bailey had a horse running at Newbury, he had let his bull mastiffs run free in the yard but the night before Blue Rondo's race he'd kept them locked up.

On Sunday 3 December the new doping – if it was one – was the front page story in the *Sunday Pictorial* which ran a cartoon of two racehorses asking if someone had doped the stewards. It was also the lead story in the *News of the World*, edging out the memoirs of Mrs Albert Pierrepoint, the wife of the former hangman, and a report on the problems afflicting the filming of *Cleopatra* in Rome. The *News Of The World* speculated on the background and make-up of the doping gang. 'Who is involved?' asked the paper, before providing what it believed were the answers. 'Some bookmakers are in the know along with two glamour girls and a handful of tough boys.' The article then queried why bookies cut the odds of horses that they knew couldn't win. The answer was that, as a consequence, the odds on the second and third favourites that they did expect to win would drift out to a bigger and more attractive price.

The doping of Blue Rondo may have had nothing to do with Bill Roper. It hardly seemed a wise or propitious moment to be breaking into another stable and Ken Bailey admitted a few weeks later, after a negative dope test, that his horse might have been suffering from a kidney infection. But at Sandown on Thursday 7 December there was an extremely crooked race in which a gambled-on favourite was either doped or hooked up by villains offering the connections more to lose than win. The horse's name was Golden Boy, an Epsom-trained five-year-old with no form to speak of, running in the Effingham Selling Hurdle over two miles. In his previous two races he had been unsighted in a handicap at Birmingham and last in a similar race at Ludlow. But here he was at Sandown, with John Sutcliffe, a bookie's son, on board, backed into 15-8 favourite in a field of nine and clearly 'off' for the first time in his life. He was in third place as they turned into the home straight but then he 'dropped out', as the race readers say, and finished a distant last. There was no stewards' inquiry afterwards but there were an awful lot of rumours.[32]

On Saturday 9 December the main meeting in the South was at Lingfield Park. The pre-Christmas fixture was one of the Queen Mother's favourites and an annual highlight at

---

32 The winner was the 4-1 third favourite La Perche, trained by Captain Ryan Price.

Fairlawne. The royal party arrived by car in time for tea on the Friday afternoon, upstairs downstairs life at the house having continued on pre-war and almost Edwardian lines with butlers, housemaids, valets and other devoted servants in close attention at all times. Guests' baths would be drawn in the early evening and then everyone would dress for dinner, the men in black tie. Peter and Zara Cazalet had their own private chef, none other than Albert Roux who was 26-years old in 1962 and had been working in England for eight years, initially at Lord Astor's house, Cliveden, where Profumo, the Secretary of State for War, met Christine Keeler.

After dinner on the Friday and Saturday nights specially invited guests like Noël Coward or Elizabeth Taylor might entertain around the piano in the drawing room. Then, the following morning, everyone would watch the horses work on the gallops in the park before going back inside for breakfast. A few hours later they would be driven ten miles through the back roads of the Weald to lovely Lingfield near Edenbridge. It could be bitterly cold there in December beneath the tall, leafless trees but to the Queen Mother every novice chase and hurdle race was clearly every bit as heart warming as the liberal measures of whisky mac and sloe gin in the Marquis of Abergavenny's box.

That December Saturday, the day of a big Ban The Bomb demonstration in London, was one of unprecedented success for the Queen Mother as Cazalet and his top jockey, Bill Rees, pulled off a treble in the royal colours. Laffy, the five-year-old French-bred that Micheline had seen in the stable on 8 November, broke his duck in the second division of the Oxted Novices Chase. Double Star upset the favourites in the two-and-a-half mile Ashdown Chase and then, half an hour later, The Rip made it three in a row, winning the three mile Eridge Chase by eight lengths. The crowd lined the rails 12 deep and cheered repeatedly as the Queen Mother patted The Rip in the unsaddling enclosure afterwards.

At the end of the afternoon, the party returned to Fairlawne for tea and hot baths, then cocktails, canapés and another one of Albert Roux's dinners. On Sunday morning the Queen Mother's routine would include going to St George's Church in Shipbourne, which had been built by Cazalet's grandfather, before returning to the house for a special Roux Sunday lunch. It was a charming weekend in a charmed and deferential setting but, whatever the view as the ladies withdrew, the rougher, cruder aspects of modern life couldn't be entirely blocked out.

Bill Roper was at Lingfield that Saturday, ignoring Bob Hill and putting bets on for clients. It didn't escape Bill's attention that Laffy was returned at even money and The Rip at 13-8 on and, in both races, the runners didn't reach double figures. By comparison, the Marsh Green Handicap Hurdle, run over two miles at three o'clock, had an 18-runner field with one red hot favourite, Sky Pink, trained by the bookmakers' old friend – and Jack Stiles's and Darkie Steward's – Captain Ryan Price and ridden by Fred Winter. Backed in from 7-4 to 11-10, he was prominent for the first mile, jumping beautifully and, in Winter's own words, 'I was as happy as a lark. But then when we had gone a mile and a half, he was suddenly dead, absolutely gone.' Winter sensibly pulled his mount up and the Captain, tight lipped for once, ordered another dope test.

The story was all over Monday's edition of the *Daily Mirror*. 'Was Ryan Price's Sky Pink doped in the fifth at Lingfield on Saturday?' it asked. 'Watched by the Queen Mother and thousands of racegoers and TV viewers, it was in a bunch of runners at the tail of the field and then suddenly stopped.' The article galloped on, giving the *Mirror*'s account of the doping gang, a version partially supplied by Bob Hill but not far off the truth for all that.

Police and Jockey Club investigators allegedly know the name of the man behind the big racehorse doping scandal. He's aged about fifty, a professional gambler who bets in four figures on horses and dogs and is known to the rest, simply, as The Boss. He's well known in racing circles in the Midlands and the south of England. Behind him is the so-called 'Paymaster General' who provides the funds to finance the gang's activities but investigators feel it will be extremely hard to prove anything against him. All the racing underworld 'grasses' have closed up and are afraid to talk for fear of being beaten up or razor slashed. Meanwhile The Boss's minder or right hand man, another big gambler, is thought to be out of the country with his attractive girlfriend.

The minder, Charlie Mitchell, was indeed out of the country and temporarily pursuing other business for the

Krays. The 'Paymaster General' was an attempt to finger Max Parker who would prove well nigh impossible to charge with any crime. (As the *Mirror* had reported the week before, Maxie was currently ill with coronary thrombosis and resting at his flat in Montagu Square.) That left The Boss, who was blatantly Bill Roper, and when the indebted, entangled and hopelessly in love Mr Racing read the *Mirror* story he was tempted to conclude that the game was up. If the newspapers were prepared to go that close to naming him and Maxie in print, the authorities must feel pretty confident about their case. Or did they?

As yet no uniformed or plain clothes officers had come calling at either Monmouth Street or Uphill Drive. Only portly, insinuating Bob Hill who may have proof of Roper's car registration but hadn't found it and never would. The key, Bill decided, lay with the loyalty, or otherwise, of the younger gang members. None of them would be foolish enough to grass up Charlie Mitchell or legal sharpies like Maxie and Cyril Stein but, under pressure and the threat of imprisonment, they might give up W. J. Roper. In the circumstances, Bill decided, it was time to close down the Notting Hill HQ, a bit like Fagin's gang abandoning their den of thieves in *Oliver Twist*.

Bill called up Darkie Steward and arranged an emergency meeting at Colville Terrace that afternoon. Roper's advice to Darkie, Sylvia Cross, Stiles, Perry and Field was simple. Pack up and clear out. Fast. They should separate and lie low outside London for the next few months. All being well the newspaper stories would die down and Bill would be in touch again after Christmas.

To the bewilderment of Mrs Robson and the watchful Major Haines, the young tenants on the third floor had all gone by morning. They'd stripped their rooms and taken their Rediffusion TV set and left behind a lot of empty bottles and overflowing ashtrays along with an envelope containing a month's rent, in cash, for each of them. Despite Bill's warning, Harry Field and Elaine Grande, who had the bedsit on the top floor, had insisted on staying on. Harry had other criminal propositions to consider as well as horse doping and, if they were successful, he hoped to get away with his girlfriend in their own time.

Bill's suspicions that the Jockey Club had a list of names but didn't yet know how to connect them, were confirmed over the next few days. On 12 December, Sir Randle Feilden reported that the Jockey Club had themselves conducted 90 dope tests over the last 18 months, including on 30 beaten favourites, and that 'not a single test taken under Jockey Club rules has proved positive'. The General admitted that 'all private tests HAVE proved positive' but insisted that 'it would be unfair to make comparisons'. The doping scandal, he felt, may 'well have been exaggerated'.

But a few nights later, Feilden was in sombre mood as he addressed the black-tied guests at the annual Gimcrack Dinner, a yearly assembly of horse racing's great and good in the Gimcrack Rooms at York racecourse. Bookmakers, not being gentlemen, hadn't been invited which may have been correct Jockey Club etiquette but was also rather pointless as Feilden's remarks were clearly aimed at the layers. 'Make no mistake,' intoned Monty's Grocer, as the General was nicknamed, 'our investigations to date show that there are a few who know much and many who know a little and they are connected with the betting ring. I divulge these facts in particular to the betting profession and would ask the bookmakers to suggest how such transactions and the passing of information might be tracked. There is no time for delay.'

Feilden's headmasterly pomposity wasn't the only thing that infuriated William Hill who had first offered his assistance after the Derby in June but had been ignored. He was now putting up a £10,000 reward, trumping the BPA and *Daily Mail* bounties, for information leading to the conviction of the dopers and no doubt hoped that his arch rivals Max Parker and Ladbrokes would be taken out as a result. But, as he grumpily observed, the 'Jockey Club can not expect the bookmakers to make out their case for them.'

On 21 December a small deputation of bookmakers, led by the endlessly helpful Archie Scott, who had issued the statement to the press on 22 November, met privately with Neville Blair and Edward Weatherby at Cavendish Square. The encounter had similarities with scenes of Conservative cabinet members meeting Trade Union leaders over beer and sandwiches, but there was still no question of the Jockey Club formally co-opting representatives of the 'betting profession' into the bosom of their enquiry. The only public reference to the meeting came in a statement printed in the *Racing Calendar* and picked up by *The Sporting Life* to the effect that Colonel Blair was now to concentrate his efforts on improving stable security. As an example of locking the stable door after the horse had not only bolted but disappeared over the horizon and into the next parish, it had scarcely ever been surpassed. In truth, the Colonel was being moved sideways. Bob Hill and Leslie Davies were doing the Jockey Club security department's work now and Ernest Barnett and his team on the Embankment were just about to weigh in too.

On 22 December Micheline Lugeon sold Ganymede II to an emotional June Downie and sold her Crawford Street shop to a friend, Peter Devon. He paid a token £2,000 and was going to try and manage it for her until 'this silly and inaccurate publicity', as she described it, 'dies down'. She retained ownership of the brand, Michelle de Paris, and was sure it would carry on in the not too distant future. That afternoon Bill Roper drove Micheline to Heathrow and put her on a Swiss Air flight to Geneva. There were tears in her eyes as she said goodbye. She wasn't leaving him, she said. She was only going home for Christmas. Roper hugged her close, his arms wrapped around the petite figure in the dark fur coat. As she walked away through the departure gate, Bill shut his eyes and imagined it was 1959 all over again and he was back in the perfumery department in Fortnum & Mason. Watching the beautiful young girl with the 50-guinea smile and breathing in the tantalising scent of Balmain, Arpège, Givenchy . . . and Michelle de Paris.

As the country broke up for Christmas, the doping stories eased off as Bill had predicted they would. Frost knocked out the big Boxing Day race meeting at Kempton and Newton Abbot was the only course able to go ahead on 26 December. The football programme was equally disrupted leaving the nation to settle down in front of their television sets and watch *The Black and White Minstrel Show*, a Norman Wisdom film and the annual Brian Rix farce.

On New Year's Eve, Bill Roper and Doris and a group of old friends went to the London Palladium to see Cliff Richard and Bill's fellow Stafford Court tenant, Alma Cogan. Mr Racing was always welcome in her dressing room. A drink with the stars. A few photographs. Clinking glasses. But did they go on anywhere afterwards? Did Doris merit a table at the Astor Club or the Pigalle? Or, as midnight struck, was Bill thinking only of Micheline? And wondering where exactly he'd be celebrating in 12 months' time?

Scholarly and bespectacled Detective Chief Inspector Barnett didn't pay much attention to holidays. He was in his office early on New Year's Day 1962. The Chief had a report waiting for him from the Metropolitan Police Forensic Laboratory. A week before Christmas, a Mrs Barbara Robson had gone into Notting Hill police station and handed in a bag of white powder that had been found in a house she owned in Colville Terrace. Her daily, Mrs Juggins, had been cleaning a bathroom next to a recently vacated bedsit on the third floor. A one-inch screw had fallen off the side of the bath and the bag had been discovered wedged behind a panel. Mrs Robson and her friend, Major Haines, thought the bag must have been left behind by some tenants who had left in a hurry. They had examined the white powder and wondered if it might be some kind of drug.

Mrs Robson and the Major were quite right. The bag contained two hundred grains of phenobarbitone, the same drug that had been found in the tests of numerous doped racehorses.

When Barnett met them the following day, Mrs Robson gave him the names of the recently departed tenants who had shared the bathroom on the third floor. Leonard Bland, John Stiles and Brian Perry. Not forgetting their friend, Alex Field, who was currently away on business but still officially a resident on the top floor. Barnett gave the names to Bob Anderson and told him to check them out with any known jockey and stable lad suspects in Newmarket and elsewhere. Then Mrs Robson told him about the older chap who had often paid the younger men's rent but never stayed. Mr Roper, his name was. So charming and always so very well dressed.

Ernie Barnett had the lead he'd been looking for.

18

A REAL DICK FRANCIS

JANUARY 1962 marked the beginning of a publishing phenomenon as Michael Joseph brought out the first Dick Francis thriller, *Dead Cert*. The former royal jockey, who still rode out at Fairlawne, had penned his autobiography, *The Sport of Queens*, and turned his hand to racing journalism with the *Sunday Express*. His first foray into fiction portrayed a racing world brimming with violence and shady dealings, and given the doping tales that had been making headlines in the papers, the timing could hardly have been more propitious.

The story is narrated by Alan York, an amateur rider determined to avenge the death of his friend Bill Davidson, who he believes to have been murdered during a steeplechase at fictitious Maidenhead racecourse.

York was the prototype of all the subsequent Dick Francis heroes. Honourable, resilient, subjected to terrible physical tortures, and yet triumphant in the end. Some of the characterisation was more Biggles and Ginger than Raymond Chandler and, while bookmakers would often be the villains of a Dick Francis novel, they rarely attained more than one-dimensional status, like the improbably named 'Bimmo Bognor' who appeared in *For Kicks* in 1965. But the basic elements of plot, narrative and page-turning drama were winners all the way and an absorbed and entertained public couldn't get enough of them.

In *Dead Cert*'s black and white universe there was never any question that good would prevail over evil but, in the grainy reality that DCI Barnett moved in, it wasn't quite as simple. Perhaps an ex-amateur rider turned investigator would have gone about it differently but Barnett, who was scrupulously honest compared to some bent coppers of that era, knew that if he wanted the information to help him break open a case and collar the suspects, he'd have to pay for it.

It was a procedure he'd followed often enough while working for his former boss, Detective Chief Superintendent Ted Greeno who had retired in 1959. Greeno was an enthusiastic betting man who often said that the criminal and racing milieus had a lot in common. 'I have been catching criminals for 38 years and backing horses for 39,' he wrote in his memoir *War on the Underworld*. 'If I had not backed so many winners I could not have caught so many criminals because at both sports you need information which costs money. A man rarely turns informant just for the money but he certainly doesn't remain one without it.'[33] The bigger

---

33 *War on the Underworld* by Edward Greeno, published by John Long, 1960. Stan Davis (see p. 68 footnote) reckoned that Greeno was no better than a villain himself and regularly took bribes.

villains like Billy Hill and Albert Dimes paid Ted Greeno to leave them alone. The smaller and more vulnerable ones took his money in return for information that might help him storyboard a crime.

Barnett was aware of Ossie Fletcher's anonymous tip-off but he couldn't arrest anyone simply on the basis of name-calling. One of the detective's problems was that there was no specific crime of doping a racehorse. To obtain convictions the police would have to prove conspiracy to defraud and that wasn't an easy charge to make stick. Barnett wanted to know who the 'tough boys' were who were pulling the strings and he turned initially to a bookmaker, Nathan Mercado, a short, stocky character whose trade name was Sid Kiki and who was allegedly an underworld grass. Mercado, who had betting shops in Acton and Shepherd's Bush, told him, off the record, exactly what a dozen other bookies would have said. Billy Roper spent 12 years working for Max Parker and it was well known that Maxie 'had all the doped horses' which meant he got the news first and framed his odds accordingly. It also meant Max would have been paying Bill for the intelligence.

Barnett could foresee immense difficulties trying to get evidence linking the chairman of Ladbrokes to the conspiracy. But what about the men who worked for Roper? The faces and the putters-on? Mercado gave him some names. There was Joe Lowry, who had been trying to fix races for years, and Jackie Dyer, who had been seriously ill in 1960 and only had one kidney. There was Jackie's nephew, Charlie Mitchell, who was a scary piece of work, and then there was 'the boy', Darkie Steward. An ex-jockey and tout. The ring knew that he'd been working for Bill on and off the course and bringing him tips and information. But it was known that Steward was also friendly with Albert Dimes who was expanding his bookmaking business and would like to have a bigger share of Bill's action if Charlie Mitchell wasn't in the way. There was a suspicion that the Blue Rondo doping and the nobbling of Golden Boy at Sandown were both initiated by Dimes.

Barnett didn't feel any more optimistic about placing Italian Albert in the frame than he did Max Parker but Steward sounded much more promising. The London and Home Counties squad had been going back over all acknowledged dopings in the south from 1953 onwards and the Central Office was collating the information from Shropshire, Yorkshire and Northumberland. Both teams were talking to trainers and their stable staff and attempting to track down lads who had been working in the yards when a horse had been got at but had since left. Hours of painstaking enquiry throughout January and February revealed that John Stiles, formerly of the Carlton Hotel, Newmarket, had been a stable boy in the town in 1960 and, before that, had been at Captain Ryan Price's Findon yard where one Emmanuel Lipman Leonard Steward had also been employed. Might Steward have been at Colville Terrace? Barnett wondered. Might Len Steward be Len Bland? And, either way, where was he now?

Barnett went up to Newmarket with Bob Hill who had been liaising with the Yard and had made contact with PC Charles Pickin, the uniformed officer who had seen the two-tone Ford Zodiac and its passengers acting suspiciously on the night of 30 March 1960, the night Jack Waugh's Treasure Hunt was doped. Pickin had his log book with the car registration number and the names of the two other men he'd seen loitering in Rous Road. Barnett studied the names in Pickin's notes. John Stiles . . . and Kenneth Santus, who was still living in Market Street with his wife and baby.

Ashen-faced and trembling, Kenny was brought in for questioning along with Michael Heffernan who had continued working and living locally after being warned off by the Jockey Club in April 1961. The pair denied knowing Bill Roper and said they couldn't even describe what he looked like. A defiant Heffernan claimed that he'd never met Len Steward or Jackie Dyer either, although they did both admit having met Joe Lowry and Heffernan said that he'd occasionally bought them a drink in exchange for tips. They also admitted knowing Philip 'Snuffy' Lawler who had been Noel Murless's 'number one lad' but they'd no idea where he was now.

The Yard ran a check on the two-tone Ford Zodiac, registration number XGH557, and found it to be owned by one Edward Charles Dyer of Lakehurst Road, Shepherd's Bush. They also found an old address for Joe Lowry in Charles Road, Forest Gate East near Upton Park. Bob Hill and Leslie Davies kept a watch on Joe's house and eventually accosted him as he was leaving home, one February morning. He agreed to come in for a 'chat' at Cavendish Square where Colonel Blair and Edward Weatherby were both present. Lowry agreed that he'd met

Michael Heffernan on occasion and said he often drank in the racing pubs in Newmarket just like any other punter on the look-out for news and tips. Yes, he'd heard the name Len Steward and thought he might have seen him around on the racecourse but not for some time. He said he didn't know Bill Roper but he'd like to because he believed he was a brilliant man. A frustrated Weatherby asked him outright. 'So who is behind these betting coups? Is it Max Parker or William Hill?' 'I don't know,' said Joe, a veteran of evasive cross-examination. 'You'd better ask them.'

That's exactly what Ernest Barnett did next. He and Bob Hill had off the record conversations with William Hill, who gave them his low opinion of the Parker/Stein family but couldn't swear to anything on oath. They talked to the bookmakers Willie Preston, who had been working for Hill since 1960, Alf Cope, Beau Goldsmith, Jack Burns and Jack Swift.[34] The police would have loved to have seen betting slips, books and accounts relating to the fixed races but none of them seemed to exist. All any of the bookies would say was that much of their trade was word of mouth and, while they suspected there had been something going on with Pinturischio, other results had been exaggerated. Yes, they may have made a profit on certain races where the favourite had lost but that was racing and, besides, they simply

---

34 Jack Burns, who began life as a marker in a billiard hall, started bookmaking after the First World War and had many aristocratic clients. Alf Cope, managing director of David Cope Ltd, took over Archie Scott's business and was, in turn, taken over by William Hill. 'Beau' Goldsmith's firm traded as Jack Wilson and Co. The very shrewd Willie Preston, who worked for William Hill, retired on Cheltenham Gold Cup day in 1964.

responded to the market. If one of their regulars kept backing second favourites and the second favourites kept winning, they'd stick a few bob on for the firm too and lay the 'jolly'. Any sensible bookmaker would do the same thing.

Bill Roper was doing his best to be a sensible bookmaker. Trading each day from his Monmouth Street office and sometimes on the racecourse. Getting his clients' money on. Chatting to them on the phone or in their boxes at the races and going home to Uphill Drive each evening. Bob Hill kept popping up, ever so friendly, for a chat but Roper managed to dead-bat his enquiries. Micheline wrote to him regularly and every few days he went to Stafford Court and she called him on the phone from her parents' house and then he rang her back. He ached to see her again and missed her desperately and she longed to return – and to finish doing up her Park Road flat so that she could put it on the market – but Bill didn't feel it was safe yet for her to come back to London.

It wasn't just the police Bill was worried about. In mid-February, Charlie Mitchell reappeared.

The hard man's Kray Twin business had gone well. His new nightclub was due to open in April but before then he wanted the gang to go back to work. Mitchell had his eye on another lucrative ante-post job like Pinturischio's Derby. The Cheltenham Festival was getting bigger each year and Ladbrokes, Max Parker, William Hill and other credit specialists were running a strong ante-post book on the Cheltenham Gold Cup and the Champion Hurdle with call-overs at the Victoria Club just like before the Lincoln, the National and the Derby. The leading contenders for the 1962 Gold Cup, Pas Seul and Fortria, were hard to separate but in the Champion Hurdle market the 1960 victor, Another Flash, was all the rage. The eight-year-old, who had been forced to miss the previous year's race due to a setback, was trained in Warwick by Arthur Thomas which meant that he was really trained in Ireland by Paddy Sleator. He'd had four runs so far that season, winning them all impressively. His jumping was fluent and, providing the ground wasn't unduly soft, the wily Sleator couldn't see him losing.

Another Flash's owner, John Byrne – a Kerry-born London impresario – and other big hitters from Ireland and England had been backing his horse all winter. It was down to 5-2 favourite with Ladbrokes and expected to start a lot shorter on the day. But, as you'd expect in a championship, there were a couple of very smart rivals in the race too. The northern challenger, Quelle Chance, was on a winning streak and then there was a promising grey called Anzio trained by the great Fulke Walwyn. Get at Another Flash, maybe the Monday night before the meeting and, with the favourite out of the running, the big ante-post layers would reward them generously. And in the thick of the Festival's burgeoning on-course market they'd be able to get a good price about Anzio or Quelle Chance.

There was no denying Mitchell's logic but when Bill got back in touch with Ted Smith to acquire the necessary drugs he was told that the Surbiton dope bank was nearly empty. The Witch Doctor explained that the frantic rate of doping attempts between October and November had all but exhausted supplies. Charlie Mitchell told Smith to get some more, and be quick about it or he'd get the same treatment as Darkie Steward. Fingers, toes, ears, bollocks. What did he want to lose first? That was motivation enough for Ted Smith but when he made contact with Richard McGee in Newcastle his old friend was horrified. He pointed out that Ted had already been sent enough gear to stop an entire army of horses and he didn't think he could safely steal any more. Smith implored him, for both their sakes, to change his mind and McGee, who was desperate to stave off another visit by Ted to the Fawdon laboratory, reluctantly agreed. A few days later Smith received another big consignment of methyl amphetamine hydrochloride in the post. He proceeded to make some of it up into doses and handed it over to Bill Roper on the platform at Baker Street station. Roper, meanwhile, began to tip off other members of the gang that there would soon be another job for them.

When Ernest Barnett had his long chat with Mrs Robson on 2 January he asked her to call his office at once if Harry Field, or any of the former tenants, returned to Colville Terrace. In late February she rang. Field was back with his girlfriend Elaine Grande and Major Haines thought that they'd already had a few visitors. Barnett put a watch on Number 24 and, a few days later, two plain-clothes officers picked up Field's trail in the Prince of Wales and followed him to Joe Cannon's Jazz Club on Westbourne Park Road. The following morning they saw him go in to the Continental Café with two other men. Discreet photographs were taken of Field and his companions as they left and when Bob Anderson showed them to Mrs Robson she identified one of the men as Leonard Bland. When Anderson showed the same photo to Nathan Mercado he said 'that's Darkie Steward'.

The police continued their surveillance of Colville Terrace but the two detectives in their grey 1962 raincoats and hats were all too conspicuous. Harry and Elaine had their own primitive early warning system and when Field came back one night, with Darkie and Brian Perry in tow, they saw the curtains of the third-floor apartment were wide open and a light was on in the window. The three men got away in a hurry, and when the detectives entered the building half an hour later and were greeted by Elaine in a dressing gown and basque, which was part of her professional wardrobe, she denied all knowledge of Harry's whereabouts.

The failed stake-out was reported back to Barnett who was furious. The dopers had gone to ground. But for how long?

On Thursday 22 February Another Flash had his final Cheltenham prep run at Wincanton in Somerset. He was sent off the 4-11 favourite for the two-mile Red April Hurdle, winning easily from the very useful Ryan Price-trained hurdler Cantab. Everything was set fair for the Festival although as Cheltenham drew nigh there was said to be mounting confidence too about the five-year-old Anzio.

There was a sudden cold snap at the end of the month but on 9 March, five days before the Champion Hurdle, the barometer reading on the weighing room wall at Newbury was 54 degrees Fahrenheit and there was a feeling that winter was over at last. But then on Sunday and Monday nights the temperature dropped again and the frost returned.

Late evening on the 12th, Darkie Steward, Jack Stiles, Jimmy Cronin and Alex Field, driven by Joe Lowry, set off for Arthur Thomas's Warwick yard. The stable was situated about a mile outside the town on the Kenilworth Road and was reached up a drive running parallel with the driveway leading to Guy's Cliffe House. The 18th-century Gothic mansion had been empty since 1947 though the chapel had been leased to the Freemasons who sometimes held ceremonies there. Paranormal sightings had been reported from time to time and the whole place, including the adjoining stable yard, had a ghostly atmosphere that must have been, quite literally, chilling at 2 a.m. on a cold March night. But the threat awaiting the dopers came not from ghouls or supernatural phenomena but from two flesh and blood Irish stable lads, Willie Burke and Jim Leigh's brother, Gerald.

Another Flash and Sleator's other Cheltenham runners were in six caged boxes near the stable office and the clock tower. There was a connecting passageway outside the boxes leading to an outer door into the cobbled yard. Alex Field, followed by Darkie and Jack Stiles, who had been to Guy's Cliffe before, climbed over the outer gate by the office and then Field picked the lock on the door to the passageway. But just as they were moving down the row of boxes – torch, twitch and dope in hand – they discovered that they'd woken up two men who'd been sleeping on cots on the floor. Burke and Leigh had been chosen by Paddy Sleator because they were stable lad boxers, brawny and fearless, and their job was to deny any access to intruders. Just to be sure, Sleator had equipped them with a double-barrelled shotgun.

When the dopers were confronted by the two lads, a 'hell of a scuffle' broke out and the racket was enough to wake up Arthur Thomas in the adjoining house. Steward, Stiles, Cronin and Field 'ran like scalded cats', as Burke and Leigh later described it, and the two Irishmen pursued them down the drive, even firing a warning shot into the air. But with a frantic screech of tyres and in a cloud of exhaust fumes, the unidentified car and its occupants got away into the night.

The news of the attempted break-in reached the Cheltenham pressroom the following day and, on Wednesday 14 March it was all over the papers. 'Stable men foil intruders,' declared the *Times* headline, adding that 'Colonel Neville Blair, who is in charge of racecourse security, was at Cheltenham but he has had a first hand report from Mr Thomas.' More likely it was from Mr Sleator. But the Colonel had apparently concluded that 'Mr Thomas's successful measures' were 'a tonic' to the security forces who would, presumably, be recommending the deployment of armed guards in all racing yards from now on.

Paddy Sleator pronounced Another Flash fit, well and untroubled by the nocturnal disturbance. With the fast ground in his favour, he went off the red hot 11-10 favourite for the Champion Hurdle but, ironically, he could only finish third, beaten three-and-a-quarter lengths by the younger Anzio who came with a strong run approaching the last hurdle and had too much speed for him up the hill. Quelle Chance finished second. The ante-post bookies had made their money with no assistance from the Roper gang and it was an extremely profitable Festival for the layers; indeed, there wasn't a single winning favourite over the three days, demonstrating racing's glorious uncertainty and that you didn't need to fix things in advance to get a result.

The day after Cheltenham ended, the focus moved on to the two-day fixture at Hurst Park which, sadly, was to be the last ever meeting there over jumps. The course's owners had sold the land for a housing development and, after the final flat racing card in October 1962, the bulldozers would move in. On Saturday 17 March the big race was the Triumph Hurdle, the championship event for four-year-olds in which Captain Ryan Price provided the 7-4 favourite, Catapult II, who had very smart form in France and had been bought for £6,000 by one of the Captain's biggest owners.[35] Price was victorious, sure enough, but it was his supposed second string, Beaver II, who stormed home by six lengths at 100-6 with Catapult runner-up.

Punters were still fulminating about the Captain's antics half an hour later as the runners went to post for the valuable Monaveen Chase for novices over two miles. The prestigious contest, named after the Queen Mother's first great chaser, was to have been the target of one of her most promising young horses, Laffy, trained at Fairlawne by Major Peter Cazalet and a course and distance winner at

---

35 Enid Chanelle, who also owned the 1961 Triumph Hurdle winner Cantab.

Hurst Park the month before. But when racegoers got to the doomed track they discovered that the royal representative, predicted to go off at 9-4 second favourite in *The Sporting Life*, was a non-runner. Cazalet had made an excuse about the horse being off colour but what the punters and press didn't know, and weren't told publicly until many years later, was that Laffy had been doped.

Bill Roper had had his eye on the six-year-old for months and the Monaveen Chase, a televised Saturday race with 11 or 12 runners and a strong betting market, had seemed like the perfect opportunity to put the intelligence that Micheline had acquired to good use. In the early hours of 17 March the gang had slipped on to the Fairlawne estate, using a footpath beyond the service drive, and had made their way stealthily up the slope through the tall trees towards the stableyard. Fairlawne was supposedly even more haunted than Guy's Cliffe and a headless man, and a nymphomaniac woman dressed in white and riding a horse, were said to roam the grounds at night. But there were no armed stable lads.

Laffy and the Major's other Hurst Park runner, Aulnoye, were in special timed security boxes separate from the main yard. At 5 a.m. the head lad, Jim Fairgrieve, got up and supervised the feeding of the horses before going over to the tack room for a cup of tea. When he returned half an hour later, Laffy was displaying the same symptoms – docility, unsteadiness, difficulty in standing up – as all the other doped horses. Peter Cazalet was summoned and when he realised what must have happened he was livid. The lock on Laffy's box had been picked and, for the dopers to have got in and out so quickly while Fairgrieve was making tea, someone on the inside must have helped them. For the moment, the Major summoned his vet and, by breakfast time, the clerk of the course at Hurst Park had been informed that Laffy had been withdrawn. Then Cazalet called the police.

Derek Ancil, the trainer and jockey of The Finn, the 7-4 favourite for the Monaveen Chase, was presented with a similarly worrying sight when he went to saddle his horse in the racecourse stables that afternoon. The six-year-old, who was owned by Mrs Selwyn Martin from Glamorgan, had nearly won the Triumph Hurdle two years before and had been impressive in his only run to date over the bigger obstacles. He was expected to be ideally suited to Hurst Park's fast track and firm going. But, an hour before the race, The Finn seemed to Ancil to be 'confused' and he blundered into a door as he was being led to his saddling box. The trainer, who was based at Middleton Stoney in Oxfordshire, asked the racecourse vet to have a look at him and then asked another vet for a second opinion. Both men thought the horse was behaving oddly but, having checked his heartbeat, said they could find nothing to justify withdrawal. It was a negligent, and very nearly fatal, decision.

The Finn fell heavily at the first fence, flinging Ancil to the ground. The horse got up, carried on and fell again, riderless, at the second fence. Getting to his feet once more, he careered across country before colliding with the running rail and falling on his back by the flat racing course. He somehow managed to slide under the rail and then, visibly distressed and completely out of control, galloped away up the track towards the Victoria Cup start where he was eventually caught. Only then did the horrified Ancil realise that his horse was almost blind. A urine test was taken there and then and Ancil, who was himself lucky to be alive, ordered saliva tests to follow. He was told it would take about ten days for the results to come through but the horse and trainer's nightmarish experience was the main story in the sports pages on Monday 19 March. 'I am convinced The Finn was nobbled,' said Ancil. 'He has recovered now but he was in a terrible state. I can not understand how he was got at.'

He was got at earlier that day, one of Ancil's stable lads administering the dope, while Darkie Steward, Alex Field and Brian Perry went to Kent. It was the gang's first and last attempt to get at two horses in the same race and it achieved a result of sorts. They didn't manage to take down the Queen Mother punters who would've backed Laffy on the day and on course but, without him, The Finn had been a heavily backed favourite in the ring and Messrs Roper, Parker, Dyer, Howard, Mitchell and, no doubt, Albert Dimes, all made money. But the distressing scenes at Hurst Park also marked a new low and another turning point in the gang's progress.

The Finn, like Pinturischio, Morland Jack and Indian Melody, never properly recovered from his abuse. Ancil's vet discovered seven rubber bands in his droppings at Hurst Park, indicative of the huge dose of drugs that had been shoved down his throat. He didn't run again that season. The following autumn he had a couple of confidence-building races over hurdles and then in November he went up to Wetherby to contest the Mackeson Novices Steeplechase, a valuable new prize over two-and-a-half miles. He was the second favourite in a 20 strong field but, maybe, the big black fences frightened him because he fell at the first, breaking a stifle joint, and was destroyed.

Laffy was luckier. The Fairlawne doping party had been in too much of a hurry, probably because a nervous local stable lad was urging them to be gone. They didn't give the Queen Mother's chaser the full quota, let alone the overdose that The Finn had been subjected to. Laffy recovered so quickly that he was able to run in a three-mile chase at Lingfield the following week, winning gamely by two lengths, and in early April Cazalet took him over to Northern Ireland to land the Ulster Harp National at Downpatrick. But the Major knew that Laffy's good fortune owed nothing to the kindness of his dopers who had ruined other horses and nearly killed their riders and might have done the same to the little French-bred if he'd made it to the starting line at Hurst Park.

That November visit by the elusive Mademoiselle Rosemarie Laumaine could no longer be categorised as a frivolous adventure or a lucky escape. She was part of the doping conspiracy rampaging through racing. It was menacing and dangerous, like the plot of a real Dick Francis novel, and now it had punctured Fairlawne's Corinthian demi-paradise. Kent and Scotland Yard detectives swarmed over the stable that March weekend, infuriating Cazalet by smoking and throwing their cigarette butts away on the ground and distressing him as they quizzed his stable staff and trawled through their rooms and possessions. The Major became more determined than ever that the culprits must be found and that the doping of the Queen Mother's horse must *never* be made public.

The following week, Cazalet spoke again to the Senior Steward of the Jockey Club, Lord Crathorne, and he spoke in turn to the Metropolitan Police Commissioner and the Home Office. Their new instructions to DCI Barnett were explicit. If you can't yet get the evidence to charge the big men, they said, the professional gamblers and bookmakers, concentrate your efforts lower down. On the low life mix of ex-jockeys, punters and stable lads carrying out the crimes. Identify the weaker vessels . . . and then get them to turn on the rest.

19

I AM THE WITCH DOCTOR

TED SMITH was partial to Brighton. He didn't mix with the smart set even though he had the money. He had a favourite bed and breakfast he always went to in Kemptown. There was a cheerful landlady who enjoyed a few drinks of an evening and gave Ted a discount for a winning tip. It wasn't the sort of place he'd take May Kibble and the kids. It was his private bolthole and reward to himself for all the risks he'd been running on Mr Roper's behalf.

His supplies replenished, Ted had been on standby throughout the summer, delivering the goods at short notice three times. On Sunday 5 August, the day after going racing at Epsom, he got another phone call. It was Darkie Steward ringing him at home on Mr Roper's business and ordering a fresh dose, to be handed over outside the Metropole at 5 p.m. on the Monday afternoon. Usual terms. Cash on delivery. Ted didn't ask which horse or race they wanted it for. Sometimes Darkie tipped him off in advance. Sometimes, following the market in his local

Surbiton betting shop, he worked it out for himself. Ted was in there most days of the week now and betting on credit over the telephone with Bernie Howard.

The Witch Doctor boarded a train at lunchtime, changing at Clapham Junction. By the time he got to Brighton, the air was heavy and there was thunder around as he walked down to the front from his digs. Holidaying families were looking up at the sky and packing up and moving off the beach, children wrapped in wet towels, clasping lilos and water wings and drifting back reluctantly towards their boarding houses in the town.

The Metropole's terracotta brick façade was warm to the touch. Ted peered in through the lounge window and saw some punters having afternoon tea. Scones, jam and cream and slices of sponge cake. The doorman was giving Ted a look but Ted just ignored him. The doorman was wearing a top hat and a frock coat and he looked like some stupid fucking coachman at Royal Ascot.

Darkie Steward, whistling cheerfully, came walking along the front right on time. Ted handed him the dope, which was in a matchbox inside a rolled-up copy of *The Sporting Life*. Darkie handed him his money which was inside a rolled up copy of the *Evening Argus*. Ted waited, pretending to read the paper, as Darkie crossed the road and got into Brian Perry's blue Cresta, the same car he'd bought on HP when they were living at Colville Terrace. As the two of them drove away, Ted looked back up at the Metropole's second and third floor balconies. He wondered if Mr Roper was up there with his sexy young girlfriend who, Darkie said, was back in town. Maybe he was ordering caviar and champagne on room service?

Ted divided up the cash he'd been given, keeping half the £50 (£500 in modern money) for May Kibble and awarding himself the rest for a good time that night and at the races. It rained all day Tuesday but Ted didn't mind. He backed a couple of winners at decent prices and, by the end of the afternoon, he was over £100 better off. When he woke up the next morning, the summer had returned, sunlight glinting off the sea. The town was filling up again and Ted spent an hour or so at the Black Rock Lido watching Max Bygraves judging the Miss Brighton beauty contest.

Maxie was in a suit and shades and taking his time to assess the charms of the various shapely contestants. Ted got an eyeful before taking a bus back to the Old Steine and cutting through the alleyways and lanes to the Cricketers for a brown and mild. He spent an hour and a half in the pub, then hailed a taxi outside Hanningtons and told the driver to take him up to the racecourse on Whitehawk Down. Joining the slow-moving queue of Southdown Coaches, open-topped buses and cars.

By the time of the first race at 2 p.m., Ted had settled down in the windowless ground-floor bar in the Tattersalls Enclosure, with his back to the counter, surveying the scene. Surveying the talent too. He had a pint glass in one hand, a cigarette in the other and his jacket and trouser pockets were stuffed with drugs.

There had been three more dopings in the first half of the 1962 flat racing season. On Friday 1 June a horse called

Twice Over started 2-1 favourite for the Shaw Maiden Stakes at Newbury. The three-year-old colt, trained at Epsom by Walter Nightingall, was dropping down in class having run creditably in the Lingfield Derby Trial the week before. He appeared to be that most enticing of betting propositions, a 'good thing', and was backed accordingly but, in a field of 22, he was never sighted.

A few weeks later, another Epsom-trained horse, Harold Wallington's Persian Crest, was a well supported 8-1 second favourite for the Queen Anne Stakes, the first race on the opening day of Royal Ascot. He wasn't expected to beat the favourite, the 2,000 Guineas winner Privy Councillor, but 'each way thieves' considered him a certainty to finish in the first three. He trailed home tenth of the 11 runners.

Ascot was the target the following month too. Henry's Choice, a consistent five-year-old trained in Yorkshire by Rufus Beasley, was running in the mile-and-a-half Sandringham Stakes on King George VI and Queen Elizabeth Stakes day. Having been a close third in the ultra competitive Bessborough Handicap over the same distance at the royal meeting in June, he was backed in from 2-1 to 5-4 favourite. He finished a never-dangerous sixth of eight.

All three dopings had gone according to plan with no bungling and no last-minute withdrawals and all the main conspirators had profited from the results. Now Bill Roper had another job in mind. A dead cert, he believed, at Lewes on Saturday 11 August. The final race on the final day of the Sussex Fortnight. It was to be Mr Racing's last throw and he'd promised his lover nothing less.

Darkie was right. Micheline Lugeon had returned to England, undetected, in May. There were no immigration or passport checks at the airport. Ernie Barnett was concentrating enquiries elsewhere and, despite *The Sporting Life* story the previous December, the Jockey Club investigators, who had been waiting patiently for her to get back in touch with them, still weren't entirely sure who they were looking for.

Micheline went back to her flat in Park Road and continued to oversee its conversion and decoration, choosing carpets, curtains and fittings. Bill bought her a smart new RCA Victor record player to while away the time and her favourite record was Acker Bilk's 'Stranger On The Shore'. She stayed away from her old shop in Crawford Street and she kept away from Stafford Court too. Some weekday afternoons when Roper was meant to be trading on the phone from his Monmouth Street office and Doris was out, he'd slip over to Park Road for an hour's passion in the half-finished bedroom or on the sofa or on the floor in the living room next door. But skulking around in three small rooms, making love in a hurry and never going out wasn't the life Micheline had imagined leading and was far from the glamorous times – dinners, nightclubs and West End shows – they'd enjoyed a few years before.

Now 25, Lugeon was impatient to resume her business career as Michelle de Paris. She also wanted Roper to promise her that his problems had been sorted out and that the financial and other pressures that had propelled them around the country the previous autumn had been addressed, or soon would be. Roper did his best to reassure her, even if he found it hard to convince himself, and said that by the end of the summer or the end of the year at the very latest, he'd have paid off his debts and his life would be in the clear. He'd still had no formal contact with the police and, whatever questions they'd been asking Joe Lowry, Jackie Dyer and the Newmarket stable lads, he didn't believe they'd found enough to link him and Micheline to an actual doping or tie them all together in a conspiracy. If he could keep them at bay for another six months, public interest in the doping scandal, and the accompanying investigation, might subside.

But Roper could also sense that Micheline wouldn't wait until 1963 to resume a full life. She needed entertaining and she needed it now. Her horse, or rather, June Downie's horse, Ganymede II, had run a few times over hurdles, finishing sixth of 11 in a small race at Plumpton on Easter Monday and down the field at Fontwell a month later. Micheline had dreamed of the day when she'd be there in the paddock beforehand in her fur coat, the jockey wearing her colours and then, afterwards, she'd return to greet her winner in the unsaddling enclosure. Eighth of 15 at Fontwell wasn't what she'd had in mind at all, especially when Bill wouldn't let her get anywhere nearer the racecourse than an audio-only commentary in a betting shop in Covent Garden.

Eventually Bill relented and by late June they had started going to restaurants together again at lunchtimes. Bill wasn't racing every day any more. He did most of his betting by phone and, if he had a good day on a Tuesday he'd treat them both to lunch on the Wednesday or the day after. The country was on the cusp of change in so many ways and fashions in eating out were changing too. Bill and Micheline's new favourite was Mario and Franco's La Terrazza on Romilly Street which is where Len Deighton sends his unnamed cockney hero – called Harry Palmer in the film and played by Michael Caine – to have lunch with his secretary Jean in *The Ipcress File*.[36]

There were no elderly, tailcoated waiters at 'the Trat' and no long and pompous French menus either. The modern Italian restaurant had white tiled floors and pink tablecloths and served tagliatelle carbonara and petti di pollo sorpresa, garlic butter oozing out on to the plate, washed down with an ice-cold bottle of Verdicchio, and Mario himself brought a bottle of grappa over to the table with the coffee. Micheline loved it and Billy Roper, 57 later that year, was willing to give it a go.

But when it was time to go down to Brighton in August for the second week of the Sussex Fortnight, Bill reverted to type and booked them a suite at the Metropole. He remembered the old bookmakers staying there in the 1920s and he had been a regular himself since his first summer with Max Parker in 1948. His fellow layers and their punters could gossip all they liked. It was still the natural billet for a London high roller with nothing to hide. Bill went racing on the Tuesday – the day after Darkie Steward rang him to confirm he'd collected the latest batch of dope from Ted Smith – and he went again on the Wednesday and

36 *The Ipcress File* was published in October 1962 to huge acclaim. The film came out three years later.

Thursday afternoons, backing two Scobie Breasley-ridden winners. Micheline didn't go to the course. She put on a head-scarf and dark glasses and went shopping in the town.

The couple had decided to stay down on the coast until after Lewes races on the Saturday. Dear, dodgy, Lewes. The ultimate south of England gaffe track. Situated high up on the downs above the county town with a great view away to Newhaven and Eastbourne and the unmistakable scent of sea mist and villainy in the air. The target was the last race on the card. The Southover Maiden Plate for three-year-old fillies over a mile and a quarter.

There were just the three runners and, by 5 p.m. on a busy August Saturday with four meetings nationwide, thousands of betting shop punters were looking to 'get out' by backing the short-priced favourite, Countess, trained at Epsom by Dick Thrale, ridden by Bobby Elliott and backed down from 4-6 to 4-11 in the ring. A close second in a better race at Kempton last time out, she looked a certainty. The second favourite, Lucky Seven, was trained by Captain Ryan Price, and had the journeyman jockey Geordie Ramshaw in the saddle. The filly had only run once in her life, finishing second over a mile at Nottingham, and was expected to improve. The outsider of three, Dear Jac, was seeing a racecourse for the first time.

Dear Jac made the running until there was about a quarter of a mile to go where Countess and Lucky Seven began to get on terms. But the favourite weakened quickly and dropped away as Lucky Seven took over and drew clear. With the dopers cheering on one of the Captain's runners for a change, rather than stopping it, Lucky Seven won easily by four lengths. Dear Jac was second and Countess another ten lengths away third.

Incredibly, and for the umpteenth time in the doping gang's story, there was no inquiry ordered afterwards by the racecourse stewards. In 1962 the job of officiating at small country tracks was still largely the preserve of good chaps on first-name terms with the racecourse chairman. There were none of the trained stipendiary, or professional, stewards who advise local panels today. At the end of the afternoon, replete after lunch and some decent port, the Lewes stewards and the racecourse vet were all keen to get away and had no desire to be kept hanging around to investigate a three-horse race.

Scotland Yard wasn't doing much better but, if officialdom was blind, the faces in the betting ring knew immediately what had happened. Some of the conspirators had been on course, placing bets on behalf of unsuspecting clients designed to shorten up the odds on Countess while Lucky Seven's price drifted out from 7-4 to 11-4 at the off. The credit offices of several big London bookmakers – including William Hill and Alf Cope – reported four-figure wagers being phoned through for Lucky Seven at SP or starting price, one of them from the Max Parker firm and one from the Monmouth Street number of Doris Curd, née Roper.

This time the gang had left a trail a mile wide but Bill didn't seem to care. It had all gone exactly as planned with Darkie and Jack Stiles carrying out the doping in Epsom on the Friday night, using Ted Smith's last consignment and making no mistake, and the second favourite winning in a canter. As well as backing the winner and laying the favourite, Roper's men had placed a string of bets on the forecast too. Lucky Seven to beat Dear Jac and it had paid £18 to a £1 unit. Bill had made money. Joe and Jackie and Charlie Mitchell and Bernie Howard and Albert Dimes had made money and the recovering Maxie Parker had cause to celebrate over another good home-cooked dinner in Montagu Square.

Bill and Micheline celebrated in Brighton with dinner at Wheelers and drinks until late in the Astor Club. The lights were sparkling on the Palace Pier and there was a phosphorescent glow on the sea. As the channel tide rolled in, the waves crashing and then receding, Bill told Micheline that the game was up and he'd fixed his last race. He may have been sincere – although Bill was always good at saying what his lover wanted to hear – but, as a statement, it was truer than he realised. Early on Sunday morning, the bedside phone rang in Bill and Micheline's suite at the Metropole Hotel. It was Joe Lowry. Had Bill heard? Ted Smith had been arrested. May Kibble had been frantically trying to get hold of Joe and Jackie Dyer when Ted hadn't arrived home from Brighton in midweek. Now it seemed Smithie had been pinched at the races on the Wednesday afternoon and, on the Friday, the police had turned up at Balaclava Road with Ted in tow, and searched the flat. They'd taken away a number of things, including an old suitcase that Ted had kept on top of a cupboard in the bedroom, and they'd told May that Ted was being taken into custody at Cannon Row.

As Bill Roper put the phone down he could feel the sky falling in.

Ted Smith had only himself to blame. He'd stood in Tatts with his back to the bar most of the afternoon. He guessed Roper was there on the rails and in the Members' Enclosure next door but it would have been unthinkable for Bill to acknowledge him in public. Ted only went outside once to watch a race. Oh yes, he loved the quick adrenalin rush of flat racing. The deep-throated roar of the punters as the horses scrambled round the edge of the downs. But this wasn't a real racing man's day. This was a holiday crowd. Mug punters clutching their Tote tickets, queuing up for whelks and mussels and asking the miserable old bastards in the ring for a shilling each way. Ted laughed at them openly, especially the girls, even as he tried to chat them up. 'You don't want to back all those blooming favourites, darling,' he'd say. 'Favourites can get beat and believe me, I know. And when they do it's us smart money boys who set it up and make a killing.' A crowd began to gather. Men as well as women, husbands and wives. 'How do you know so much?' one of them asked. Ted winking. Ted smirking. Ted showing them the cash in his top pocket, the reward for deeds done. 'You've heard about horses being doped haven't you, sweetheart?' he said to one blonde in a billowing summer dress. 'Well, I'm carrying enough dope to stop all the horses running on this racecourse today.'

Ted swung round, acknowledging more listeners on either side and bringing the barman into his confidence too. It was drinks on him, drinks for all the girls and 'drinks for all the better looking blokes too'. The gawping, giggling crowd pressed closer as Ted drew himself up to his full height and pronounced: 'I . . . am the Witch Doctor.' The girls laughed, men scoffed and the barman frowned as he served the beers and the cider and the lager and limes and then he went through to the back to have a word with the catering manager who listened and nodded and then picked up the telephone and dialled 999.

It was 4.30 p.m. and the sixth race, the Downs Maiden Stakes, was about to begin. Ted sending his fans outside with instructions to 'back Lester on the John Goldsmith thing. My mate Mr Roper knows all the top jockeys and trainers too'[37] – just as Superintendent Marshall and Detective Chief Inspector George Dunstan of Brighton CID walked into the bar. They were accompanied by two uniformed officers and when Ted saw them, he tried to turn his back as if they must be looking for someone else. Marshall asked him to step outside with them for a moment. Ted asked if he could finish his drink first. As he raised his glass, he was seen putting his other hand in his jacket pocket. The two constables immediately seized his arms and Dunstan forced open the fingers of his left hand, revealing a small bottle of white powder, which Ted said was medicine for a migraine. It was, in fact, luminal sodium.

Dunstan took the bottle and the constables took Ted out of the bar through the caterers' door at the back and walked

---

37 The trainer John Goldsmith, who had been in the SOE during the war, won the Downs Maiden Stakes with Jour de France, ridden by Lester Piggott and returned at 4-1.

him round to the old racecourse police station, a relic of *Brighton Rock* and the razor gangs. When they searched Ted's pockets they found another bottle containing a capsule, which turned out to be gelatine – which dissolves quickly in a horse's mouth – with a quantity of methyl amphetamine hydrochloride inside. Ted said that he'd found the bottle on the ground at Epsom racecourse about three weeks ago and had forgotten all about it. They also caught him trying to slip a matchbox under some old beer crates that had been stored in the corner of the room. Inside the matchbox was a bolus wrapped in silver paper and bound with rubber bands.

The Witch Doctor was drunk, too drunk, Dunstan decided, to start interrogating him there and then. So they bundled him into a car and drove him down to the main police station in the town which was in the basement of the Town Hall building on Bartholomew Square. Ted was locked up in a cell in the same basement block where prisoners were held before an appearance upstairs before the magistrates or the recorder at the Quarter Sessions.[38] Throughout the evening he kept up a tuneless dirge of abuse supplemented with intoxicated demands to see his wife and a solicitor. He was sick several times. Dunstan let him stew overnight and then, when he was taken a mug of tea in the morning, looking pale and hungover, he asked if he could see the Detective Chief Inspector in private.

---

38 Mods and rockers were held in the same cells after fighting on Brighton seafront in May 1964.

Ted said that he'd been thinking things over during the night and had decided to 'tell you all about it. The only thing is, I'm afraid my wife might get hurt.' It was thinking about his lady, May, and her children and what they meant to him that had convinced Ted that he didn't want to go on with it any more. 'Go on with what?' asked Dunstan. 'The horse doping,' said Ted. 'The gang has kept on to me about getting the stuff for them. Initially I thought that I could make a bit of money but then I acted like a fool and gave them some drugs and then I kept being pestered and became too frightened to stop.' 'Who was pestering you?' Dunstan asked him. 'Who's behind it?' Ted looked at him. 'I know the lot,' he said. 'The horses, the races, the names . . . and if you look after my lady and her kids . . . I'll tell you everything.'

Dunstan put a call through to the London and Home Counties Squad at Scotland Yard who immediately contacted Ernie Barnett and, on the morning of Friday 10 August, the Brighton police drove Ted Smith back to Surbiton in handcuffs. Barnett met them as arranged at Balaclava Road and they searched the flat in the presence of the anguished May Kibble. When they went into the couple's bedroom, they noticed the old suitcase on top of the cupboard and, on opening it up, found a huge arsenal of drugs. Packets of white powder, capsules, tablets, medicine bottles and countless ready-made doses in silver paper. The director of the Metropolitan Police Forensic Laboratory, Lewis Nickalls, later estimated that Ted had enough dope under his suburban roof to stop between 600 and 900 racehorses.

The Witch Doctor had indeed been holding out on Bill Roper and Charlie Mitchell. Hoarding supplies and sometimes diluting doses and selling them, if approached, to other speculative characters trying to emulate the Roper Gang's success. So far from being chastened or contrite, Ted seemed proud of his stash as if the diabolical evidence was conclusive proof of the scale of his achievements.

Smith was formally arrested and cautioned by Barnett and then handcuffed again and taken in a different car to Cannon Row police station where the DCI proceeded to question him at length. Ted was as good as his word and by Monday morning, when he appeared briefly in court and was remanded in custody, he'd already given Barnett's team a fascinating insight into how the dopings had been carried out. Ted wasted no time in placing his 'best pal' Richard McGee in the frame and, following a call from Barnett on 13 August, Detective Superintendent Robert Scott of Northumberland CID, who had been investigating the doped horses from the Verley Bewicke and Ken Oliver stables, called at the Winthrop Laboratory with a party of officers.

It was the moment that McGee had dreaded, but half expected, for a long time. He was interviewed on his own and in the presence of his manager John Eversley and, although he admitted knowing Ted Smith and being visited by him at Fawdon, he initially denied any wrongdoing. He was cautioned and told to expect to be summoned for further questioning in both Newcastle and London. After the police had gone, a distressed Eversley told McGee that he'd had his suspicions, but had not wanted to believe them, ever since a stock check in April had disclosed a shortfall of two kilograms of luminal sodium. Two empty bottles had subsequently been discovered on McGee's desk and when the numbers were checked with the missing stock they were found to match.

McGee broke down and told Eversley that he'd been caught up in something that he couldn't easily escape. Eversley, who liked McGee and valued his work, reluctantly informed him that he would have to leave Winthrop's employ that day but that he would arrange for him to be paid two months' salary. He also suggested that McGee get in touch with MedoPharma, a laboratory in Tooting in South London, where he believed work might be available, albeit at a lower rate. The grateful McGee left Newcastle on the train that afternoon and never returned. But when DS Scott returned to Fawdon a few days later, Eversley, pricked by guilt, told the detective where their suspect could most likely be found.

Armed with Teddy Smith's testimony, Ernest Barnett went to work. He'd begun to divide the conspiracy into four major, interconnecting strands. There was Ted Smith, the supplier, in Balaclava Road and his connection to Richard McGee and the dopers like Darkie Steward. There was the network of corrupted stable lads in Newmarket and the evidence of PC Pickin on the night Treasure Hunt was got at in Jack Waugh's yard. There was evidence of the gang living, meeting and plotting, regularly, at 24 Colville Terrace, and then there was Bill Roper and his mistress Micheline Lugeon and their journey around the country in October and November 1961. Barnett was confident that the Balaclava Road story was in the bag. Now he was determined to sew up the Newmarket connection too.

The DCI had some top detectives working with him now like the Flying Squad operatives Terence O'Connell and Pat Sugrue, who was one of the hardest men in the Yard. The two London Irishmen were racing enthusiasts, as familiar with Kempton and Hurst Park as any racecourse bookie and, earlier that summer, they'd enjoyed a major breakthrough. Philip 'Snuffy' Lawler had been discovered living on the edges of Newmarket and working on a fruit farm. When Barnett and O'Connell first had him in for questioning he insisted that he'd never personally doped any of Noel Murless's horses and maintained that he'd always thrown the drugs away. He'd been unable to escape the attention of the gang, he said, and although he hadn't asked for money, they'd sometimes given it to him. He said he'd been too frightened to tell his guvnor what was going on.

After Ted Smith's arrest, Barnett brought Lawler and the other Newmarket stable lads – Heffernan, Hilliard and Kenny Santus – down to Cannon Row, locked them in separate interview rooms and shredded their alibis bit by bit. Each of them was told that their erstwhile colleagues were going to incriminate them and reveal the whole story. Stern Barnett warned Snuffy that he was going to take the fall for a lot of people and go to prison. But kindly Bob Anderson, cigarettes to hand, left the door ajar. If they co-operated and told the police the names of the men who'd paid them and how much, they could still get off. All four lads admitted knowing Joe Lowry and Jackie Dyer but claimed they'd never met Bill Roper or Max Parker or Charlie Mitchell or Albert Dimes.

Snuffy Lawler, quizzed particularly about St Paddy, admitted discussing the horse's chances with the man he called Len, rather than Darkie, Steward but when he was pressed about Pinturischio he clammed up. But after 24 hours of intense interrogation – with no lawyers present, not in 1962 – Kenny Santus cracked, as Barnett had expected him to, and told them all about being recruited in March 1960 and about the doping of Treasure Hunt. He said he hadn't seen Jack Stiles for over a year and claimed not to know where Darkie Steward lived either. But then Barnett got another lead as the increasingly loquacious Ted Smith gave him an old address for Darkie's mother in Tolworth. When the police called at the house, she confessed that she thought her boy was living in Harrow in North London, renting two rooms from a Mr Power. The landlord was traced to Number 69 The Avenue, a modest suburban street a short walk from Rayners Lane tube station.

They sent portly Bob Hill in first to check that their suspect really was there and then, at 7 p.m. on Monday 4 September, Detective Chief Inspector Ernest Barnett and Detective Inspector Bob Anderson knocked on Steward's door. Ever the cheeky chappie, Darkie did his best to play the role of a fully co-operative but innocent man. Barnett began by asking him about his career as a stable lad, especially the nine years and nine months that he'd spent with Harold Wallington at Epsom. Had he ever had to give medicine to a racehorse? Yes, replied Steward, but only ever from a bottle. Barnett asked him about the practice of 'balling' where a horse's tongue was twisted in one hand and a physic ball pushed down its throat with the other. Darkie said it was only ever done by a head lad and reiterated that he'd only given medicines from a bottle. Barnett asked him if it was true that balling was a risky operation and could lead to a stable lad getting his fingers or hand bitten? Darkie said he'd heard of that happening but had never seen it. Barnett asked him if he'd ever been bitten on the hand by a racehorse. Darkie shook his head.

Then the detectives moved on to Darkie's time working for Captain Ryan Price at Findon. Was that where he met John Stiles? Darkie couldn't remember but thought it sounded likely. When did he last see Stiles? Darkie had a think. About six weeks ago, he said. In a chemmy Club in Windmill Street. Stiles was a good friend of his, wasn't he? Darkie saw him around, as you do, but Jack was a moody character and always restless about one thing or another. When did you leave Captain Price's employ? asked Anderson. Darkie hesitated so Barnett answered the question for him: 3 April 1959. Jack Stiles had left a few days before on 27 March. Barnett put it to Steward that the two lads were both sacked for sloppy work and a bad attitude. Darkie denied it. Barnett asked him how he'd felt when he read that the Captain's horse, Scarron, had been got at before a race at Fontwell the previous November? No, said, Darkie, all wide-eyed innocence. Was that one doped?

Anderson wanted to know how Darkie had been making a living since he'd ceased to be a stable lad. Steward said he still knew all the lads and jockeys and they gave him tips and information and he tried to use that to make a few quid on the side. Selling information? asked Barnett. That's right, said Darkie. Like the Faultless Speech race at Redcar in 1959? asked Anderson. Darkie admitted that he'd been paid well for tipping that winner. Barnett was incredulous. Why would anyone pay him for tipping them a short-priced favourite? Darkie said it always helped to know that a horse was fit and well. Who did he tip it to? asked Anderson? The usual faces, said Darkie. Like Bill Roper? asked Barnett. And Joe Lowry? And Jackie Dyer? And Charlie Mitchell? And Albert Dimes? Darkie struggled. I don't know all those people, he said. But Bill Roper and Joe Lowry and Albert Dimes all paid you for tipping them Faultless Speech? asked the detective. They may have done a bit, said Darkie, but I made a few quid from bets on it too.

You don't deny you know Bill Roper? asked Anderson. You used to work for him, didn't you? I worked for him for a while, admitted Darkie. What do you know about Roper and his office in Monmouth Street? asked Barnett. I know that the business is in his wife's name, Doris, replied Darkie. And I know that he sits up there a lot placing bets over the telephone. Did you ever see Roper talking to Max Parker? asked Barnett. I know Bill used to work for Mr Parker at one time, said Darkie. But I didn't know their business and they wouldn't have told me about it. Did you ever fall out with Bill Roper? asked Anderson. I may have tipped him a few horses that didn't win, agreed Darkie. Did you meet his girlfriend? asked Barnett. A couple of times, said Darkie. What did you think of her? Very smart, very pretty, said Darkie. But not really my type. Did she and Roper ever come round to 24 Colville Terrace together when you were living there? asked Anderson. Not that I remember, said Darkie.

It was after 11 p.m. when the questioning ended and, three days later, the police returned. Terence O'Connell and Pat Sugrue picking up Darkie in an unmarked car and driving him down to Cannon Row. This time O'Connell sat in on the interview and Barnett started by asking Darkie how often he went to Newmarket. I go sometimes, said Darkie. I've got some money there in the post office. Have you ever been there with Joe Lowry, Jackie Dyer and John Stiles? asked Barnett. No, said Darkie. I did go there once with Jack Stiles and a couple of birds. I think Jimmy Cronin was with us too. Do you know a stable lad called Kenny Santus? asked O'Connell. Never heard of him, said Darkie. He says he knows you, said O'Connell. He says you and him and John Stiles climbed over the wall at Jack Waugh's stable and doped the colt Treasure Hunt. That's not so, insisted Darkie. I love animals too much. I've never been asked to do anything improper.

What about Edward Smith? asked Barnett, changing tack. How well do you know him? We're good friends, said Darkie. When did you last see him? asked the DCI. I can't remember, said Darkie. I think I spoke to him on the phone about six weeks ago. Did you ring him on 5 August? asked O'Connell. No, said Darkie. Did Bill Roper tell you to ring him on 5 August? No, said Darkie. Did you meet him outside the Metropole Hotel in Brighton on 7 August? No, said Darkie. Where did you first meet Smith? asked Barnett.

Pubs, said Darkie. Which ones? asked Barnett. The Toby Jug in Kingston, said Darkie. Then at the Richmond ice rink. Then at Sandown races. Did you know he was called the Witch Doctor? asked O'Connell. I heard, said Darkie. Why do you think he was called that? asked O'Connell. He always had tablets, said Darkie. He gave me some Panadol once for a migraine. What else did he give you? asked Barnett. A tonic, once, said Darkie. Some red stuff. Metatone? asked Barnett. Darkie nodded. And you gave it to a horse? Not on my life, said Darkie. Did Ted Smith ever talk to you about doping? asked Barnett. He threw out some hints, said Darkie. And what did you think? asked Barnett. I thought it was a liberty, said Darkie.

Did you ever go to Ted Smith's flat in Surbiton? asked O'Connell. Lots of times, said Darkie. Did you ever go there with Bill Roper or Charlie Mitchell? asked O'Connell. No, said Darkie. I went once with Jackie Dyer and I went with my lady, Sylvia. But no one else came. Tell us about Ted, said Barnett. What's he like? He can be a bit excitable sometimes, said Darkie. And a bit ratty with his missus. Did Ted introduce you to Roper, Lowry and Dyer? asked Barnett. At Sandown and Hurst Park he did, said Darkie. But I never saw Mr Roper at Ted's flat. Did Ted ever go to Number 24 Colville Terrace? asked O'Connell. Sometimes, said Darkie. He'd get lost around Portobello and I'd have to go out and meet him. Did Ted Smith ever introduce you to Richard McGee? asked Barnett. I've never heard of him, said Darkie.

It was an all-day session and it wasn't until 7 p.m. when Darkie was told he was free to go. But there was no taxi

ride back to North London. He had to go by underground
to Rayners Lane and, unbeknown to Steward, the police
continued to keep a watch on Number 69 The Avenue over
the next few weeks.

Barnett and his fellow detectives were reviewing the evidence
and discussing various options with the office of the Director
of Public Prosecutions. In the meantime Bill Roper, Joe Lowry,
Jackie Dyer and the other conspirators had got wind of Darkie's
interrogation and were sweating on the outcome. It was all too
much for Micheline Lugeon. The press had made a big story
of the arrest of Ted Smith and the uncovering of the 'Dope
Bank' at Balaclava Road and the quantity of drugs in Smith's
possession told Micheline that Bill had been lying to her and
that, so far from closing the gang down, more dopings were
being planned for that autumn and winter.

She tried to tackle Bill about it and challenged him to
repeat his assurance that the racket was really over. When
he became evasive – ducking and diving, a bit of this, a bit
of that – she became increasingly anxious about her own
position. Lunches were cut short or cancelled and 'intimacy'
discontinued as, for the first time, her relationship with
the ex-RAF sergeant went into a tailspin. Finally, the
prospect of arrest, and even imprisonment, looming large,
her patience snapped. The week after Darkie was brought
into Cannon Row, Bill and Micheline had a furious row
at Stafford Court. Micheline accused Roper of placing her
in an intolerably dangerous situation and said she couldn't
take it any longer. She left his flat on her own and went
back to Park Road. When Bill went over there the next

day, he found that she'd packed up and gone, leaving him a note to say that she loved him but that she was going home to Switzerland and that this time she wouldn't be back. She'd left behind a number of things that Bill had given her including a gold signet ring, some clothes and the RCA record player. When Roper looked, there was still a stack of records on the turntable including 'Telstar' by the Tornadoes and 'I Can't Stop Loving You' by Ray Charles.

Roper jumped into a car and tried frantically to catch up with her at Heathrow but by the time he got there, she was airborne. Their love affair, it seemed, was over.

Bill was bereft and alone. He couldn't understand why the Yard hadn't come for him yet. He'd been so busy worrying about his mistress that he'd taken his eye off some of the other gang members. But Mr Racing should have remembered what happened to Stanley Baker in *The Criminal* who was grassed up and betrayed by a former partner. What Bill didn't realise was that the police had decided to prosecute the tools of the conspiracy first, as Barnett put it, and then turn their attention to the organisers. What he also didn't know was that Ted Smith had been telling them all about Bill's visits to Balaclava Road, and about Charlie Mitchell and the Newcastle trips and the exchanges of money and drugs on Baker Street station, and, when the case came to court, the Witch Doctor was going to turn Queen's Evidence.

20

ATTEMPTED MURDER

SATURDAY 10 November was the final day of the flat racing season and the Manchester November Handicap – almost as big a betting race in its prime as the Lincoln and the Grand National – was the traditional end-of-season highlight. The 1962 renewal, run in the usual Mancunian fog, was won by a 20-1 chance, Damredub, trained down at Lewes by 'Towser' Gosden, father of John, with the well-backed Dalnamein, ridden by Lester Piggott, four lengths away second. Elsewhere jump racing was in the ascendant. The future Cheltenham Gold Cup winner Mill House won a three-mile steeplechase at Sandown and, up at Wetherby, Peter Cazalet's Kapeno landed the valuable Mackeson Novices Chase, the race in which The Finn, a victim of the dopers at Hurst Park back in February, fell at the first fence and was destroyed.

At 9.30 that morning, Emmanuel Lipman Leonard Steward, one of the principal abusers, was arrested at Number 69 The Avenue. When the police searched his bedroom they found a book called 'Practical Animal Husbandry' on the windowsill. It was open at page 143, a section on how to administer boluses to racehorses.

Darkie was taken back to Cannon Row police station. Richard McGee, who had been arrested at his ex-wife's home in Harlesden, was already there along with their old friend and ally turned accuser, Edward Smith. There was some tension in the charge room as Ted and Darkie were reunited, the older man berating the former jockey for calling him the Witch Doctor in his police interviews. McGee looked on in silence.

The three men were all formally charged with being part of 'a conspiracy to cheat and defraud owners and trainers of racehorses, bookmakers and such other persons as should wager money on the results of horse races by means of the administration of drugs to racehorses in order to affect the performance of such horses when running in races.' McGee was also charged with five counts of stealing from Winthrop Laboratories and Ted Smith and Darkie Steward were charged with 'counselling and procuring him to commit the said offences' and of being 'an accessory before the fact to receiving stolen property'. On top of that Ted faced a separate charge of being in possession of 21 grains of methyl amphetamine hydrochloride at Brighton racecourse on 8 August. It might not have been the scale of charges or the range of defendants that Ernie Barnett would've liked, but the police and the DPP were confident of securing convictions and, with the Witch Doctor as their ace in the hole for future proceedings, it would get them off to a good start.

The three appeared in court on Monday 12 November and were all remanded in custody after the Yard vigorously opposed bail, on the grounds that key witnesses might be interfered with. The case now switched to Brighton, which had been chosen as the venue for the trial, and the committal proceedings took place at Brighton Magistrates Court from 28 to 30 November. The prosecutor, Brian McDermott QC, told the court that while Smith and McGee had procured and stolen the drugs, Darkie Steward, 'an erstwhile stable boy and jockey at Epsom and other places', was an active member of the doping gang and 'an expert in the theory and practice of administering dope to racehorses'. Steward was 'the only member of the gang before the court today', said Mr McDermott, leaving no doubt that further prosecutions were to come, including of as yet unnamed bookmakers who, he said, were the chief beneficiaries of the conspiracy. The gang made their money, he informed an enthralled press and public gallery, by 'telling bookmakers which horses had been doped. The bookies could then lay bets safe in the knowledge which, in a peculiarly sinister way, came straight from the horse's mouth.'

The police and prosecution were under no obligation to show all their cards, as they would be today, and only a handful of witnesses were called at this stage. Jack Waugh came down from Newmarket to testify to the doping of Treasure Hunt and McDermott hinted that a former gang member – Kenny Santus – would describe the break-in at Heath House and, along with one of the accused – Ted Smith – would place Lipman Leonard Steward firmly at the scene of the crime.

To give some idea of how long the conspiracy had been going on, the prosecution had dug up Norman Pope who said he was no longer a stable lad but a scrap metal dealer. Pope, who had agreed to testify in return for immunity from prosecution, claimed that Ted Smith had approached him in 1956, told him the names of some horses he wanted to have stopped and given him some tablets to dissolve in water. But the brave Popey insisted he'd wanted nothing to do with it and had 'flushed the tablets down the toilet and pulled the chain'.

Pope's testimony angered Ted Smith who took to the witness box and denied that he'd ever given the Epsom stable lad tablets. He said that he'd only ever given him drugs in powder form and that it was Pope who came to him, wanting money in return for doping horses where he worked.

Ted's performance was loud and fretful, though not inarticulate, but what was picked up immediately by Bill Roper and the gang, when they heard about it, was that he didn't have a brief. Ted Smith, it seemed, was going to represent himself. A shocking mistake in Roper's view, but not half as shocking as the realisation that gradually came his way on the grapevine that the Witch Doctor was going to stitch them all up.

Roper had been distracted. Roper had been negligent. He should have been aware of Ted's behaviour at Brighton in August and stopped him then. Now he tried frantically to get a good solicitor in to see him in Lewes jail where the three men were being held. But all visits, and all attempts to remonstrate with Smith via other sympathetic prisoners, were rebuffed. For Bill it was an appalling dilemma. If Ted talked in court not only Roper's liberty or Micheline Lugeon's or Joe Lowry's or Jackie Dyer's would be at risk. Maxie Parker would be implicated and so too would Charlie Mitchell and Albert Dimes. When Roper met Mitchell to discuss what they should do, the strong man's response was unequivocal: if Ted Smith wouldn't shut his mouth, he said, they'd have to shut it for him.

A good barrister could possibly have construed Smith's willingness to tell all in the witness box as evidence not so much of a repentant sinner as of galloping insanity. Why else would he place himself in such mortal peril? Ernest Barnett's old guvnor, Ted Greeno, used to say that a man could get his throat cut in the West End of London just as quickly and easily as on a pirate ship in the South China Seas. That was certainly the case in the gambling underworld in the winter of 1962/63. With big money at stake now in the new betting shops and gaming clubs, some of the leading players were resorting, increasingly, to violence to protect their share.

Nathan Mercado's West London shops for example, were the target of a protection racket broken by a police undercover operation in which the celebrated detective Leonard 'Nipper' Read, who would later take down the Kray Twins, posed as a cashier behind the counter and disarmed one of the gangsters who was holding a shotgun.

Up west, Albert Dimes had been involved in a feud with the Jewish bookmaker Moishe Cohen, or Major Collins, as he insisted on being called. The Major, who had no military credentials that anyone knew of but felt the title added class, had a betting shop in Percy Street, north of the Oxford Street divide. It was not far from Albert's Soho demesne and Albert's shop hedged money with the Major on a regular basis. By the autumn of 1962, Dimes had run up a slate of £16,000. The Major decided it was time for settlement and he sent a character called 'Groucho' down to Frith Street to collect. Groucho was, by all accounts, a man most debtors went in fear of, the Luca Brasi of North Soho, but he didn't scare Albert's boys. They welcomed him politely into their office but then, just as they were all sitting down to talk, he was jumped on and beaten up. The police were called – corrupt West End detectives in the pay of Italian Albert – and told that Groucho had tried to rob the shop. The unfortunate debt collector got two years in prison and that wasn't the end of it.

Major Collins already had a second shop on Rathbone Place and was planning to open a third in Greek Street, even nearer to Albert Dimes's territory. But on the night of Yom Kippur, 8 October 1962, the front of the new Greek Street office was blown out with gelignite. The Major got the message and never ventured south of Oxford Street again. It was said that Dimes quite liked Moishe Cohen and enjoyed having a chat with him now and again over a milky espresso and an eclair. But if he was prepared to blow up his betting shops to prevent him poaching his punters, what might he do to a grass like Teddy Smith who was about to implicate him in the doping scandal?

Charlie Mitchell was an even more present danger. In April 1962 he had opened his new gambling club in Fulham, partly financed by Bill Roper and the doping racket. For several days and nights, plain clothes policemen working for Ernest Barnett maintained a vigil outside the club, building up a picture of who came and went. Eventually Mitchell, complaining of harassment, went outside and punched one of the detectives in the eye. But the Flying Squad continued to chip away at Charlie and, a month later, he was had up for drink driving and fined £50.

Unlike Albert Dimes, Mitchell had been to Balaclava Road several times in company with Bill Roper and had threatened Ted Smith with the severest imaginable consequences if he double-crossed them. The Witch Doctor had reported those conversations to Barnett and Anderson and they provided the only real evidence linking Mitchell to the conspiracy.

The decision on how to respond was out of Bill Roper's hands. He may have clung to the hope that Ted could be dissuaded from talking or bought off but for Charlie Mitchell it was unthinkable that Smith should bring them down.

If you needed to lean on a witness in 1962, or tamper with a jury or get at someone behind bars, there was, apparently, one man in particular who could fix things. His name was Billy Howard and, according to the ex-boxer Gerry Parker, who wasn't easily cowed, 'he was *the* face. A hard bastard and the best street fighter in London. If you went into a club and he was there, you left.' Howard had good connections in Brighton and had allegedly been behind the intimidation of a female witness during the 1957 trial of the Chief Constable, Charles Ridge, and two detectives who were facing corruption charges. Howard didn't need to confront a witness personally. He left the rough stuff to others but, if silence in court was what was needed, he could arrange it.

What was planned for Ted Smith was probably similar to the treatment meted out in *The Criminal* to a grass who returns to prison at the beginning of the film. Co-operative warders, led by the chief officer, Patrick Magee, are suddenly nowhere to be seen as a violent, half-witted convict, egged on by sharper tools, closes in on the whimpering informant. In the film the grass lives, just. But if Billy Howard did indeed know sympathetic officers at Lewes and inmates who owed him a few favours, the Witch Doctor was in grave danger.

The trial was due to begin on Monday 31 December at the outset of the Quarter Sessions at Brighton Town Hall. Until then Smith, Steward and McGee were held in what was supposed to be close confinement. The high walls and flinty façade of HMP Lewes were all of a piece with its reputation as one of the grimmest places of incarceration in the country. In the 1920s its Victorian cell blocks had housed Irish Republican prisoners like Eamonn de Valera and Thomas Ashe and, between then and Ted Smith's arrival 40 years later, not a lot had changed.

Christmas in prison was bad enough at the best of times but Christmas 1962 coincided with the onset of the severe weather that would bind the country in one of the harshest winters in British history. The blizzards began on Boxing Day with 12 inches of snow in London and the south-east. Temperatures plunged below freezing and then, on 29 December, there was another 24 hours of continuous snow, accompanied by gale force winds leading to 15- to 20-foot snowdrifts in places. Many towns and villages were cut off and road and rail traffic was severely disrupted.

There was to be no horse racing in England between 22 December and 7 March 1963. The *Express* racing pages had to make do with a photo of Lester Piggott sweeping snow from his driveway in Newmarket – Lester was about to set off on a Florida holiday – while their correspondent, Charles Benson, tried to keep himself warm with thoughts of his long-range fancy, Frenchman's Cove, winning the Grand National in March.

Despite the terrible weather, the business of the law went on as usual and the various barristers involved in the doping trial were all present in Brighton Town Hall at 10 a.m. on Monday 31 December. But the atmosphere in the improvised courthouse was unusually tense and the Recorder, Charles Doughty, who was hearing the case, began by summoning the defence and prosecution teams to tell them about 'certain events that took place in Lewes Prison last night'.

During the evening of Sunday 30 December, Edward Smith had fallen from a top-floor landing. No protective netting had been in place at the time and no prison officers, or fellow inmates, had been present or had witnessed the incident. Smith had landed on a stone floor and had fractured his skull and broken his thigh. He had been taken to Brighton General Hospital where he was under police guard and described as 'deeply unconscious and critically ill'.

The competing barristers, all experienced criminal lawyers, had few illusions as to what had really happened. The immediate question was whether the trial of the others should go ahead as scheduled and, after much hand wringing, Doughty decided that it should. The chief prosecutor Owen Stable QC, who had replaced Brian McDermott, admitted that 'the absence of Smith does place the prosecution in some difficulty'. For Ernest Barnett too, Smith's accident was a bitter blow. If Ted didn't recover – and that seemed highly likely – it would make it much harder to proceed against the other leading gang members and their backers.

So why hadn't the police done more to protect their star witness behind bars? It seems that Barnett thought, or had been assured, that Ted was safe and his death, or attempted suicide, was a shock even to the Yard and demonstrated to them just how deadly the gang's reach could be.

Darkie Steward and Richard McGee had already been brought to Brighton from Lewes and were being held in the old police cells in the basement. They were white faced and fearful as they were led up the steps to the dock. They may not have seen Ted's fall the previous night but they had certainly heard it, and Darkie didn't believe it was an accident any more than it was attempted suicide, as some of the screws were suggesting. Attempted murder, more like, and Darkie, his cheeky chappie aura now long gone, was terrified that he might be next.

The jury of nine men and three women were sworn in and then the charges were read out. McGee pleaded guilty on all counts. Darkie pleaded innocent on all counts. Anthony Scrivener represented McGee while Darkie was defended by Montague Sherborne QC. The crown dealt with McGee first and it didn't take long. The 48-year-old said that he'd stolen the drugs at Ted Smith's request. He described how he 'went to pieces' in 1954 and how Ted befriended him. 'I got caught up with him and could not easily escape,' he said. 'However, I accept responsibility for my own actions. I can only say that I am sorry.' Scrivener told the recorder that McGee was 'an outsider' and not a full member of the doping gang. Smith knew that he'd been in financial trouble and had paid him between £20 and £25 a time for the thefts, amounting to some £200 (£12,600 in modern money) in total, but had never told him the names of the horses that were to be got at. Doughty sentenced him to two years' imprisonment.

On 1 January Owen Stable outlined the crown's case against Steward. The prosecutor, who went on to become a High Court judge, is remembered by some other barristers of the time as a rather humourless, self-important individual and, having been given a leading role in such a newsworthy case, he seems to have been determined to make the most of it. He started by warning the jury that they should dismiss from their minds anything that they might have read in the press 'about the man, Edward Smith'. This couldn't have been easy as the newspapers were full of lurid descriptions of Ted's fall and the supposedly scandalous conditions inside Lewes jail. 'Where was the netting?' asked the banner headline in the *Daily Sketch*. The Labour MP Alice Bacon, an opposition home affairs spokeswoman, was demanding a probe into the prison, pointing out that Ted Smith's was the second fall there of a man about to be tried in a month. She was referring to Harvey Holford, the Brighton club owner accused of the capital murder of his wife, who had fallen 15 feet in Lewes on 2 December and fractured his skull the day before he was due to appear at Sussex Assizes.

Mr Stable attempted to brush aside these 'tawdry matters' as he sought to portray a conspiracy going back at least five years. He called the police forensics expert Lewis Nickalls who confirmed that when Ted Smith had been arrested he'd had enough drugs in his possession – including luminal sodium, methyl amphetamine hydrochloride and over 600 Trancopal tablets – to stop nearly 1,000 horses. Norman Pope was wheeled out again and Jack Waugh and the Newmarket police constable, Charles Pickin, who gave his account of the events of the night of Thursday 31 March 1960. Then Stable called little Kenny Santus who was unable to stop shaking as he entered the witness box.

Stable described him as an accomplice but said that the DPP had decided not to proceed against him. Santus's evidence was damning. He told the court of the midnight car ride he'd been taken on in Newmarket in 1960 and the arrangement whereby he was to find out where certain horses were stabled in return for £50 (around £900 in modern money) 'every time we done a horse'. He said that John Stiles had told him the names of horses that had been doped and he identified Darkie Steward as being in the car with him on the ride to Heath House and when they climbed over the wall to get at Treasure Hunt. He recalled that Darkie wore rubber gloves to protect his fingers and had the dope in little balls of silver paper. But when he was pressed to say more about the other members of the gang, he dried up and said that he was frightened that they'd 'catch up' with him. Owen Stable applauded him for giving evidence at all and said that he wanted the court to keep a 'fatherly eye' on him.

When it was Mr Sherborne's turn, he recalled Richard McGee who testified that, other than his friendship with Ted Smith, he'd never met any of the other members of the gang and had never been enjoined by any of them to place a bet on any of the fixed races. McGee said the only time he ever placed a bet on a horse race was a shilling each way on the Derby. The barrister drew the jury's attention to the fact that the first time McGee saw Darkie Steward was in the charge room at Cannon Row police station, so how could Steward possibly have been involved in a conspiracy with him?

Then Sherborne put his client on the stand. Darkie claimed that he'd borrowed the book on Practical Animal Husbandry from his landlord, Mr Power. He said that he'd 'found it interesting' because he'd formerly worked for a bloodstock agency, transporting horses from stud farms to stables and sometimes it had been necessary to sedate them. He was hoping to work for the agency again and he needed to do a bit of homework. He also said that in March 1960 he'd been suffering from a bad leg as a result of an old riding accident and couldn't possibly have climbed over a seven-foot wall. He denied going to Newmarket with Joe Lowry and Jackie Dyer and again denied knowing Kenny Santus. In short, he denied all knowledge of horse doping and said he would never get involved in it as he loved animals too much.

Owen Stable mocked Darkie's protestations of innocence and accused him of 'talking so much rubbish'. He then intrigued the jury and excited the public by introducing the names of characters that were not yet in police custody. He asked Darkie about his relationship with 'the bookmaker and moneylender Charlie Mitchell'. Was it true that Mitchell had assaulted him and kicked him 'in the testicles' and had also given Edward Smith and Darkie's girlfriend Sylvia Cross 'a backhander or two?' Darkie admitted that Mitchell had a short temper and that he didn't like him much. Stable asked why Mitchell had been so cross with him. Darkie claimed it was because he'd tipped him a horse that lost when it should have won and Mitchell had lost his money. The prosecutor, following Ernie Barnett's line, suggested Mitchell was angry because Darkie had assured him that a horse he'd doped would lose but instead it won. Darkie shook his head. 'It was no drawing-room affair when Mitchell was angry was it?' observed Stable. Darkie looked confused.

Stable moved on to the £1,200 (over £20,000 in modern money) that Darkie said he'd made from tips when Faultless Speech won the William Hill Gold Cup at Redcar in 1959. Who were the grateful punters who'd paid him so generously? asked the prosecutor. Darkie couldn't remember. Was not one of them 'the bookmaker and gambler William John Roper?' Darkie nodded. And the others, who were they? Friends of Mr Roper, said Darkie. What kind of friends?

asked Stable. Bookmaking friends, said Darkie. Like Joe Lowry? asked Stable. Darkie nodded. And Jackie Dyer? Darkie nodded again. And who was the other friend who paid you £100? asked Stable. A bookmaker, said Darkie. What was his name? asked Stable. Darkie shook his head. He stammered. 'I am not going to reveal the other bookmaker's name,' he said. 'That's not fair.' 'Who was Mr Roper's other bookmaking friend?' asked Stable again. Darkie mumbled. The recorder told him to speak up. 'Albert Dimes,' he said. 'His name was Albert Dimes.' And he gave you £100? asked Stable again. 'That's correct,' said Darkie.

Stable asked Darkie about the time when he was employed by Bill Roper in 'his bookmaking business in Covent Garden'. Did he know 'Miss Micheline Lugeon who it is alleged was Roper's girlfriend?' Darkie said he'd seen her photograph in the paper. Did he know that she had visited 30 different training establishments up and down Britain? 'Not that I'm aware of,' said Darkie. Mr Roper had just said that she was trying to find a stable for her horse. 'You must have known the moment he told you that it was a lie?' said Stable. 'Why should I dispute it?' asked Darkie. 'To add tone to the enterprise she was set up as the owner of Ganymede II and registered her own racing colours,' said Stable. 'I wouldn't know,' said Darkie.

The cross-examination lasted a day and a half and when it was over and Darkie was returned to the dock, he had to ask to be taken out first to be sick.

At 10.30 a.m. on Monday 7 January, Recorder Charles Doughty began his summing up. He reminded the jury that 'conspiracy is an agreement of two or more persons to do an unlawful act'. He said that many people mentioned in the case had not been before the court but that there was no evidence that Steward had conspired with McGee and Smith and that, although Santus had identified him, Santus was an accomplice and it was dangerous to convict on the uncorroborated evidence of an accomplice alone. The jury retired at 11.45 a.m. and returned at 12.18 to make a request. They wanted to study more fully a statement that Darkie had made to DCI Barnett at Cannon Row police station but Doughty pointed out that there was no statement, only an account of an interview which was taken down and had been given orally to the court. The Recorder read out the account of the interview and then the jury retired again.

When the jury returned that afternoon, they found Darkie not guilty, as instructed, of the charges of conspiring to procure drugs with Smith and McGee, but guilty of the main charge of conspiring to cheat and defraud owners and trainers of racehorses along with bookmakers and the betting public. At Stable's and Ernie Barnett's request, the Recorder then agreed to an hour-long adjournment during which Darkie was taken back down to the cells where Barnett went to talk to him. With Ted Smith gone, the DCI was desperate for another crown witness to help him get Roper, Mitchell, Dimes and the rest of the gang and he urged Darkie Steward to play that role. But the former jockey was already convinced he'd said too much and was petrified of the consequences of going any further.

The court returned to hear Montague Sherborne's plea of

mitigation. His client, he said, was 'in a great state of fear not only for himself but also for his family'. He described the 'dissatisfaction of many apprentice jockeys who don't do awfully well financially' and depicted Darkie as 'a tool in a conspiracy dominated by persons other than the defendant himself'. The real 'villains of the conspiracy, the bookmakers, are still not in the dock', he went on, 'and it is they who have reaped a rich harvest'. He had counselled the defendant to co-operate with the crown in their attempts to bring those villains to book but, unfortunately, his client was 'in a considerable state of agitation and can give no further assistance in the matter'.

Charles Doughty allowed that Darkie was 'only a tool in a highly organised business which is quite capable of threatening and obviously has threatened witnesses. I also accept that there are people or persons who must be bookmakers who are behind all this.' But then he took a harsher line. 'You were playing for high stakes and lost,' he told Darkie theatrically. 'Now it's time to pay for your crimes. Being a stable lad is too much like hard work for you. You are too big for the job so you decided to undermine and wreck the whole occupation which up until then you had been engaged in. You will be sent to corrective training for four years.'

Doughty finished by asking Mr Stable for a report on the condition of Edward Smith and, when told that he was in a coma and unlikely to recover consciousness, declared sombrely that the whole case had cast 'a very great stain on racing'. The court was about to rise when there was an unexpected postscript in the form of a public statement by John Alliott

QC who rose to say that he had been instructed by his client, Mr Albert Dimes, to say that he 'denies categorically any complicity in this matter'. The recorder observed that Mr Dimes was a bookmaker and that he would 'no doubt wish to give the authorities any assistance that he could'.

It was neither the first nor the last time that Italian Albert – who was always sensitive about what was said about him – issued a statement through the courts. But, so far from clearing his name, these interventions merely served to confirm the public's lurid image of him.

When Ernie Barnett was questioned afterwards about the gang's underworld backers and declared solemnly 'their day will come', everyone assumed he was referring to Albert Dimes. The following day's *Daily Mirror* titillated readers with a description of 'Racing's Mr Fixit: the gangster who gravitated from point-to-points and can be seen most days of the week in the West End of London.'

Doping was front and back page news once again. The Conservative government was reeling from the embarrassment caused by the Vassall espionage case in which a gay civil servant had been blackmailed into spying for the Russians. On 6 January the *News of the World* ran a story about how Harold Macmillan had appointed a special medical expert to advise him 'on the prevalence of perverts in public life and how to recognise them'. But not even sex and the Cold War could oust racecourse racketeering from the headlines. 'Fear sealed the lips of Lipman Leonard "Darkie" Steward,' reported the *Mirror*. 'Fear of the vengeance of the racing underworld against him and his girlfriend.' Darkie's mother confirmed that Lennie was 'a frightened boy. His lips were trembling as I spoke to him. He didn't make much out of this racket but he won't split on the others for fear of what they might do.'

The *Mirror* said 'a new worldwide hunt' was underway for the dope gang while running an interview with Darkie's girlfriend Sylvia Cross, which stoked the drama still more. 'If I knew anything I wouldn't tell,' reported Sylvia. 'I don't want to have my face slashed. The big men behind this racing racket are ruthless. I'm sure they will stop at nothing.' She told of her feelings for the imprisoned Darkie. 'Len is a pretty rough diamond,' she said, 'but I love him. He's the only man I have ever really loved. We both share the gambling bug and I went to card games with him and to the races. We've been engaged for a year now but I don't know whether we will marry.'

The future didn't look too promising given that Darkie was now in Wormwood Scrubs although he was planning to appeal. When his old sidekick Ted Smith died in hospital on 10 February, 42 days after his fall in Lewes Prison, the Brighton coroner ruled that the cause of death was probably suicide while of unsound mind. He referred to 'upsetting letters' Ted had received in prison and to the warnings of fellow inmates who had told prison officials that Ted had been threatened with violence several times.

Jackie Dyer, for one, is still convinced that Smith killed himself to avoid having to testify against his friends, and recalls the governor of Lewes Prison referring to a letter from Smith that he kept locked up in his office safe. In it, Ted supposedly confirmed that he was planning to end it all and expressed his regret at ever having co-operated with the police. But Ernest Barnett, Bob Anderson and Terence O'Connell didn't think it was suicide. They were as certain as they could be that Smith had been murdered, not just to shut him up but in order to dissuade Darkie and the others from 'getting milky'. It had done the job. Kenny Santus had barely managed to get through a single morning of cross-examination without fainting and there was little likelihood of the other stable lads, like Philip 'Snuffy' Lawler, testifying on oath about Pinturischio as long as they feared they'd suffer the same fate as the Witch Doctor.

Barnett still had hopes of arresting Bill Roper and his backers for conspiracy to murder but, by the time the ice and snow had finally melted and another Cheltenham Festival was under way, the DCI had decided – belatedly, you might think – that Roper's lover could be the key. She sounded like a sensible young woman, keen to get on, and she surely wouldn't want to go to prison on behalf of a corrupt bookmaker twice her age. If he could find the young lady, be she in London, Paris or Switzerland, and press her to reveal the whole story, including what she knew about Teddy Smith, he could maybe put Roper away for years.

It was the right strategy but the only problem was that Bill had thought of it first. The week after Ted Smith's death, Mr Racing, still at liberty, took a plane to Geneva and went in search of Micheline. He wanted to tell her that he still loved her and that he needed her . . . and he wanted to try and persuade her to return with him to the UK.

21

I CAN'T STOP LOVING YOU

BILL SPENT a week in Switzerland. After a few days of terse, tearful telephone conversations from his hotel room, Micheline agreed to meet him at lunchtime in a brasserie near the station. Roper, the continental traveller, tried the Sion wine and the choucroute and pronounced it just the job to have in London this bloody awful winter.

Bill told her that he adored her and couldn't live without her. He said that the British police were going to try and find her and use her against him. He'd been a bloody fool, he knew that. He'd got in too far and he'd always regret it. He was sorry. Bitterly sorry. But everything he'd done since Shropshire in October 1961 had been to try and protect them both and Doris and the boys. He described the long hours of questioning he'd now been subjected to in Monmouth Street and at Scotland Yard. Barnett and Anderson had been to Uphill Drive and talked to Doris and, the day after the Brighton case ended, they turned up in Covent Garden. They had a warrant to search the office but Bill had already cleared out his safe and destroyed any incriminating records.

Between 10 January and 5 February, Bill had been taken into West End Central on three separate occasions and quizzed relentlessly about everyone from Ted Smith and Charlie Mitchell to Max Parker, Cyril Stein and Albert Dimes. He gave away absolutely nothing. He knew the score and he knew what would happen if he talked. He said a lot about his well-to-do clients and connections and Ernie Barnett noticed how important they seemed to be to his image and self-esteem. The DCI asked him about Micheline Lugeon and her whereabouts – at least they had the name right now – but Bill feigned ignorance. Bizarrely the police hadn't taken his passport away. Not yet.

Bill was still Bill and he didn't tell Micheline everything. He didn't say that Barnett was still threatening him with a murder charge. Nor did he mention what Charlie Mitchell had said about shutting Smith up. He just said that, whatever was going to happen to him, if they stuck together and told the same story, they had a chance. That would be the easiest way through it for her and the least painful for Doris and the children too . . . and, when it was all over, they could maybe go away and try again . . . in another country.

Micheline made him wait for her answer. One afternoon she let him come out to her parents' house in Nyon. Bill had never been short of chutzpah and self-belief but it must have been one of his biggest ever challenges as he sat on the sofa in his Savile Row suit, sipping tea and talking politely to her mother and father. He told them Micheline still had a big future ahead of her in business and he wanted to help her if he could. When they asked him about the trouble he was in back in London, he said it had all been exaggerated and that the police were only after him because the press had made a fuss. He expected it all to die down soon.

On the morning before he left, Micheline took him for a long walk by the lake. Bill noticed that she still had her sealskin coat. He'd brought the gold signet ring with him from Park Road and he insisted that she keep it.

When Roper got back to London, the temperature was lower than Geneva and parts of the Thames had frozen over at Hampton and Hurst Park. The thaw finally began in early March. Racing resumed at Newbury on the 8th and, the following week, Bill went up to Cheltenham as usual – undeterred by the speculation in the press box and betting ring – and laid bets to his remaining clients. He saw Arkle win the Broadway Chase by 20 lengths and Mill House win the Gold Cup by 12 and, for three days and nights, surrounded by old friends and colleagues, he carried on as if it was life as normal.[39]

Micheline had returned to England on 28 February, the day before the police issued a warrant for her arrest. This time she may have travelled on a false passport supplied by Roper (something she presumably didn't tell her parents

---

39 The following year Arkle won the Gold Cup, beating Mill House by five lengths in one of the most famous races of all time. The greatest steeplechaser who ever lived, Arkle won the Gold Cup again in 1965 and 1966.

about). But the police and immigration services were no wiser as to her movements than they had been the previous year and she passed through Heathrow undetected. Number 27 Park Road had been sold and the money banked. Micheline was unsure how long her new stay would last or how it would end but, for the moment, she rented a bed-sittingroom in a large, comfortable, detached house on Platts Lane in Hampstead. The owners, Mr and Mrs Barbour, were friends of a couple she had been an au pair for six years before. She told them she was now married and that her name was Mrs Bell. Her husband, she said, had been based in Switzerland but was working for the British government in some indeterminate capacity and she had come to London to be closer to him.

Bill gave her the money for the rent and, although he suspected he was being watched, he tried to get out and meet her at a hotel or a friend's house and occasionally at Platts Lane when the Barbours were away. Micheline may have been using a pseudonym but neither of them was planning to run away. Roper had a good idea what was in store and was trying to prepare for it as best he could. He'd taken Doris into his confidence up to a point, assuring her that he'd salted money away for her and the boys and, that whatever happened to him, they'd always be looked after. He may have sought some kind of absolution for his sins because, in the weeks that followed, Doris never had a bad word to say about him in public despite receiving plenty of encouragement.

Bill had consulted his solicitor Harry Goodrich who was based in the City. He'd liked to have talked to some of his old customers, the Ladbrokes punters, who knew a thing or two about the law. He'd tried talking again to Max Parker, who'd encouraged him every step of the way. Maybe Maxie's ingenious mind could come up with a defence Bill hadn't thought of. But it was no good. Bill knew the older man was cunning and wouldn't help if it meant appearing in court. As far as Maxie was concerned, Bill's activities were all eminently deniable. He hadn't told him to dope horses. If he'd heard things, like bookmakers do, and reacted accordingly, that was another matter. But, no, unfortunately all his records and ledgers concerning those races seemed to have been thrown away and, as for Ladbrokes, that was an entirely separate and perfectly respectable company run by his nephew Cyril.

The truncated jumping season gave way to the flat. Only For Life, ridden by the big race specialist Jimmy Lindley, won the 2,000 Guineas by a short head and the ace French filly Hula Dancer landed the 1,000 by a length. It was the season of Derby trials, of rumours, whispers and Victoria Club call-overs with the French colt Relko attracting most of the money and, by the weekend before the race, he was trading at 4-1 favourite.

That year the Derby was due to be run, not on the first Wednesday in June, but on the last Wednesday in May and it was at the beginning of that week that the police finally moved in. Ernest Barnett came in person for Bill at Stafford Court at 7 a.m. on Whit Monday, 27 May. Even on a bank holiday Roper was always an early riser but the police gave him time to change into a smart suit and tie, as he would on any working day, and pack a small overnight bag. But when it was time to take him downstairs, he was handcuffed humiliatingly to two uniformed constables. How high he had risen. The self-made Catford boy who had aspired to Kensington penthouse luxury. And how far he had to fall.

As Bill came out of the lift with his police escort, they passed the milkman on his way up.

'Good morning, Mr Roper.'

'Good morning, Frank.'

'Shall I cancel your usual delivery?'

'I think you'd better.'

'Got any tips, Mr Roper?'

'Not today, Frank. Not today.'

Outside on the street, the police bundled Bill into a waiting car and drove him off towards Cannon Row. Simultaneously, the London Irishmen, Terence O'Connell and Pat Sugrue, were arresting their fellow hard man, Charlie Mitchell, at his home in Rannoch Road, Fulham. Charlie laughed at them when they arrived but he got into the car without a fuss. Other groups of detectives rounded up Joe Lowry and Jackie Dyer, who had been advised by Bill to make arrangements of their own, but not Bernie Howard or moody Jack Stiles who could not be found and were believed to be in Spain. In their absence, the other four men were taken to Cannon Row police station and charged and then driven down to Brighton and remanded in custody after a brief appearance in the Magistrates' Court.

A week later the quartet appeared before the magistrates again. It was a fine, sunny early summer's day – five days after Relko had won the Derby in a canter – and the Brighton police were in their traditional summer uniforms with white helmets. There were plenty of reporters and photographers on hand as Bill, Charlie, Jackie and Joe, all smartly dressed and handcuffed in pairs, arrived at the Town Hall in a green prison van. They laughed and talked among themselves but, as was customary at the time, they tried to shield their faces with pages of newspaper when the cameras came near.

The police categorically opposed bail for all four men lest there should be further witness intimidation. Mr Stable explained that some enquiries couldn't proceed until the arrests of the suspects 'for fear of causing ripples in the pool'. But he said that Interpol was now involved and that he would be calling over a hundred witnesses from England, Ireland, Scotland and France and would establish that the gang had doped more than forty racehorses while possessing enough stolen drugs to dope hundreds more. The chairman of the magistrates, Mr Herbert Ripper, deemed that the committal proceedings should begin on 24 June. By then, both Alex Field and Brian Perry had been added to the haul. Perry had been arrested at his mother's home in Ewell but Field, the master locksmith and cracksman, was already in police custody, having been convicted of house breaking in Stoke-on-Trent. He had a five-year prison sentence hanging over him in that case but first he would have to face the music in Brighton with Bill Roper.

The dopers were held in Lewes prison and, initially, the conditions were harsh. Jackie Dyer says they were all treated like murderers which was, basically, what the police suspected them to be. Despite this they formed good relationships with the governor and some of his staff with Bill Roper playing the Robin Hood role and arranging for money to be paid to the family of one warder whose daughter was seriously ill and needed expensive medical treatment which was only available at a hospital in Germany.

On 16 June the prisoners all tried to crowd around a radio to listen to the big fight at Wembley Stadium as Cassius Clay, as he was then, took on Henry Cooper, the British heavyweight champion. Clay's career almost ended there as 'Enery, cheered on by thousands of East End fans and faces, landed a colossal left hook at the end of the fourth round. Clay was saved by the intervention of his quick-witted manager Angelo Dundee, who slit his man's left glove to buy time. Clay came back strongly in the fifth round and the referee stopped the bout in his favour. The controversial left glove came into the possession of that noted boxing enthusiast Albert Dimes, who kept it on the wall behind the counter in his betting shop in Frith Street.[40]

While Bill Roper and his gang kicked their heels in jail, Ernest Barnett continued his hunt for Micheline Lugeon. On 12 June Barnett flew to Paris, accompanied by portly Bob Hill, and the two men went in search of 18 Avenue de la Roche, the address that 'Mademoiselle Rosemarie Laumaine' had given Neville Crump and others. The Jockey

---

40 Clay changed his name to Muhammad Ali in 1964 after his first World Heavyweight title victory against Sonny Liston.

Club Secretary Edward Weatherby had assured them it didn't exist and so had the French police. But Barnett still wanted to check the area in person and it took a morning of fruitless, flat-footed research to convince him that Les Flics were right.

The investigators went on to the Lamorlaye stable of Max Bonaventure, the original trainer of Ganymede II, satisfying themselves that Mademoiselle had not been a regular owner there, and then had a rather stiff meeting – not helped by mutual linguistic incomprehension – with Jean Romanet, the top man at the Société d'Encouragement. The frustrated DCI returned to London empty handed, a bit like Jack Slipper after his abortive attempt to bring Ronnie Biggs back from Rio, but Bob Hill continued to feed tantalising snippets of information to the racing press.

There was a tangible air of excitement as the public waited for the court proceedings to begin and the atmosphere chimed with the general sense of melodrama that prevailed that summer. On 5 June John Profumo had resigned after admitting lying to the House of Commons about the nature of his relationship with Christine Keeler. Less than a month later Kim Philby was unmasked as 'The Third Man' and the backbench Labour MPs George Wigg and Marcus Lipton intensified their pursuit of Prime Minister Harold Macmillan, who had approved Philby's security clearance when he was Foreign Secretary seven years before.

The blunderings and convolutions of the government found a reflection in the embarrassment of the Jockey Club as they tried to deal with racing's latest public relations disaster. Five horses had apparently failed post-race dope tests including, sensationally, the Derby laureate Relko, and the gambled-on 1963 Victoria Cup winner Tudor Treasure, who was owned by Bill Roper's old punter Ian Murray.[41] There was no suggestion that any of them had been got at with stopping drugs. It was more a case of the Jockey Club hinting that, shades of Talma II, the sneaky French might have given Relko something to enable him to run faster and his connections, the brilliant but haughty trainer François Mathet, owner François Dupré and jockey Yves Saint-Martin were summoned to a July enquiry in London.

By then Mr Stable had had another run-out in Brighton. On 24 and 25 June he gave a *tour d'horizon* of the prosecution case. 'The story I am going to tell and ultimately prove,' he began with a flourish, 'is a story of large-scale horse doping by a gang, the chief men of which are in front of you now.' It was, he avowed, one of 'the blackest chapters in the long history of the Turf. Doping undermines racing completely and converts it from a sport to a racket. If not stamped out, it would very materially alter the bloodstock industry in this country and endanger the reputation of its dealers for producing some of the finest thoroughbred horses in the world.'

Intriguingly, Stable's submission contained almost no reference to the betting and bookmaking angle, which

---

41 The Victoria Cup, a seven-furlong handicap on the flat, used to be one of the biggest betting races of the season and was run at Hurst Park until the track closed in 1962. It is now staged at Ascot.

had been central to the plot as far as the protagonists were concerned. With no Ted Smith to make their case and no chance of getting Max Parker in the dock, the crown seemed to have decided to concentrate on the threat posed to the prestige of British racing, which also suited the Jockey Club whose knowledge of the gambling industry was still pitifully small.

On 28 June Captain Neville Crump gave evidence, describing the 'extremely attractive young lady who spoke English well with a French accent' who came to look around his yard. Mark Myers QC, representing Roper, asked him if he didn't regularly have female visitors to his stable. 'Not like this one,' replied the Captain.

Stable produced all four of the English stable lads, the 'frightened accomplices' who were permitted to write down their full names and addresses rather than reveal them in open court and who were then referred to throughout by their Christian names. Michael Heffernan said that between 1958 and 1960 he'd been asked by the dopers to pinpoint between twenty and thirty horses and he identified 'Joe and Jacky', the two men who approached him, as two of the defendants in the dock.

Jimmy Hilliard described the doping of Providence at Fergie Sutherland's yard in 1959. 'Were you nervous?' asked Stable. 'I sure was,' replied the lad who was barely tall enough to be seen over the top of the witness box.

Philip 'Snuffy' Lawler told of being approached by the same two defendants, Joe and Jackie, and of how they had wanted to know the position of St Paddy's box at Warren

Place. It was a shattering revelation for the racing community to discover that St Paddy's lad had been offered £500 to give the horse a physic ball before the 1960 Dante and twice as much to do it before the Derby itself. Lawler described how the balling procedure would have purged St Paddy violently and stopped him running at Epsom but he claimed that he had, honourably, resisted temptation and thrown the ball away. No mention was made of Pinturischio.

The most dramatic moment came on 3 July when Owen Stable declared that Harry Field's girlfriend, the auburn-haired stripper Elaine Grande, may have attempted to interfere with a witness. 'That's not true at all,' she cried from the public gallery, resulting in her removal from the court. Stable went on to allude, darkly, to information that had supposedly come to the prosecution's notice since the case had begun and which he may have to ask to be considered in closed court. There was intense speculation that he was referring to Ted Smith's former lady, May Kibble, who was going to testify for the crown that she had seen Bill Roper and Charlie Mitchell 'regularly visit' Ted at his 'Dope Bank' at Balaclava Road.

The crown evidence ended on 11 July after more than a hundred witnesses had been called. Mark Myers for Roper and Leonard Lewis QC, representing Jackie Dyer, again sought bail for their clients. Myers described Roper as 'a man of some importance in racing circles' and claimed that keeping him in custody would jeopardise his defence as he would 'not have access to his papers, cheques and records of phone calls'. Lewis based his appeal on health grounds, explaining that Jackie only had one kidney and had been seriously ill in 1960, but in both cases Stable was 'resolutely opposed' and the magistrates agreed with him. They ruled that the six should go for trial at Sussex Assizes.

With the men now safely back under lock and key in Lewes, the police intensified their search for Micheline Lugeon. There had been numerous references in Brighton to 'the mysterious Frenchwoman' who was said to be a 'key figure in the plot' and the newspapers had run with the idea of a James Bond femme fatale. The coverage eventually came to the attention of Mr and Mrs Barbour in Platts Lane, Hampstead. The couple had been away on holiday in Devon but, when they returned on the afternoon of 22 July they confronted their lodger, the reclusive Mrs Bell, with their suspicions. Either she phoned the police, they said, or they would. Micheline didn't attempt to deny it. She rang Bill Roper's solicitors according to a pre-arranged plan, and a member of their staff telephoned Scotland Yard. The solicitor then drove out to Platts Lane and collected Micheline, who bade a tearful farewell to her landlords, and then allowed herself to be taken to Cannon Row police station where Ernest Barnett was waiting.

Barnett said later that Micheline was given every chance to save herself by testifying against Roper on behalf of the crown but that she refused. She was formally charged with conspiring to dope racehorses and held overnight in the cells at Cannon Row. The following day she was driven down to Brighton where the 'Swiss beauty specialist', as she was now described, made a 30 minute appearance in court. She had been denied access to her normal Michelle de Paris cosmetics and hairspray but she was still smartly dressed in a dark blue suit and white blouse. 'I am innocent and I know nothing about it,' she said of the charges against her. The magistrates remanded her in custody for a week.

On the same day that Micheline appeared in court in Brighton, Mandy Rice-Davies was giving evidence at the Old Bailey in the trial of Stephen Ward for living off immoral earnings. She famously remarked: 'He would, wouldn't he?' when told that Lord Astor denied that he'd had sex with her in Christine Keeler's flat in Wimpole Mews. The one with the two-way mirror, installed by Peter Rachman (Rice-Davies's former lover), so that voyeurs could watch what was happening in the bedroom. The possible link between the slum landlord, a government minister and another of Keeler's lovers, the Russian naval attaché Yevgeni Ivanov, had shocked and enthralled the nation.

The coincidence of two court cases featuring sex, crime and gorgeous young women was not lost on the newspapers and, if Bill Roper was the leading man, Micheline was going to be the real star of their trial which Mr Justice McNair ruled would begin at Lewes Crown Court on 2 October. Until then she faced two months in Holloway Prison.

The death, or murder, of Teddy Smith wasn't the only setback to the successful prosecution of the dopers. On 30 July the Appeal Court quashed the four-year sentence that had been handed down to Darkie Steward in Brighton in January. Mr Justice Paull, sitting with Justices Nield and

Stephenson, ruled that a conversation between two other conspirators (Kenny Santus and Jack Stiles) had been wrongly admitted as evidence. It was possible, they said, that Steward would have been properly convicted even without that evidence but, they added, the conversation in which it was claimed he had doped five or six horses might have been fatal to his chances of being acquitted.

Darkie, wearing a smart suit and tie and a clean white shirt, blew kisses to Sylvia Cross, who was in the gallery, during the lunch adjournment and left court with her later, Sylvia carrying a huge bunch of flowers. The sight of one of the biggest, and most guilty, dopers walking free unsurprisingly enraged the Jockey Club as well as DCI Barnett and his men. Establishment tempers were probably not improved when, besides Darkie's story in the following day's papers, they saw a picture of the Grand National-winning owner and celebrity hairdresser, Teasy Weasy Raymond, arriving at Cowes in a pink helicopter.[42]

Darkie, for all his promises of rehabilitation, soon slipped back into the gambling demi-monde and wherever bookmakers, faces and touts gathered that summer there were mutterings that very soon there was going to be an awful lot of money floating around on the racecourse. Bruce Reynolds, Charlie Wilson, Gordon Goody and their friends were planning 'The Train' and the racecourse bookie Tommy Wisbey was one of their team. A sizeable portion of

42 Teasy Weasy, whose real name was Raymond Bessone, loved to shock, calculating correctly that the publicity it brought him would boost his business.

the £2.4million haul from the robbery was never recovered. Darkie Steward was not involved directly but the bookie's clerk, Tommy Lawrence, remembers that there was much talk of 'how cash could be laundered through the betting ring' and that a good deal of it was supposedly cleaned and legitimised on Britain's racetracks.[43]

It was the sort of scam that would assuredly have appealed to Bill Roper as it did to another gambler and villain, Brian Wright, 30 years later.[44] But, as summer drew to an end and Detective Chief Superintendent Tommy Butler closed in on the train robbers, Bill was otherwise engaged and shaping up for the climactic weeks of his career.

43 Tommy Lawrence remembers one racecourse face describing how he literally washed banknotes from the robbery in Blue Daz in his bath in South London.
44 Brian Wright, nicknamed 'The Milkman' allegedly because he always delivered, was a high-stakes punter and racing enthusiast who was allegedly behind the doping of at least 20 horses in the 1990s. In 2007 he was convicted of international drug smuggling and sentenced to 30 years in prison. He still follows the racing from behind bars.

22

THE PRICE TO PAY

LEWES CROWN Court has a forbidding aura as befits a place of grave, judicial reckoning. The imposing three-storey building was constructed from Portland stone in the early 19th century and sits at the bottom end of the high street, opposite the White Hart Hotel. A flight of seven steps leads up from the pavement to the colonnades and white, double-fronted doors through which witnesses, journalists and spectators passed on the opening morning of the Assizes on 2 October 1963. They entered a wide, red-carpeted corridor where bewigged barristers, solicitors and court officials were hurrying up and down. There was a waiting room for the defence witnesses and another for the prosecution witnesses and, with more than 100 of them summoned to appear over the next fortnight, it turned into a sort of impromptu racecourse weighing room and was soon thick with cigarette smoke.

Micheline Lugeon was brought in and out through the front entrance, having been driven down from Holloway in a black, police Humber Hawk. But Bill Roper and the other male defendants arrived at the back of the building in the Lewes Prison van and were held in the cells below the courtroom before the trial was ready to proceed. Walking up the steps into the dock, Bill and his men were confronted by a setting of classical Agatha Christie proportions complete with a polished, wooden witness box and brown public benches covered in red upholstery and looking deceptively like something out of a Victorian church or pub. The judge's bench was straight ahead of them, the defence and prosecution teams were in the well of the court below, the jury to the left and the public galleries either side. A clock ticked above their heads but they couldn't see it.

It was small enough to be intimate, yet grand enough to intimidate and connoisseurs of courtroom drama would have known that many dramatic scenes had taken place there. The trial of the Brighton Trunk Murderer in 1935. The trial of the acid bath murderer, John George Haigh, who was sentenced to death at Lewes in 1949 and subsequently hanged, and the committal proceedings of the suspected serial-killing Eastbourne doctor, John Bodkin Adams, who somehow escaped the gallows but was convicted of fraud and forgery at Lewes in 1957.

Bill Roper's brief, David Weitzmann QC assisted by Mark Myers, and the barristers appearing for the other men, would have left their clients in no doubt that the presiding judge, Aubrey Melford Steed Stevenson, would have quite happily recommended hanging for horse doping if the law had allowed. The 62-year-old (who as a barrister had defended

Ruth Ellis and been part of the unsuccessful prosecution of Bodkin Adams) had a house near Uckfield called 'Truncheons' and was notorious both for the severity of his sentences and the number of times his judgements were challenged in the Court of Appeal. He was most definitely not a racing enthusiast.

Roper, Charlie Mitchell, Joe Lowry, Jackie Dyer, Alex Field and Brian Perry took their seats in the dock under Melford Stevenson's stern gaze. Micheline Lugeon was allowed to sit just outside and to the right of the dock in a chair normally reserved for the governor of Lewes Prison. She was flanked on either side by a wardress and, each day of the trial, she began by looking across at the dock to catch Bill's eye and smiling at him warmly. The wives and girlfriends of the other men travelled down to Lewes from Victoria on the train and took their seats in the gallery which was packed, not only with members of the general public but journalists from both the racing and the national press.

It was another unseasonably warm early autumn and Lewes and the surrounding Sussex countryside were bathed in sunshine. But the public mood in the town was fractious as the railway line from Brighton to Tunbridge Wells, via Lewes and Uckfield, was one of the many hundreds recommended for closure by the infamous Dr Beeching and local opposition was strong.[45] On the national stage, Harold Macmillan, diagnosed

45 Dr Richard Beeching was the chairman of British Rail. His report on the future of the railways, first published on 27 March 1963, resulted in the closure of over 4,000 miles of track and hundreds of stations. The Lewes to Uckfield line closed in 1969 though there are currently plans to reopen it.

with prostate cancer, was contemplating retirement as his possible successors – Butler, Hailsham, Maudling – jockeyed for position. And, on the racetrack, the champion jockey, Scobie Breasley, was engaged in a thrilling, neck-and-neck duel with Lester Piggott for the 1963 title.

After a day or two of legal argument, the early pace in Court Number One was set by Owen Stable as he launched, for the second time in three months, into an overview of the dopers' crimes. But this time Mr Stable, who needed to make the conspiracy case watertight, had an extra defendant to target, the 'pretty, intelligent and resourceful' but, in his view, 'unquestionably guilty' Miss Micheline Lugeon, and he set out to attack both her character and her alibi. So virulent was his onslaught that in the eyes of many onlookers, the Swiss femme fatale became an object of sympathy, as much a victim as an agent of crime.

Stable sketched a picture of what he called 'Micheline's journey' during which she visited 21 racing stables, as far apart as Kent and Roxburghshire, in 41 days. In the course of her travels, said the prosecutor, doping 'followed her about as if it was a contagious disease and she was the carrier'. Of the stables she called at, he said, five subsequently suffered an outbreak of doping – it was, of course, many more than that but not all of them were detected – and it was Roper, who 'was often there in nearby hotels' who 'exploited her good looks and personality to get her into places where she had no authority to be'.

Micheline had 'acted as a front for the gang', said Stable, charming the stable staff she came into contact with and then noting down the boxes where the horses the accused wished to dope were standing. The gang needed stable lads and traded on their low pay. Joe Lowry, in particular, had been free with his money in Newmarket and had found it easy to gain the lads' confidence and information. Stable called the four Newmarket stable lads again – Snuffy, Santus, Michael and Jimmy – and they repeated their stories. But, just as at Brighton in July and in accordance with the deal struck with Philip Lawler in advance, there wasn't a single mention of the doping of Pinturischio.

In keeping with Stable's promise, other witnesses came from far and wide. Kenny English, a stable lad at Verley Bewicke's Northumberland yard, remembered seeing the 'mysterious French girl' at Glanton House and then again in the racecourse stabling area at Kelso. Arthur Stephenson's housekeeper, Mrs Redfern, was called along with the jockeys Harry East, Bobby Beasley and Johnny Lehane, while Jean Romanet delivered a characteristically lofty exposition of the Société d'Encouragement's procedures for correctly registering as a racehorse owner.

Micheline's PR girl, June Downie, testified that Miss Lugeon had asked her if she thought it would be a good idea for her to buy a racehorse and use it to publicise her cosmetics business as Chanel and Teasy Weasy had done. Under cross-examination by Micheline's counsel, Mr W. R. Hudson, she spoke glowingly of Micheline's hard work and enterprise and, when pressed by Stable, was adamant that she hadn't doubted her then and still didn't now.

On Thursday 10 October it was the turn of the Fairlawne head lad, Jim Fairgrieve, and a clipped Peter Cazalet, who was clearly irritated to be taken away from a day's racing.

Cazalet confirmed that 'the French girl' had come to visit his stable in November 1961 but, as agreed in advance with the Jockey Club, the Metropolitan Police commissioner and the Home Office, he said nothing about the doping of the Queen Mother's horse.

Numerous other trainers took the stand including Roy Whiston, Chris Nesfield and, painfully, Roper's old friend Tim Molony, as well as Jack Waugh and Neville Crump. For the Jockey Club, it was out of the question that any of the stewards should submit to questioning but Colonel Blair made a brief appearance and then, on Friday 11 October, the Jockey Club Secretary Edward Weatherby was involved in a surreal exchange with Leonard Lewis QC for the defendants.

'Do I understand it is your evidence that you know nothing about racing?' asked Lewis.

'I did not say racing. I said betting,' said Weatherby.

'Betting is closely associated with racing, is it not?' asked Lewis.

'Yes,' said Weatherby.

'Are you telling the judge and jury that you know nothing about it?' asked Lewis.

'In a rule the stewards of the Jockey Club take no cognisance of betting as such,' said Weatherby. 'I am their servant.'

'And you know nothing about it?' confirmed Lewis.

'Nothing,' agreed Weatherby.

Lewis shook his head in disbelief and in the press gallery, racing correspondents exchanged meaningful glances.

The closest the prosecution case came to alluding to the mechanics of the betting side of the plot was when Clive Graham, Peter O'Sullevan's colleague at the *Express* and, like him, a dedicated punter, explained that some bookmakers would pay good money for information that a certain favourite couldn't win. But other than the men in the dock, not a single bookie, on or off course, or bookmaker's clerk or workman or tic-tac operative was asked to account for their activities during the years of the conspiracy or even shed light on how the betting ring worked.

Stable moved on to the plotters at Colville Terrace and the court heard from Major Haines about the horse bite on the absent Darkie Steward's hand and the stable maps in Brian Perry's bedroom. The cleaner, Mrs Juggins, testified to finding the bag of luminal sodium behind the dislodged panel in the bathroom on the third floor and then Mrs Robson took the stand to describe the comings and goings of the various tenants in and outside the flat. She got into something of a muddle when it came to identifying the defendants in the dock and mistakenly labelled Joe Lowry as Bill Roper's brother which made both men laugh. But she swore on oath that she saw Charlie Mitchell outside the house with Roper and about to join a convoy of cars with the others and that evidence was crucial.

The crown may have lost their prize catch, Teddy Smith, but they had great hopes of Ted's lady, May Kibble, who had testified in Brighton in July that Mitchell always accompanied Bill Roper to Balaclava Road. But when May was put on the stand at Lewes, she sensationally contradicted and changed her own testimony. She was sorry, she said, but she'd made a terrible mistake and could no longer identify or even recognise Charlie Mitchell.

There was a tense interlude while the court rose and Mrs Kibble was interviewed again within the court buildings by Ernest Barnett who was waiting to testify himself. The DCI had absolutely no doubt that his witness had been intimidated – no doubt by the same men who had arranged Teddy Smith's murder – but, despite being threatened with a perjury charge, she refused to retract.

As she left the court at the end of the afternoon, May Kibble was surrounded by reporters. 'I've got three other children besides the one at home,' she told one of them while running tearfully towards the station. 'I have only just got a council house and the other three are coming home soon. Have you ever heard of vengeance?' The newspapers lapped it up. 'The frightened woman' was the *Mirror's* lead the following day. 'Her fear of the razor slashers.'

The May Kibble testimony came at the end of the prosecution case and marked a suitably dramatic halfway stage in the proceedings. On 16 October the case for the defence began and Joe Lowry was first up in the witness box. He admitted that he had seen Bill Roper at the races and had tried to become friendly with him. 'He was an inspired man,' he said of Roper, 'and always to be seen with the highest in the land.' When asked by his barrister to explain whom exactly he was referring to, Joe said that Roper was 'known to do commissions for some of the biggest people in racing'. But he insisted that he'd never spoken to either Bill or Charlie

Mitchell before the case and, that while he had occasionally paid Brian Perry £5 for tips, he had never met either Alex Field or Micheline Lugeon.

'Would it be right that Roper was a bookmaker with the brothers Parker?' asked Mr Stable, grandly. 'I know he used to work for them on the rails,' said Joe. The prosecutor sniffed which was about as close as he came to publicly implicating Maxie and Cyril in the plot. Stable asked Joe about Darkie Steward and Teddy Smith. He admitted knowing them but denied ever visiting Colville Terrace. Then Stable asked him about the three Newmarket stable lads, Snuffy, Michael and Jimmy. Yes, agreed Joe, he had known them and had tips from them and bet on horses on their behalf but he claimed it was 'a diabolical lie' for any of them to say that he and Jackie Dyer had ever been on a doping expedition with them. He had his own explanation for the night he was stopped by the police in Newmarket in March 1960. He had met some US servicemen stationed in Suffolk who had invited him and Jackie to a party in the Carlton Hotel. They had made a bit of a night of it and then Joe had driven them back to London, dropping them off in Coventry Street in the early hours.

Joe recalled that he had once taken Jackie Dyer to Balaclava Road in Surbiton but said he'd never entered the house himself. Guided by his brief, he told the court that he had written to the Jockey Club stewards offering to help them in any way he could but denied that this had anything to do with doping. 'I don't believe there was any doping going on,' he declared. 'I think it was all sensational paper talk.'

Mr Stable wasn't going to let him finish on such a confident note. He wanted to leave the jury in no doubt about Lowry's criminal associations. He showed him a piece of paper with a name on it and asked him if he knew the person. Joe, unfazed, replied that he did. He had met him dog racing and had a few drinks with him and a very nice man he was too. 'The King of the Underworld tried to cut him up,' he said to the courtroom at large, 'but he defended himself, got tried and was acquitted.'[46] The name on the piece of paper – not revealed to the jury or the public – was Albert Dimes.

Then it was Jackie Dyer's turn. He said that, at the time of his arrest, he was a 'bookmaker's assistant' and that he spent most of his time at the racetrack and at one time had owned a betting shop of his own. He confirmed that he was Charlie Mitchell's uncle and agreed that he knew Joe Lowry but said that he didn't know any of Brian Perry, Alex Field or Micheline Lugeon. He told his counsel, Mr Hudson, that he had met the former stable lad, Michael, 'about ten to 12 years ago' and had been introduced to him as someone who might be able to give him tips.

As to Bill Roper, well, of course, 'everybody knows about him on the racecourse', he said. 'Roper was Mr Racing and they all used to follow him.' Owen Stable wanted to know if Roper went around 'with five pound notes in his pockets'.

---

46 Joe Lowry was referring to Jack Spot, aka 'The King of the Underworld' and his famous knife fight with Albert Dimes on the corner of Frith Street and Old Compton Street in August 1955. Both men were subsequently acquitted in court and the incident became known as 'the fight that never was'.

Jackie shook his head, smiling at Stable's naivety. 'Roper has so much credit,' he said, 'he could put £10,000 or £20,000 on a horse without a penny in his pocket.' Stable pressed him about his own relationship with Roper. Jackie said that he'd tried to get to know him but had never met him until they were unfortunate enough to be in prison together before the trial.

Mr Hudson asked Jackie about the illness he'd had since 1958 and his client confirmed he'd been in hospital several times and only had one kidney. Hudson invited him to explain how he had made his living since then. Dyer replied that he was 'satisfied to go to the races to earn a few pounds' any way he could. 'Are there no scruples about it?' asked Stable. 'There are no scruples in racing, are there?' replied Jackie, which led Melford Stevenson to intervene. 'You say there are no scruples in racing?' he asked, frowning. 'Suppose you heard of someone doping a horse? Would that shock you?' 'No, sir,' replied Jackie, honestly. 'It has been going on for hundreds of years. It's been going on since we were charged.'

There was an audible intake of breath in the courtroom as the public and the press digested Dyer's comments. At which point Melford Stevenson decided to break for lunch.

The case for Alex Field and Brian Perry was a brief one. Field, described as 'a key man in the organisation' by the prosecution, avowed that he had 'nothing whatsoever to do with doping' which was true in the limited sense that he had picked the stable locks rather than administered the drugs. He said that he had gone to meet Roper in

Newcastle because he was hoping to interest him in buying or investing in some property with him. Perry also denied any knowledge of doping and claimed that his only connection with the other defendants was his friendship with Len Steward who had encouraged him to take a room at Colville Terrace.

Charlie Mitchell, as was his right, declined to go into the witness box and almost the only words he was heard to utter at Lewes were 'Not guilty, my Lord' when the indictment was read out.

However guilty all the seven defendants were, the prosecution was not making a great job of proving it or demonstrating that they all acted together as conspirators. Without Ted Smith's evidence – or May Kibble's – Mr Stable's case was a thin one and he knew it. Summoning over a hundred witnesses was all very well and he'd made a lot of sound and fury but, as the trial approached its climax, he needed a match winner. He needed to try and break Micheline Lugeon and persuade her to betray Roper and admit their guilt.

Each day the 'startlingly attractive' Micheline, as one newspaper had taken to describing her, came to court looking impeccably turned out. Sitting between two women prison officers, she usually wore a suit of midnight blue with a white blouse, flesh-coloured stockings and black shoes. Her dark brown bouffant hair was always smartly groomed over her head and she wore her gold signet ring on her right hand. She was kept apart from the male defendants and lunched alone in a small room beneath the court, usually on a salad brought over from the hotel across the street. But when she stepped into the witness box on Friday 18 October, taking the oath confidently in fluent English, her magnetism eclipsed everyone else in the room.

Micheline's barrister, Mr Elton, took her through the details of her career since leaving her job as the Ropers' au pair in 1956 and moving on to become a beauty culture student and then setting up in business as a 'rival to other leading specialists'. She said that she had been in the north of England with Mr Roper in October 1961 because she was attempting to put her cosmetics on the market and wanted to get publicity for her products and beauty creams. They had initially gone to Shropshire but then an old flame called Jean Pierre, who was 'a vendor of lace', had followed her to the Buckatree Hotel and made a scene. She and Mr Roper had had a row but then they had made up and decided to leave Shrewsbury and go to the North East instead.

Micheline was asked why she had 'told a few lies', as Elton put it. She smiled and sighed and replied, 'I just boasted and put on a bit of window dressing, that's all. I didn't tell everyone my proper name because so many of the men were trying to get friendly and ring me.' Two women members of the jury nodded and smiled too as if they completely understood.

Mr Elton asked Micheline if it was indeed true that she had visited Major Peter Cazalet's stable and with a chauffeur in tow. Micheline admitted that she had been to Fairlawne, to see if Major Cazalet might be able to take her horse. 'It was such a beautiful stable,' she said directly to the jury.

And the chauffeur? asked Elton. Micheline laughed. She'd met a friend of hers, a student called Adrian, in a coffee bar in the King's Road. He just happened to have a black car outside so he had driven her down to Tonbridge and worn a chauffeur's hat as 'a big joke'. Some of the jury members smiled again. Others looked unconvinced.

Mr Stable was smiling as he rose to begin his cross-examination. He walked right up to the witness box and began by complimenting Micheline and telling the jury that she had used her good looks and intelligence to 'play a difficult role with incredible skill'. But then he reminded them that her role had been not at all humorous or romantic, as she was suggesting, but to assist a man who drugs racehorses. A man, he said, who 'plays fast and loose with the life of the jockey who has to ride the horse and adds considerably to the danger of the other jockeys in the race'.

Now Stable itemised various dates in Micheline's career, building up to the moment in 1959 when she and Bill became lovers. 'When you were first . . . *intimate* . . . with Roper,' he said, emphasising the word distastefully, '. . . did you love him?' Micheline smiled at Bill in the dock and lied. 'No,' she said. 'I did not.' Stable turned to look at Roper. 'Do you love him now?' he asked. 'I am fond of him,' she replied. Then she looked across at Melford Stevenson. 'Am I being tried here?' she asked. 'Or the moral issue?' The judge coughed. 'You and Mr Roper were very close and prepared to share bedrooms at hotels,' he said. 'He was known as Mr Racing. Why were you chasing up and down the country asking questions of stable lads when the trainer was away?' It was a better question than any that Stable had put but Micheline just brushed it aside. 'I was hoping to get tips for Mr Roper for when we went racing,' she said. Melford Stevenson invited Stable to continue.

'Can you explain why horses in different parts of the country – Fresh Winds, Irish Honour and Bronze Warrior among them – were found doped after you had visited their stables?' asked the prosecutor. 'I would not know,' replied Micheline. 'You are trying to cover the dirty work of stable boys and trainers.' 'You think it was all stable boys and trainers?' asked Stable with a sneer. 'Yes,' said Micheline firmly. 'I do.'

The court rose for the weekend and on Saturday 19 October there were photographs of Micheline in all the national newspapers. When they returned on Monday 21 October, it was time for Bill Roper to be called to account.

Six feet tall and smartly dressed in one of his best Savile Row suits, Bill cut an imposing figure. If he was going to go down, he'd decided, he would go down in style. He rested his hands on the edge of the witness box and responded to his brief, Mr Weitzman,[47] in the clear, confident tones of a man with long experience of calling the odds. 'I was very well known on the racecourse,' he began. 'I knew everybody who was anybody.' He agreed that he had 'hobnobbed with the great', as Joe and Jackie had put it, and been called 'an inspired man'. He explained that, since January 1960,

---

47 David Weitzmann QC was also Labour MP for Hackney North and Stoke Newington.

when he left Max Parker's employ, he had acted as a punter on his own account while continuing to get bets on for big clients. 'I put money on for as high as Lord and Lady Rosebery down to the Newmarket paper boy,' he boasted.

There were more gasps in the courtroom and racing journalists, such as Norman Pegg of the *Daily Herald* who had seen it all (and remembered the downfall of Snouty Parker in 1941),[48] imagined they could almost hear the furious reaction forty miles away in Jockey Club headquarters in Cavendish Square. 'How dare this bookmaker, this cockney upstart, this mountebank and chancer, link his name with one of the Turf's finest and premier peers of the realm?' they'd splutter. 'He presumably thought he had what his sort would call "sauce".' But they'd slap him down. They'd see him off and no two ways about it.

Bill knew he was making a splash and he was enjoying it and not about to stop. He talked about putting as much as £15,000 on a horse for men like Ian Murray and Prince Aly Khan and helpfully explained to Melford how he got the bets on, using up to 16 friends or faces who, at a signal from him, would all step in and wager up to £500 with different bookmakers. He talked about his lifestyle and 'flying to night meetings in summer with Lester, Scobie and Doug Smith in a plane I used to organise'. Lester and Scobie and Doug weren't there in person to confirm or deny Bill's claims but the spectators in the gallery, and the shilling-

---

48 Norman Pegg worked for the *Daily Herald* for 38 years and was still contributing in his eighties. He died in 1980.

each-way punters reading about it in the following day's papers, were riveted. Here they were in conservative, nine-to-five Britain in 1963, less than a decade after rationing had ended, hearing about what sounded the unimaginably glamorous existence of a man who had lived the racing and gambling dream to the hilt.

Mr Weitzman moved on to the potentially trickier area of Roper's relationship with Micheline, the married man and father of two, seducing and corrupting a lovely young woman half his age. Bill recalled when she first came to his house as a mother's help when she was nineteen years old and how she stayed for six months. He described the next time he saw her at Ascot in 1959 and how, by the following year, she was running her own beauty shop in Knightsbridge and he admitted, somewhat sheepishly, that by then he had 'formed an association' with her. He claimed he knew of only four visits she had made to racing stables and that he first heard of them after her interview at the Jockey Club. He said she'd told him that she was trying to get tips and he'd 'told her off and said she must be crazy'.

Bill denied having anything to do with the purchase of Ganymede II. It was entirely Micheline's project, he said. 'She just wanted to emulate Elizabeth Arden and Chanel who bought racehorses for publicity purposes.' He also denied ever having been concerned with doping. 'I have told the truth,' he assured Weitzman and the court.

Owen Stable, giving Roper a dismissive look, asked him if he knew the late Edward Smith. Bill agreed he did but claimed he knew nothing about 'the vast quantity of dope' stored in Smith's house, enough to dope at least 600 racehorses. 'I'm not suggesting it was you who wore the rubber glove or anything of that sort' said Stable. 'Thank you' said Bill. 'But don't you think it's funny that you just happened to be at Uttoxeter on the day that Fresh Winds was doped?' 'It's not funny,' said Bill. 'I go to lots of racemeetings.' 'Yes' said Stable. 'Mr Dyer has called you "Mr Racing himself".' 'Much obliged to him' said Bill. Some of the jury members laughed. Stable asked Bill if he knew about Micheline Lugeon being observed by the lad Kenny English looking at Bronze Warrior in the stabling area at Kelso racecourse. Bill said he didn't. Stable asked him if he felt responsible for Micheline being in court. 'No. Not at all,' said Bill. 'Why not?' asked Stable. 'She has committed no crime,' said Bill. The prosecutor asked him if he and Micheline had not stayed in the Royal Station Hotel in Newcastle the night before Hiawatha II was doped. 'That wasn't her,' said Bill. 'You signed the register W. Roper and wife,' said Stable. 'Yes,' said Bill, 'but that was someone else . . . a friend.' 'What friend?' asked Stable. 'Maria,' said Bill. 'Maria who?' persisted Stable. 'Maria Callas,' said Bill, smiling. His fellow defendants laughed. The public gallery laughed. Bill winked at Micheline. 'Was this Maria Callas an opera singer?' asked Stable. 'No,' said Bill quietly.

Stable went right up close to the witness box as he had done with Micheline. 'Have you held yourself up as a man of exemplary character?' he asked. There was a pause. 'I have got my love affairs mixed up a bit,' said Bill looking up sadly at Doris who was in the gallery. 'I've been a bit foolish regarding them . . .' Melford Stevenson, uncomfortable with any emotional or sexual overtones, interrupted. 'We are concerned with doping,' he reminded Stable. 'If we start going into the defendant's love life we may be here for another month.' Bill smiled. Micheline smiled at Bill. 'No more questions, my lord,' said Stable.

The next day the papers reported Bill's testimony along with more photos of Micheline, the object of his love, or his folly. The rest of the week and the following Monday was taken up with legal arguments as the defence attempted to have Mrs Robson's confused identification evidence struck out and again challenged the honesty and motives of the Newmarket stable lads.

It wasn't until Tuesday 29 October that Melford Stevenson finally began his summing up. He started by saying that the characters he felt most sympathy for were the racehorses, a sentiment that no true lover of the sport could disagree with. He didn't seem to think much of the four stable lads – Snuffy, Santus, Michael and Jimmy – and warned the jury that 'accomplices testifying for the crown have a strong incentive to distort the truth'. Snuffy, he said, had been prepared to double cross the other parties in the conspiracy. Santus 'couldn't have been less impressive.' Michael had 'yielded to the blandishments of Lowry' and Jimmy had been 'trying hard not to tell the truth'. The judge stressed that there must be 'independent evidence to corroborate an accomplice's evidence' and that, for the conspiracy charge to be proved, the jury must be satisfied that 'there was an agreement between the accused' to act together. He made a rather confusing comparison between the defendants and the small boys camped out on the pavement outside the court during their half-term holiday and asking for a penny for the guy – for a legitimate firework night bonfire or just for sweets, he wondered?

At 10.47 a.m. on 30 October, the 21st full day of the trial, Melford Stevenson sent the jury out to consider their verdict. They returned after twenty minutes seeking yet further clarification of the identification evidence and then retired a second time at 12.27 p.m. The six men were taken to the cells. Micheline was taken back to the small room beneath the court.

Bill Roper asked a prison officer to find him a newspaper to help him pass the time and he was given an old copy of the *Daily Sketch* with Micheline's photograph in it. The other main story in the paper was about the 14th Earl of Home – Sir Alec Douglas-Home as he was about to become – who, to the astonishment of many, had 'emerged' as the new Prime Minister and leader of the Conservative Party. There was also coverage of the ever more exciting duel between Lester Piggott and Scobie Breasley, who were now tied on 170 winners apiece, and a story about The Beatles who were to appear at the Royal Variety Show the following month. The tune on Bill Roper's lips was 'You'll Never Walk Alone' by Gerry and the Pacemakers.[49]

---

49 'You'll Never Walk Alone' entered the charts in October 1963 and was number two by 26 October and number one by 2 November.

At 2.55 p.m. the jury returned and the prisoners were brought back up to hear their fate. All seven of them were found guilty on all counts. Watching from the public gallery, Ernie Barnett and portly Bob Hill were exultant. Some of the wives and girlfriends were in tears.

Before sentencing, counsel for the accused entered pleas of mitigation. Mr Hudson, for Joe Lowry, said that his client was not a bookmaker and had 'been tempted by others'. Jackie Dyer had also been tempted but he was living in a council flat and could hardly be said to have profited from the conspiracy. Jackie, who had a wife and child and kidney trouble, was basically 'a decent citizen', said Hudson, and had already been in custody since 27 May.

Mr Elton, speaking for Micheline Lugeon, said she had been in custody for 14 weeks and that what had happened to her was 'a tragedy'. He urged the court to 'help her to restart her life as soon as possible'.

Mark Myers, for Roper, began by exonerating Micheline of any part in Bill's crimes. He accepted that evidence had been given on Roper's behalf that the two acted independently but said that his client now wished to make clear that 'it was his association with her which had brought her to the dock'.

Myers said that, in his time, Roper had been a 'respected figure on racecourses throughout the country' and he cited the evidence of Doris Curd who had spoken, movingly, of her undiminished affection for Bill, despite his affair, and had testified that over the twenty years that she had known him, he had shown her 'nothing but kindness'. Myers referred briefly to the couple's two sons, who were now at public school, to Bill's unstinting support for them as a father and to 'the tragedy that now awaits him'.

Bill was sentenced first. Mr Racing stood up as directed, leaning forward and gripping the bar of the dock with his hands. He imagined that he was looking not only at the judge but at all his clients, past and present. The Rich Charlies and the Lords and Ladies who had always thought Bill Roper was 'a bit of a card' but had liked him all the same, but who now saw him revealed as an arch doper and villain. 'It is perfectly obvious that you were the brains behind this plot,' said Melford Stevenson. 'You organised all that was done and you were quick to see and turn to profit, every opportunity that presented itself to corrupt those who were corruptible, and you succeeded in corrupting a very large number of people. You used a strong intelligence to obtain that result and behind it all was the motive of most unpleasant greed. You will go to prison for three years.' Dapper Bill, so confident and larger than life on the racecourse, rocked on his heels. It was his 58th birthday and, although the sentence allowed by law was much shorter than the police would have liked, Roper knew that his British racing and bookmaking career was in ruins.

The judge moved on to Joe Lowry, Jackie Dyer and Charlie Mitchell, sentencing each of them to two years in prison. 'Thank you, sir,' said Mitchell, the otherwise silent strong man. But there were no thanks from Joe, for whom a third prison sentence was already one too many, or from

Jackie with his kidney condition and a wife and child who depended on him.

Alex Field was given 12 months to run concurrently with his five-year sentence for house breaking. Brian Perry got two years' probation.

Finally Melford Stevenson came to Micheline. 'I have not any doubt,' he said, 'that you not only lent yourself to this wicked conspiracy but that you have made use of a generous endowment of charm and intelligence which could have been turned to account in honest work, to embark on this disgraceful course of fraudulent events. You will go to prison for 12 months.'

The men were taken down first, Micheline giving Bill one last desperate smile as he turned to walk down the steps. Minutes later she was taken out and held in the small room beneath the court while Bill, Joe, Jackie, Charlie and Alex were loaded up into the prison van and each locked into their own small, claustrophobic compartment, ready for the journey to Wandsworth which, it had already been decided, would be their next destination.

Before the court was cleared, there was one last theatrical moment. First the barrister Mr Charles Bathurst rose to say that 'on behalf of Lord Rosebery' he wished to make clear that his Lordship 'had no recollection of ever meeting the man Roper and believed that all of his bets had been placed with the Parker firm'. There was no comeback or retort or contradiction. The judge simply noted Mr Bathurst's comments, as did the press, which were entered in the trial transcript and widely reported in the papers the next day.

Then, just when it all seemed over, up stood Mr Elton, who had appeared for Micheline Lugeon, to say that he had been instructed by 'Mr Albert Dimes, the London bookmaker, to make it clear that he is in no way connected to the doping conspiracy.'

Melford Stevenson gave Elton a withering look and briefly noted his interjection, much as the Brighton recorder had done nine months before.

The press, when released by the judge, dashed from the courtroom to begin working on their copy, deadlines imminent. Some two hours later, his *Daily Herald* story complete, Norman Pegg walked outside on to Lewes high street to see a smart, black, police Humber Hawk parked by the kerb. Sitting in the back seat, flanked by a policewoman and a woman prison officer, was Micheline. Her departure for Holloway had been delayed until the photographers and general throng had dispersed. Pegg noticed that she was wearing a black fur coat. It was the same sealskin coat that she had worn when she visited Fairlawne in November 1961.

As Pegg watched, the police driver, or should it have been chauffeur, switched on the ignition and the Humber Hawk pulled away down the hill into the dusk. The last that Pegg saw of the mysterious young woman was her looking back at him out of the rear window.

The show was over.

23

A CERTAIN CHARISMA

FLEET STREET loved the doping trial. 'The biggest plot in Turf history,' proclaimed the front page of the *Daily Herald* on Thursday 31 October. There was a photograph of Micheline Lugeon beneath the headline and a breathless account of the 'five men and a beautiful woman' who had 'brought British horse racing to its knees'.

The paper recounted the downfall of Bill Roper with lip-smacking relish, describing how 'balding Bill' had taken to doping to support his extravagant lifestyle which 'centred around Kensington's exclusive Stafford Court and included keeping two mistresses'. But now the law had caught up with him. The bookmaker had 'swapped his penthouse for a cell in Lewes prison' (actually he was back in South London) and his lover was in Holloway.

There were more photographs of Micheline in a double-page centre spread in the *Sketch*, while, on Sunday 3 November the *News of the World* ran an interview with Zoe Progl, the former shoplifter and so-called 'Queen of the

Underworld' who had first-hand experience of Holloway. She warned that Micheline would have to beware of the prison's DX Block, the so-called 'married quarters' occupied by 'aggressively dominant females'. Pretty new arrivals could expect to be sent messages written on scraps of lavatory paper. Some would offer friendship and support but others would be predatory and threatening. All in all Progl painted a bleak picture of life inside. Newly convicted inmates (as opposed to prisoners on remand) would spend much of the time on their hands and knees scrubbing the jail's stone floors, breathing in the stench of carbolic soap and listening to jangling keys and clanking buckets. They would have to subsist on a meagre diet and watch one notoriously sadistic wardress feeding tinned salmon to her cats while the prisoners queued up for mush.

The worst moment of the week though, said Progl, had been Saturday nights when she knew the rest of the city was at play. Locked up in her cell, cold and hungry, she had found the loneliness overpowering. It would all be very different to dinner at the Coq d'Or and a show at the Astor Club.

Some of the papers had a story supplied to them by portly Bob Hill in which he claimed to have identified Micheline after seeing photographs of her 'thin legs'. But the conspirators dismissed this as a fantasy of Hill's designed to exaggerate his role in the case. Micheline Lugeon, they said, had very fine legs.

Where the Sundays mostly emphasised the human angle, other coverage revolved around 'the guilty men' who were not in the dock at Lewes and should have been. 'Now Yard hunts crooked bookies,' thundered the *Herald*. Its racing correspondent, Norman Pegg, drew a contrast between the '10,000 odd licensed bookmakers, on course and off, in Britain and the small handful who have given any kind of assistance to the authorities'. He claimed the Jockey Club had drawn up a blacklist of at least 20 high-rolling bookmakers and professional backers who had paid Bill Roper and his gang for information.

Arthur Tietjens, in the *Daily Mail*, followed a similar theme but warned readers that, while the police had identified more of the top bookies they'd like to see behind bars, obtaining the evidence to successfully prosecute them wouldn't be easy. Bookmaking continued to be a closed world – secretive, sly and self-supporting – and conspiracies were still the hardest thing to prove. Even the case against the seven at Lewes had been a tenuous one and Scotland Yard was disappointed, but not surprised, when Charlie Mitchell managed to get his conviction overturned on appeal in February 1964. Mr Justice Finnemore, while dismissing appeals by Lowry, Dyer and Field, ruled that there was no evidence associating Mitchell with the others on a doping expedition and that he couldn't safely be convicted on the uncorroborated evidence of accomplices alone.

With Mitchell out and Darkie Steward at large, it was probably no coincidence that, at around the same time, doping resumed. Antiar, a promising hurdler trained by Peter Cazalet, started 4-11 favourite for a Champion Hurdle trial at Wincanton but fell at the last flight when well beaten. The seven-runner race was won by the 3-1 second favourite, Satchmo.

The Wincanton race concentrated minds at the Jockey Club where the stewards had just received a report by a three-man committee, headed by Sir Randle Feilden, which had been charged with enquiring into 'the security of the racehorse'. The committee's findings convinced the Jockey Club that Colonel Blair and portly Bob Hill would no longer do and that they needed a new full-time inspector of security. To nobody's surprise, they chose a man of their own class and background, appointing Brigadier Henry Green, CBE, officer commanding the London District Brigade of Guards and a former MI5 officer.

'Gumshoe' Green's first task was to conduct a review of stable security arrangements at Britain's racecourses and he co-opted ex-Detective Chief Superintendent George Davis, who had been the titular head of the Bill Roper inquiry but had now retired from the Yard, to assist him. In the summer of 1964 the pair visited all of Britain's sixty-eight racetracks and, the following year, Securicor was awarded a contract to provide a round-the-clock guard at racecourse stables when meetings were taking place. The £350,000 cost of the arrangements would be met by the Horserace Betting Levy Board whose chairman, George Wigg (the former persecutor of Harold Macmillan), loathed racing's aristocratic rulers and was himself cordially detested by the Jockey Club.

Green's second priority was to hire an experienced detective as his chief investigations officer. The Brigadier may have emerged from racing's magic circle – much as Lord Home had emerged as Tory PM – and like his predecessor, Colonel Blair, be largely ignorant of bookmaking and gambling. But his time with MI5 had taught him the importance of good police work and he understood that if he was to succeed in preventing further dopings, he needed a proper criminal investigator who would know how to follow the money from the betting ring to the underworld.

The Brigadier's establishment connections were every bit as pukka as Peter Cazalet's and it was an obvious step for him to consult with his old friend Sir Ranulph Bacon, who spoke in turn to Tommy Butler, who had rounded up most of the Train Robbers by now. The 'Grey Fox' recommended his former number two, Bob Anderson, who had spent nearly 30 years in the Met, eighteen of them with the Flying Squad, and who had worked with Ernest Barnett on the 1962 inquiry leading up to the arrests of Ted Smith, Darkie Steward and Richard McGee.

Anderson was offered the post and accepted, arranging to retire from the police and start his new job as Chief Investigations Officer at the beginning of 1965 when the Jockey Club moved into their new London offices in Portman Square. Incidences of doping to lose had undoubtedly diminished since the Lewes and Brighton trials but they hadn't altogether gone away and, in the early months of the 1965 flat racing season, there were two disturbing results. Night Appeal, a filly owned by the Jockey Club member Sonny Richmond-Watson and ridden by Jimmy Lindley, was strongly fancied for the 1,000 Guineas at Newmarket but trailed in a well-beaten last of the 16 runners. The racecourse stewards, incomprehensibly, failed to order a dope test on the day but a subsequent private test, arranged by her trainer Arthur Budgett, confirmed that Night Appeal had been nobbled with a depressant drug called phenothiazine.

Ten days later, Night Off, the 1,000 Guineas winner and the 5-1 ante-post favourite for the Oaks at Epsom, finished almost 200 yards behind the others in the Musidora Stakes at York. The filly's furious owner, Major Lionel B. Holliday, said that Night Off was trembling and distressed when they got her back to the racecourse stables and he was certain she too had been got at. The winner of the Musidora was the heavily backed second favourite, Arctic Melody.

Rumours were rife as to who might be behind the doping with the name of Max Parker, who died the following year, once again in the frame. Clive Graham, writing in the *Express*, wondered if 'our racecourse security agents have been tracking the activities and movements of a certain bookmaker' and suggested that if Night Off's dope test was upheld – and it wasn't – it 'must be the death knell for bookmakers in this country'. The bookmakers' trade body took offence at Graham's remarks and complained to the Press Council, who found in their favour, leading the unrepentant journalist to comment that such action 'ill becomes such a body of plaster saints'.

Whatever the laws of libel might be, Graham was only saying in print what others were saying in private. But Bob Anderson, whose task was to try and stop the doping and who suspected Charlie Mitchell and Albert Dimes, needed a positive lead, like

Ernie Barnett three years before. It came in the shape of a tip-off from a detective sergeant at Bow Street, a racing enthusiast and ally of Anderson's, who had an informant with links to the old Roper gang. The two men met in the Horseshoe pub in Tottenham Court Road, where Anderson was told that the grass, who wanted cash for his assistance, had said that Darkie Steward and Joe Lowry, who had been released from prison earlier that summer, were both involved.

In order to test the accuracy of the information, Anderson wanted the grass to tell him the name of any horse that the gang had 'done' but that had not been publicised. A few days later, the detective sergeant called to say that his man had told him that Mary Barr, the even-money favourite for the Walmer Plate at Folkestone on 20 July, had been doped. When Anderson looked the race up in the formbook, he saw that Mary Barr had indeed run unaccountably badly and when he telephoned her trainer, John Bartholomew, the Kent handler admitted that, although he hadn't reported his suspicions at the time, he was convinced that his horse had been got at.

A month later another Bartholomew runner, Kracadour, competing in a modest handicap at Windsor, performed equally badly, starting 5-2 favourite in a small field but finishing well beaten by a 3-1 shot ridden by Lester Piggott. The Windsor racecourse stewards, like their colleagues at Newmarket and at Lewes in 1962, didn't order an official dope test but a private test, organised by the trainer, confirmed the presence of phenothiazine in the horse's bloodstream.

The informant got back in touch and said that the same gang that doped Mary Barr had got at Kracadour but that he hadn't known about it in advance. Next time, he said, he'd give Anderson early warning. The Jockey Club's man didn't have to wait long.

The horse chosen for the gang's next job was Spare Filly, a three-year-old trained at Lambourn by Bob Read whose Silver Kumar had been nobbled by the Roper firm in the summer of 1960. Spare Filly was due to run in the Florizel Handicap at Kempton Park on Saturday 18 September and, when the Friday evening papers confirmed that the race had only attracted seven runners, the informant rang Bob Anderson and told him that the doping was on. The ex-detective chief inspector had already been to see the Flying Squad's Commander Ernie Millen at New Scotland Yard and a special team had been put on standby led by Terry O'Connell and Pat Sugrue who were also veterans of the Bill Roper enquiry.

This was the era when The Sweeney was in its prime and O'Connell, Sugrue and their squad, real Regan and Carter hard men ready for a rumble, set off at high speed for Newbury where Anderson met them at the police station. Then, accompanied by Detective Superintendent Lawson of Thames Valley CID and a group of uniformed constables, they all drove on to Lambourn where the understandably startled Bob Read was about to go to bed. They explained the situation to him and told him that he should stay safely out of harm's way while they staked out the yard.

At 11.15 p.m. the Flying Squad officers, veterans of robbery ambushes, took up their positions. Four of them were concealed at each end of the yard while another – who was armed – lay in the ditch that ran parallel to Mill Lane at the other side of the stable paddock. Another detective was in a Dutch barn on the eastern side of the yard. All four observation points were equipped with two-way radios but, as no police officer from that time will be surprised to hear, they failed to work when needed.

It was a dark and windy night with heavy rain and the detectives spent a wet and uncomfortable few hours lying in wait for the dopers. Finally, at around 1.50 a.m., the officer in the ditch saw a two-tone Ford Zodiac drive slowly along Mill Lane. Within a few minutes it returned and stopped, facing the direction in which it had come. Ten minutes later another car, a dark Hillman saloon, pulled up, and the officer saw three or four men get out and heard a voice say 'half an hour then'. The car drove away and the men walked a short way along the lane and then climbed over the fence into the paddock at the rear of the stables.

A malfunctioning radio meant that O'Connell and Sugrue could not be forewarned of the gang's arrival but they were alert anyway and they heard the sound of the men clambering over the gate and then of the bolt being drawn back on Spare Filly's box. The light was switched on in the box and then, on a count of three, O'Connell and Sugrue charged forward. The stable door was wide open and one man was in the act of putting a head collar on the horse. Another stood by his side holding a large stick, or twitch, and a third was in the shadows outside holding a milk bottle.

When the men realised they'd been discovered they tried to run for it, one of them dropping the bottle which smashed on the ground. More police officers stormed into the yard from the Mill Lane exit and a violent struggle began in the yard and in the paddock with some of the over-enthusiastic locals attacking their fellow constables by mistake in the darkness. The man that Terry O'Connell had hoped to find, and had come prepared for – hence the firearm – was Charlie Mitchell but, like Bill Roper, Mitchell was always too smart to actually take part in a doping. Instead O'Connell and Sugrue found themselves fighting Bill's old minder Johnny Barnham, an ex-boxer turned taxi driver, and a formidable man in a scrap. Barnham was eventually subdued but Darkie Steward – whom O'Connell had recognised in the torchlight – escaped along with Jimmy Cronin. But when the Hillman saloon returned to try and pick up the fugitives, the police in the lane arrested the driver at gunpoint and the man behind the wheel was Joe Lowry. O'Connell reminded him that he'd known him for over ten years and had first met him at Kempton and Hurst Park in the 1950s when Uncle Joe used to try and sell the policeman tips.

Darkie Steward was arrested early the following morning at a house in Cobham in Surrey. The tenant was May Kibble and the same grass who had given Anderson the information about the doping had also told him that Darkie was now living with Ted Smith's 'widow'.

The three men were remanded in custody at Oxford and eventually came to trial at Berkshire Assizes the following

February. This time there was no murdered witness or retracted testimony and no escape for Darkie Steward. They had all been caught red-handed and Steward and Barnham were sent down for four years each and Joe Lowry, five. It was hard time too in Parkhurst and it was too much for Joe whose health was already poor and whose comment that he was 'too old for villainy' was all too true. He died of a heart attack in his early fifties.

In 1969 Jimmy Cronin, who had gone on the run in Ireland, returned to London and was arrested by O'Connell, after another stake-out, coming out of a pub on the Marylebone Road. He got two years.

The dramatic events more than vindicated 'Gumshoe' Green's appointment of Bob Anderson, while the publicity afforded to the trial added further to the public's perception that Dick Francis was spot on and racing was beset with skulduggery. Two more Francis thrillers had followed *Dead Cert* to the top of the bestseller lists: *For Kicks*, which came out in 1965, had a particularly colourful cast of Machiavellian horse dopers and frightened stable lads although the chief villain was not a bookmaker but an upper-class psychopath in hunting boots.

The jockey turned author continued to be popular with his former royal patron who enjoyed all his books and also enjoyed further successes at Fairlawne until Major Peter Cazalet's death in 1973. No racehorses have been trained at the stables since Cazalet's day and the house and estate now belong to Frankel's owner, Prince Khalid Abdullah.

The chief remaining villain in Bob Anderson's book was Charlie Mitchell but he proved too big and elusive a catch for the racecourse security service. In April 1966 he turned up in two dog-doping trials at the Old Bailey where a kennel maid at Walthamstow Stadium testified that she had been paid to give greyhounds sausagemeat with phenobarbitone inside. She described a farcical scenario in 1965 where, one night, the traps opened for a race and only two of the six runners came out while, on another occasion, there were eight dogs on the track at the conclusion of a six-dog contest. Mitchell was acquitted the first time after a female witness retracted her identification evidence, much like May Kibble had done at Lewes in 1963. But the witness subsequently admitted perjuring herself to get Charlie off and, at the second trial, he was sent to prison for two years.

The big man next made the headlines in May 1968 when he was one of the 15 men arrested with the Kray Brothers by Nipper Read and his squad. But when the Twins were committed for trial at Bow Street Magistrates' Court in July of that year, the charges against Charlie Mitchell were dropped. It transpired that he had given the police a substantial amount of information about the proposed murder of two witnesses that the Twins had asked him to take care of.

Grassing up the Krays seemed to many to be a suicidal move.[50] In 1969 the Twins were jailed for 30 years, Melford Stevenson presiding at the Old Bailey. But when two shotgun blasts were fired at Charlie Mitchell in broad

---

50 Stan Davis (see footnotes on pp. 68 and 231) says he was summoned to Brixton Prison by Ronnie Kray, whilst Ronnie was on remand, and asked to try and find out where Mitchell was so that the Twins could arrange to have him killed.

daylight outside his Fulham home in September 1971, the gunman firing from the back of a blue Ford Cortina, it was assumed, wrongly as it turned out, to be a revenge attack. The bookmaker, club owner and moneylender had other enemies in West London, men who had had their chance and missed, but a violent death was not far away.

In the mid-1970s Charlie was one of many London villains to relocate to the Costa Del Crime and, one sweltering night in a bar in Marbella, a waiter hit him over the head with a bottle. Some said the waiter was acting in self-defence and trying to break up a drunken brawl. Others say it was a contract killing.

By contrast, Mitchell's uncle, Jackie Dyer, lives on in London to this day. Materially, life hasn't been too kind to the veteran oddsmaker for whom home is a 1940s council estate in Fulham. But he takes consolation from the thought that when he walks on to a racecourse, like Epsom or Ascot, he can still see 'over a hundred people' who count him as a friend.

Mitchell's fellow gangster Albert Dimes never faced charges for the doping conspiracy and nobody was ever brave, or foolish, enough to point a gun at him either. He died of lung cancer in November 1972 and his good friend Stanley Baker, who would die of the same disease four years later, was one of the several hundred mourners at his funeral.

Edward 'Teddy' Smith's name resurfaced briefly in March 1966 when Frankie Fraser and Eddie Richardson were involved in a dramatic OK Corral-style shoot-out with members of the Hayward and Hennessy families in Mr Smith's Club in South London. The gambling joint had been opened by Diana Dors the previous autumn and its full name was 'Mr Smith and the Witch Doctor'. It was situated on Rushey Green in Catford, Bill Roper's old manor, and Bill had not only known the Haywards for many years but had also met the club's real owner Paddy McGrath, the proprietor of Manchester's Cromford Club. For some there were too many coincidences.

Not that Bill Roper ever mixed again with the London underworld. He had contracted jaundice and hepatitis while on remand in Lewes and his first few months in Wandsworth were painful ones. He at least had Charlie Mitchell to protect him until February 1964, and with other inmates keen to demand a share of Bill's profits from the horse doping business, some protection was necessary.

Roper was later transferred to Ford Open Prison in West Sussex where he made a lasting impact on the teenage Tony Gilks whose father was one of the prison officers. Gilks junior wanted to join the West Sussex police but needed to pass the entrance exam and feared his English and maths skills were not up to scratch. His father arranged for him to have private coaching by 'just the right person' and Bill Roper, the man with two brains, gave him lessons twice a week in a garden shed behind the prison greenhouses. Gilks had heard all about Roper's doping gang and his 'stunning girlfriend' but what particularly impressed him was the older man's immaculate appearance. Bill, the former RAF sergeant and racecourse bookmaker, was always the smartest looking inmate, not a hair out of place, his trousers pressed and prison-issue shoes spotlessly clean. The lessons – and for the arithmetic section, Bill taught him racecourse odds and percentages – were a big success and Gilks went on to become a thirty year officer with the West Sussex force.

The positive impression of Roper resonates with Sir Peter O'Sullevan who placed many winning bets with the Max Parker firm and remembers Bill vividly. 'Oh, yes,' he says with a smile. 'You could say he had a certain charisma.'

The man who aspired to be Mr Racing was one of many rogues and chancers who saw an opening in the great gambling boom of post-war Britain. A time when the aristocracy still had money and liked to spend it on horses and cards and a time when betting and racing enlivened and brightened an otherwise rigidly class-divided world. Many of Bill's contemporaries took advantage of the folly of their rich clients but Roper went further, from profiting on races he knew to be fixed to fixing the races himself. Once he'd embarked on that journey and let the gangsters set the pace, there was no way back. The thought of a racehorse under the influence of drugs being asked to jump fences and hurdles without the trainer or jockey knowing about it, is still enough to send a shiver down the spine of any horse lover. The irony of Bill's life is that he loved horses and racing with the best of them . . . but he loved Micheline Lugeon even more.

Bill read the first few Dick Francis novels while in prison and enjoyed them although he told Gilks they could've been a 'bit more realistic in places'. He also continued to follow the racing in the newspapers, enthusing regularly about Arkle, and urging his pupil to back Sea Bird, the brilliant winner of the 1965 Derby and Prix de l'Arc de Triomphe.[51]

When Bill left Ford at the beginning of 1966, 'Mickey' had already been released and she was waiting for him on the outside. There was no law at the time confiscating the financial gains of convicted fraudsters and Roper seems to have kept some back for their future. The police believed that the gang made around £4.5 million in modern money between 1959 and 1962 and that wasn't counting the sum Bill paid Charlie Mitchell or what the big bookmakers made from the doping of Pinturischio.

Having been warned off all racecourses indefinitely, Roper decided there was no future for him in England and he and Micheline left for South Africa where they started a new life, Bill working for a bookmaker and Micheline as a beautician. Doris Curd, who was taken care of as Bill had promised she would be, lived on in North London and her two sons, after leaving public school, set out on their own private lives. But then in the 1970s their father and his lover returned to the UK. In the eyes of the racing world Bill would forever be 'Roper the Doper', part myth, part legend. But that was still better than being an enigmatic bookmaker in exile. Even

---

51 Sea Bird II won the Arc by six lengths beating a top-class international field. But Bill Roper always said the best horse he ever saw was the Italian colt Ribot, who was undefeated in 16 races and won the Arc in both 1955 and 1956. Ribot was also a favourite of 'Italian Albert' Dimes.

though he couldn't go to the track anymore he could still bet on the horses and watch them on television and the lure of his old life proved strong. But racing wasn't the only consideration. By staying in England Bill left Micheline free, as he saw it, to start again with a much younger man. She went back to South Africa on her own and this time there was no reunion.

Jackie Dyer believes that Bill Roper died in London a few months short of his 90th birthday.

The end of Micheline Lugeon's story remains a mystery. Was she happy in South Africa? Did she marry and have children? And did she ever return to London or Paris or Geneva? She was so much more than just a clothes horse and pin-up. Hard working, ambitious and capable of making a success of any business she turned her hand to. But the motley cast of characters she encountered in British racing stables would always remember her in a particular light. Their sentiments summed up by Peter Cazalet's head lad Jim Fairgrieve, who wrote a 12-verse poem about her – with a little help from Rudyard Kipling – warning his fellow lads and trainers to be wary of exotic foreign visitors. Especially when they were 'well groomed, sweet and serene'.

'I've learned my lesson. Now I know
Why great men sometimes fail.
The female species, to my woe,
Is deadlier than the male.' [52]

---

52 The poem 'The Female of the Species' by Rudyard Kipling was written in 1911.

Postscript

OF THE stable lads who appeared at Lewes Crown Court in 1963, Philip 'Snuffy' Lawler ended his days back in Newmarket living, ironically, in Jim Joel Court which was named after one of the greatest patrons of the Noel Murless stable where he wreaked so much havoc.

Kenneth Santus successfully put the Lewes trial behind him and worked for more than thirty years as a stud groom and travelling head lad. He denies that he ever personally went 'over the wall' at Jack Waugh's yard in March 1960.

Sir Mark Prescott, who now trains at Heath House stables, started out as Jack Waugh's assistant and remembers an incident at Tattersalls Sales Paddocks in Newmarket in 1965 when Mr Waugh caught up with 'the lad that did Treasure Hunt.'

Darkie Steward's sidekick Brian Perry, who received a suspended sentence at Lewes, went on to become a professional criminal. He was suspected of being involved in the 1983 Brinks-Mat gold bullion robbery and in 1992 he was convicted of handling stolen goods. In November

2001 Perry was shot dead in broad daylight as he got out of his car in Bermondsey in South East London.

Alex Field's brother Lennie played a small but crucial role in the Great Train Robbery. He had control of Alex's money while his brother was in custody in the summer of 1963 and he used it to act as nominal purchaser of Leatherslade Farm which became the train robber's hideout.

Nicholas Gregory, now a retired District Judge, was the junior member of Bill Roper's defence team at Lewes in 1963. He remembers 'Mr Racing' as 'an amiable and highly intelligent man who liked to be liked.'

After each day of the trial Bill's barrister, David Weitzman, his number two, Mark Myers, and Gregory would have a brief conference with their client in one of the cells beneath the court. Apparently the conversations were nearly always about racing. Weitzman was a bit of a punter himself and would ask Roper if there was anything he fancied running the following day? Bill would give him a few tips and that evening the barrister would ring up his bookmaker and place a bet. Most of them won and Roper joked that Weitzman should give him a discount on his fee in return for the information.

Gregory believes Roper was resigned to his fate and almost relieved when he was only sentenced to three years as he'd been warned to expect more like five or six. Gregory had to visit Bill twice in Ford Open Prison to discuss various legal issues. Roper seemed to be leading something of a social life behind bars and once a week was allowed out to play bridge at a local country house. Extraordinarily a prison officer would drive him over there and wait around patiently to take him back after the game was over.

On one occasion Roper asked Gregory if he could send him two books: Fowler's Use Of The English Language and the Dictionary of Antonyms and Synonyms. 'Why in heaven do you need those?' asked Gregory. 'You're banged up in gaol.' 'You don't understand' Bill replied. 'This is Ford. In my block alone there are five solicitors and 17 accountants.'

Gregory's last meeting with Bill was after he'd been released from prison when he was trying to get some possessions back from Doris. Over a conversation in a pub he seemed anxious to assure Gregory that he was a very different kind of man to Charlie Mitchell and had never wanted to get caught up in Mitchell's 'sordid and violent' schemes.

Bill Roper's niece, Sheila McLauchlan, remembers her uncle and his lover with affection. She says that Bill's father was an alcoholic and she felt that Roper's character was formed by his experiences as a boy when he had to provide for his mother and siblings from an early age. Sheila describes Bill as 'soft spoken and charming' and recalls that by the early 1960s he had lost his Cockney accent.

Micheline Lugeon stayed with Sheila's mother and her family when she came out of Holloway and while she was waiting for Bill to be released.

Sheila contradicts Jackie Dyer and believes that Micheline stayed with Bill until the end of his life. Micheline used to write to Sheila regularly from South Africa and Sheila last heard from her in 2004.

Acknowledgements

THERE ARE many people I would like to thank for all the help and encouragement they gave me in the writing of this book. Victor Chandler kindly put me in touch with a number of old colleagues and family friends who were working on the racecourse in the 1950s and 1960s and Eamon Evans took the time and trouble to track down one of the leading players. As a result, a distinguished coterie of former bookmaking and betting ring faces were good enough to share with me their memories of the heroes and villains of Bill Roper's era. Tommy Lawrence, Benno Miller, Bobbie Edwards, Charlie Maskey, Jackie Dyer. I thank them all.

James Morton, the doyenne of underworld chroniclers, introduced me to several fascinating characters. Gerry Parker was an engaging host over breakfast at Claridges and a fund of colourful and incisive portraits and Stan Davis, though now troubled by lameness, was equally helpful and generous with his time.

I am deeply grateful to Alan Byrne, Bruce Millington and everyone at the *Racing Post* for backing the project and to James de Wesselow for his tireless support and enthusiasm.

It would have been a much poorer book without the invaluable editorial input of Ian Preece, who brought an outsider's experienced eye to bear on both the racing details and the human angle. I am also indebted to Brough Scott who provided telling comment at an important juncture. I should like to thank Julian Brown, Liz Ampairee and John Westerby for all their hard work and assistance and Sean Magee both for reading the manuscript and introducing me to Tim Cox and his wonderful library. James Lambie, author of a masterful history of *The Sporting Life*, called *The Story of Your Life*, answered queries and provided advice at an early stage.

Long hours were spent going through the police and court records in the National Archives and trawling through old editions in the British Newspaper Library and I am lucky to have a friend like Jan Hollway who provided me with a base during these London forays and also gave up her office during a visit to France.

I have been inspired as always by the incomparable Sir Peter O'Sullevan who was the voice of racing throughout my childhood and long after and knew many of the personalities described in the story. Sir Peter has always been a punter par excellence. It was also a pleasure to talk to the lovely Penny Graham about her father Clive Graham who was Sir Peter's colleague both on the BBC and at the *Daily Express* in the 1950s and 1960s.

One man who I think would have enjoyed this book is my old friend Mel Smith who sadly died in July. He was the best, funniest and most generous companion a betting and racing lover could ever have and I hope he is looking down from the great Members Enclosure in the sky. RIP Mel.

Finally, I can not say enough about the wonderful support I have had from my wife, Sara. At a time of great stress for herself and her family, she has borne my obsession with tolerance and fortitude. I couldn't have done this without her.

Bibliography

Beasley, Bobby. *Second Start* (WH Allen, 1976)

Bromley, Peter. *The Price of Success* (Hutchinson/Stanley Paul, 1982)

Curling, Bill. *Royal Champion* (Michael Joseph, 1980)

Deighton, Len. *The Ipcress File* (Hodder and Stoughton, 1962)

Fitzgeorge-Parker, Tim. *The Guv'nor* (Collins, 1980)

Francis, Dick. *The Sport of Queens* (Michael Joseph, 1957); *Dead Cert* (Michael Joseph, 1962); *For Kicks* (Michael Joseph, 1965)

Greeno, Edward. *War on the Underworld* (John Long, 1960)

Hamlyn, Geoffrey. *My Sixty Years In The Ring* (Sporting Garland Press, 1994)

Herbert, Ivor. *The Queen Mother's Horses* (Pelham Books, 1967)

Johnstone, Rae. *The Rae Johnstone Story* (Stanley Paul, 1958)

Kaye, Richard. *The Ladbrokes Story* (Pelham Books, 1969)

Lambie, James. *The Story of Your Life* (Matador/Troubador Publishing Ltd, 2010)

Mortimer, Roger. *The History of the Derby Stakes* (Michael Joseph, 1973)

Morton, James. *Gangland Soho* (Piatkus/Little Brown, 2008)

Nicholson, David and Powell, Jonathan. *The Duke* (Hodder and Stoughton, 1995)

Pearson, John. *The Gamblers* (Century, 2005)

Pegg, Norman. *Focus On Racing* (Robert Hale Ltd, 1963)

Rickman, Eric. *Come Racing With Me* (Chatto and Windus, 1951)

Rimell, Fred and Mercy. *Aintree Iron* (WH Allen, 1977)

Sandbrook, Dominic. *Never Had It So Good* (Little Brown, 2005)

Smith, Sean. *Royal Racing* (BBC, 2001)

Index

INDEX